EX LIBRIS

PACE
UNIVERSITY

THE HENRY BIRNBAUM
LIBRARY

PACE PLAZA, NEW YORK

A Life of Emily Brontë

A Life of Emily Brontë

Edward Chitham

Basil Blackwell

Copyright © Edward Chitham 1987

First published 1987

Basil Blackwell Ltd
108 Cowley Road, Oxford OX4 1JF, UK

Basil Blackwell Inc.
432 Park Avenue South, Suite 1503
New York, NY 10016, USA

All rights reserved. Except for the quotation of short passages for the purposes of criticism and review, no part of this publication may be reproduced, stored in a retrieval system, or transmitted, in any form or by any means, electronic, mechanical, photocopying, recording or otherwise, without the prior permission of the publisher.

Except in the United States of America, this book is sold subject to the condition that it shall not, by way of trade or otherwise, be lent, re-sold, hired out, or otherwise circulated without the publisher's prior consent in any form of binding or cover other than that in which it is published and without a similar condition including this condition being imposed on the subsequent purchaser.

British Library Cataloguing in Publication Data

Chitham, Edward
A life of Emily Brontë
1. Brontë, Emily——Biography 2. Authors.
English——19th Century——Biography
I. Title
823'.8 PR4173

ISBN 0-631-14751-9

Library of Congress Cataloging-in-Publication Data

Chitham, Edward.
A life of Emily Brontë.

Bibliography: p.
Includes index.
1. Brontë, Emily, 1818–1848—Biography. 2. Authors, English—19th century—Biography. I. Title.
PR4173.C45 1987 823'.8 87-6582
ISBN 0-631-14751-9

Typeset in 11/12pt Bembo by Columns of Reading
Printed in Great Britain by Billing & Sons Ltd, Worcester

PR
4173
.C45
1987

Contents

Illustrations

Plates

(between pages 160 and 161)

Maps *page*

Acknowledgements

Anyone writing on the Brontës must acknowledge the work of many predecessors. My bibliography shows how far I have followed in the footsteps of dedicated researchers and commentators.

Of previous writers on Emily Brontë, I have found Muriel Spark, John Hewish and Romer Wilson the most valuable secondary sources. Hilda Marsden's published material on the Halifax area compelled me to look very closely at Law Hill and High Sunderland. The Shakespeare Head *Lives and Letters* volumes, reissued in 1980, have been used as the basis of my knowledge of Charlotte's letters. I have checked the manuscripts and dating in some cases, but readers should note that precise dates are sometimes disputable. We still need an authoritative edition of these letters; the task of providing one is a lifetime's work.

Among many others, I should like to acknowledge the help given me by letter from the following:

John H. Patchett, of Queensbury, for points about the life of Elizabeth Patchett; Dr A. Betteridge of Calderdale District Archives; Dr Jennifer Cox, who helped to pinpoint material relating to Law Hill; Miss S. J. MacPherson of Cumbria Record Office; Miss M. E. Burkett of Abbot Hall Museum, Kendal; Miss Pauline Millward of Shibden Hall Museum; Mrs Joanna Hutton of Haworth; as always, the Brontë Society, and in particular Dr Juliet Barker and Ms Sally Johnson. Thanks are due to the Council of the Brontë Society for their special permission to print a transcript of the hitherto untranscribed accountbook stub. Thanks are also due to the Headmaster of

Casterton School for his help in acquiring a photograph of the 'ledger', and to Dr Betteridge of Calderdale archives for assistance in selecting an illustration of High Sunderland.

Quotations at chapter headings are by Emily Brontë unless otherwise stated.

Illustrations

Plates 3, 4, 5, 8, 10, 11, 12, 13, and 14 © Brontë Society are reproduced by kind permission. Plate 1 is by courtesy of G. Walker, The Parish Church of St James, Thornton, and thanks are also due to Revd Patrick Foreman. Plate 2 is reproduced by kind permission of Calderdale District Archives. Plate 6 is reproduced by kind permission of G. Vinestock, Headmaster of Casterton School, Kirkby Lonsdale and thanks are also due to Cumbria County Record Office. Plate 7 Edward Chitham. Plate 9 is reproduced by kind permission of the National Portrait Gallery, London. The maps on pages 286, 287, and 288 are reproduced by kind permission of Birmingham Public Libraries.

Introduction

Thy sweet, low voice waked in my heart
Dead memories of my mother's love;
My long-lost sister's artless art
Lived in thy smiles, my gentle dove.

– attributed to Hugh Brunty of Ballynaskeagh

Emily,
I love thee; . . .
Would we two had been twins of the same mother!
. . . Ah me!
I am not thine: I am a part of thee.
. . . We shall become the same, we shall be one
Spirit within two frames, oh! Wherefore two?
One passion in twin hearts, which grows and grew . . .
One hope within two wills, one will beneath
Two overshadowing minds, one life, one death,
One Heaven, one Hell, one immortality,
And one annihilation.

– P. B. Shelley, *Epipsychidion*

Emily Brontë's life and character are full of fascination. How could a young woman without much formal education and with little experience of life produce such an extraordinary work as *Wuthering Heights*?

She certainly sets the biographer a difficult task. There is so little external material that the temptation to use imagination is strong. Some of her biographers have admitted this, and produced credible portraits using an authorial sixth sense. But some biographies which appear to be factual have slipped in imaginary details without warning. Where legend is so strong, this seems dangerous.

I prefer to regard this book as investigative biography. Some factual matters about Emily's life can be settled once and for all; a number have been finally clarified within the last few years. I shall be able to state these as facts and draw conclusions from them. Many questions cannot be answered. In these cases I shall present the evidence as clearly as possible and try to weigh it. Complete references will be given, even though these may seem distracting; only in this way can the reader follow up and check my assertions.

There is a third category, between fact and theory. This includes places, objects and people we know Emily must have seen, but of which we have no independent record. For instance, we can still go and visit Law Hill, or Cowan Bridge, and see with our own eyes what Emily must have seen with hers. In dealing with such places, I shall write 'Emily would see' or 'Emily would have seen' rather than 'did see' if there is no external record of her at that point. Not all her biographers have been so careful, and legendary material has crept into the record.

The rest of this introduction discusses how we come to understand anything at all about Emily Brontë's life. In it I shall describe the sources for our knowledge in detail that might be thought fussy unless one has had to wade through the quantity of inaccuracies which has passed for biographical data on the Brontës. This is even more evident in the case of Emily than the others; as Muriel Spark and Derek Stanford pointed out years ago, after her death her acquaintances began to think she was 'no normal being'. Later accounts of the mature Emily have to be scrutinized very carefully; this caution applies also to the accounts given by her elder sister, Charlotte.

Charlotte was by far the best placed of anyone to offer detail about Emily's life and thought. She did so in several ways, fact and fiction. She wrote

1 A 'Biographical Notice of Ellis and Acton Bell' (dated 19 September 1850);
2 An 'Editor's Preface to the new 1850 edition' of *Wuthering Heights*;
3 An introduction to her selections from Poems by 'Ellis Bell'.

Charlotte also talked of Emily to Mrs Gaskell, her own subsequent biographer, and she wrote Emily into parts of *Shirley*, after having perhaps also used her sister to some extent in *Jane Eyre*. This fictionalized evidence cannot be rejected out of hand, and we shall examine the relation between 'Lowood' and Cowan Bridge School in Chapter 4. As for *Shirley*, the interweaving of imaginative material is hard to disentangle.

Mrs Gaskell wrote:

> The character of Shirley herself, is Charlotte's representation of Emily. I mention this, because all that I, a stranger, have been able to learn about her has not tended to give either me, or my readers, a pleasant impression of her. But we must remember how little we are acquainted with her, compared to that sister, who, out of her more intimate knowledge, says that she "was genuinely good, and truly great", and who tried to depict her character in Shirley Keeldar, as what Emily Brontë would have been, had she been placed in health and prosperity.[1]

We shall be following Charlotte's relations with Emily and seeing how 'intimately' Charlotte was acquainted with her at different periods of their lives. They shared a good deal, but not everything. On the face of it, Charlotte's aim of presenting her sister 'as she would have been' if in health and prosperity is ridiculous. If Emily had been an heiress, she would not have been herself.

But it seems from her letters of late 1848 onwards that Charlotte became obsessed with her dying and dead sister. Emily worked her way into the character of Shirley whether Charlotte wished it or not. So it was after Shirley's station in life and cluster of ancillary characters had been established that elements of Emily Brontë grafted themselves on to her. In creating Shirley, Charlotte seems to be trying to plumb Emily, trying to understand her and record her, not giving a cut-and-dried view of a character she could read clearly. We have two major passages in which Shirley's attitude to nature is illustrated. These certainly seem to reflect Emily's trance-like appreciation of nature, but they do not attempt a rational theology (which Emily might have been quite capable of supplying) and they may over-romanticize. Charlotte wrote and talked of Emily, just as she wrote and talked of Maria and Elizabeth, through a haze of feeling, the very haze which makes her books so popular. She was indignant about their fate; similarly everything she wrote about Emily in 1849–50 was affected by what Jane Eyre calls her 'organ of veneration'.

However, Charlotte was a close observer of external habits. She includes in *Shirley* some habitual characteristics of Emily, here and there confirmed from other sources. We shall be justified in taking some of Shirley's mannerisms, perhaps some of her aphorisms, as Emily's. For example, Shirley lay on the hearthrug to read; so did Emily. Shirley doted on her rough dog; so did Emily. I shall use such vignettes, with acknowledgement and caution, in filling out the evidence for Emily Brontë's character.

Anne could have told us a good deal about Emily. From about 1830 she had been closer to her than anyone else. But Emily does not appear in *Agnes Grey* or *Wildfell Hall*. Anne was less obsessed with Emily, because she knew her better. In her late poetry she tells us something about the progress of their alliance and how it broke down. Anne was a more conservative moralist than Emily. She must have argued with her sister as both tried to make sense of Branwell's collapse. *Wildfell Hall* conveys implicit criticism of *Wuthering Heights*, but it does accept some of Emily's predispositions, and does not attack her personally. We shall use Anne's late work to illuminate Emily's own statements of belief in the period 1845–8.

Ellen Nussey is the most copious source of our knowledge of the Brontës. She was totally loyal to the memory of her life-long friend, and regarded herself as the guardian of Charlotte's reputation. She kept hundreds of Charlotte's letters, but ran a black pen through anything she considered embarrassing. Every biographer from Mrs Gaskell to Clement Shorter consulted Ellen, over a period of forty years. She wrote back politely and interminably, telling remarkably consistent stories, but she edited her material mentally. In any case, Ellen did not know Emily very well, though the two did achieve a friendly relationship. What little Ellen does say, we can build on.

We shall need to use Charlotte's letters again, though every biographer has used them. Their dating and editing is very faulty, and some are lost.[2] Ellen seems to have gone over them in retrospect and misdated them through lapses of memory. There are huge gaps, for example for 1837, when Emily was just creating her *altera ego*, 'A. G. A.'. Non-literary records in Emily's own hand are trivial.

For about sixty years after the death of Emily in 1849 there were old Haworth residents who had known her. They were constantly badgered by seekers after Brontë lore. Some enjoyed the process. Most of their names are easily discovered, but we are still lacking a few. It is important to find and assess these very various eye-witnesses, who added a great deal of local colour to the works of the nineteenth-century biographers. They talk of the everyday Emily, not the one concerned with Gondal or Heathcliff, but the dog-taming, bread-making Emily who was kind to children but wouldn't teach in the Sunday School. From one witness, however, a pistol-shooting Emily emerges, and another tells of a long-legged young Emily climbing out of a top-floor window and smashing a cherry tree.

Four of the witnesses to the lives of the Brontës were servants. Nancy and Sarah Garrs were two young girls taken on by Mr Brontë at Thornton. Nancy had been at the Bradford Industrial School and was recommended to the family. She transferred to Haworth with them and stayed until the children went to Cowan Bridge. She died in 1886, aged eighty-two, being known then as Nancy Wainwright; her husband Pat having predeceased her. She had spent some of her time in Sheffield, and was not consulted by all the nineteenth-century biographers, but Mrs Chadwick did speak to her some time in the 1880s. Sarah also helped to nurse the children. She married a Mr Newsome and moved to Crawfordsville, USA. About 1886 she wrote to Erskine Stuart and confirmed some details. A third sister, Martha Taylor, 'contributed some interesting anecdotes of Haworth Parsonage' to Erskine Stuart; these seem to have concerned Branwell, and may have been second-hand, since we have no direct record of Martha Garrs working in the parsonage.[3]

Two other girls were taken on at the parsonage later. They were Martha and Tabitha Brown, daughters of the sexton whose influence on Branwell may not have been all good.[4] The latter is not to be confused with Tabitha Aykroyd, the old servant of whom all the Brontës were very fond, but who died in 1855. Tabitha Brown married and became Mrs Ratcliffe.

She was consulted by Miss A. M. F. Robinson and Mrs Chadwick, and by Whiteley Turner, whose *Spring-Time Saunter* was written in 1905, though published later. Tabitha was very firm on the authorship of *Wuthering Heights*. Her sister, Martha, who had been christened by Mr Brontë on 8 June 1828, owned many Brontë relics and was an informant of Mrs Gaskell. She was also interviewed by a Mrs Cortazzo, who visited Haworth in 1866 and 1882. Some reminiscences of Martha Brown appeared in the *Cornhill Magazine* for July 1910.[5]

William Wood the carpenter visited the Brontës frequently and was involved in making anything they needed out of wood. He talked to Mrs Gaskell and Miss Robinson. To Mrs Chadwick, he observed that he had made all the Brontë coffins except Anne's.[6] Some of his financial accounts have been published, giving contemporary evidence of some external matters concerning the family.[7]

John Greenwood, the Haworth stationer, became Mrs Gaskell's right-hand man during her visits to Haworth to collect material for her book. He must have told her a great deal, some of which she did not record. He himself wrote a notebook of reminiscences, and saved a tracing of a picture of the three girls which would otherwise have been lost.[8]

During the controversy over Cowan Bridge, several eye-witnesses wrote to the *Halifax Guardian*. They included the two superintendents, Mrs Hill (formerly Andrews) and Mrs Connor (formerly Evans). (Mrs Harben, who also wrote to the *Halifax Guardian*, turned out not to have been at Cowan Bridge during the Brontës' stay.)[9] Some of the pupils in Belgium, including the Wheelwrights, emerged quite late on and gave material to Mrs Chadwick.[10] A Mrs Watkinson proved an important witness to Law Hill.[11] Souvenir hunters journeyed to Haworth from the 1850s, and occasionally brought back scraps of knowledge which may be important. They are often secondary sources, deriving their knowledge from one of the Haworth villagers already mentioned.

I shall try to track to its source every piece of information occurring in the biographies, and to evaluate it. This has to be done, since some outrageous liberties have been taken with the evidence. I shall also make cautious use of the internal evidence in the poems Emily wrote. In them autobiographical and fictional material is closely intertwined. An unorthodox way into discovering the limits of actual autobiography has proved to be contemporary weather records, a method first advocated by Herbert Dingle.[12] In *Brontë Facts and Brontë Problems*[13] I investigated the stages by which Emily turned her observations and feelings about weather and season into poetry. In doing so I built up a picture of her methods and felt I was gaining expertise in understanding where autobiography ceases and fiction begins. The reader will judge whether my suggestions accord with facts.

Early biographers of Charlotte steered clear of Emily, and it was not until 1883 that A. M. F. Robinson produced the first book devoted to her. The decreed scope of her book was little help to her, and many questions went unasked. Ellen Nussey's emollient view is paramount, disregarding the cauldron of jarring feelings that so often threatened to blow off its lid and destroy Emily's sanity. A complete reconstruction is never going to be possible, but by patient delving and thought – especially about the neglected area of Emily's childhood – an approximation to a fair portrait of Emily Brontë can be slowly built up. In life, she took few pains to be understood. I should like to think she might recognize herself in this portrait more easily than in most of the others.

1

'Papish Pat' Goes to Yorkshire

There are a few Novels . . . which are not only harmless, but very entertaining and instructive.

– Patrick Brontë, 1818

The Brontës were not born at Haworth. They were not even of Yorkshire ancestry. Yorkshire moorland scenery so stamped itself into *Wuthering Heights* that it is easy to believe so, yet Mr and Mrs Brontë were from Ireland and Cornwall respectively. Emily was born at Thornton and did not see the parsonage at Haworth until she was almost two.

The Irish background mattered.[1] Some may see reflections of Irish 'national character' in the Brontës. Whether we accept such concepts or not, some of their qualities seem to stem from their ancestry. Emily's grandfather was a traditional storyteller, with a fund of old legends, family history, ballads and folksongs in his head. He electrified his listeners when he told tales of the devil avenging faithless lovers, or of Irish wars, or perhaps recited long sagas based on Irish tradition. He may have had political theories too, which he declaimed to a mixed audience of Catholics and Protestants in his corn kiln, during the dangerous years of the late 1790s. Emily's uncle went out to fight at Ballynahinch, presumably taking the good wishes of Patrick with him. In retreat, he was chased through the gorse by the redcoats. Later, they arrived in Ballynaskeagh and set fire to Patrick's home. His father allegedly dissuaded the Welsh soldiers by talking to them in what seems to have been his own native tongue, Irish Gaelic.

Emily's grandmother, 'Ayles', was a great beauty, according to those who had known her. She remained loyal to Catholic religion even after marrying the apparently religionless Hugh Brunty. Uncle James played the fiddle and came over to England on a tour of harvest work. We shall meet him and Uncle Hugh in these pages. With Walsh and William, they played practical jokes on their neighbours, pretending there were ghosts in the old mill at Ballynaskeagh. Clannish and strong-minded, the Bruntys of County Down danced the old dances and sang the old songs, calling to each other through an aurochs horn discovered in a bog. They all had sharp ears and persuasive tongues. There was also a family mystery.

The eldest of the brothers and sisters was Patrick, born on St Patrick's Day, 17 March 1777. His poor but gifted parents were soon talking and singing to him as the baby lay by the scorching fire which served to roast the corn in the little cabin at Imdel. (Fire was always held in great respect by the adult Patrick.) The boy soon began to fend for himself. He was blacksmith's assistant, weaver, and then local schoolteacher. He read by firelight, we may suppose, just as he read on the top of Imdel fort on a summer's day. His charming way with children is shown by the fact that the Presbyterians employed him, a part-Papist, to teach their children, even (in at least one case) when they could have had a choice of teachers, being rich enough to travel a distance. The impression made on local people by Patrick Brunty in his youth suggests that he was an extraordinary man. He had a very advanced view of education, and has surely been given far too little credit for the freedom of self-expression and development he gave to his children. Long afterwards, it was recalled in Ulster that he had fostered the education of *girls*, as he undoubtedly fostered that of his own five daughters.[2]

Ellen Nussey, Charlotte's friend, remembered Patrick telling stories to the children at breakfast-time. They were then in their teens, but there is a clear implication that he had always done so. Emily's first biographer, Miss A. M. F. Robinson, understood that it was Emily who most appreciated these wild stories and 'at five years of age used to startle the nursery with her fantastic fairy stories'.[3]

We now enter the field of speculation concerning the mystery of the origin of the Brontës. Local people in County Down had heard the older Hugh, Patrick's father, tell a tale about his own childhood. He had been brought up near the Boyne river, some miles out of Drogheda, right at the centre of a web of Irish oral culture. Here a wicked uncle, Welsh or Walsh, had oppressed him and taken away his birthright. It seems possible that Hugh told that this uncle had been a foundling, discovered on a Liverpool boat. In the *The Brontës' Irish Background* I have suggested a possible origin for this fairy tale, which is quite impossible to prove. However, what seems clear is that this 'foundling' story *was* told by Hugh, and that Patrick knew it. In Celtic countries, family origins have always been important.

Patrick Brunty went to Cambridge, a remarkable feat. He began to spell his name differently, mixed with aristocrats, and perhaps thought he would be a great man. He had the intelligence and thoughtfulness necessary for greatness, but he was not a flatterer, and his awkward honesty did not win friends in high places. His own word for himself is 'eccentrick'. As a young clergyman, he met a bright girl from Cornwall, Maria Branwell, and married her.[4] His works show that he had a high and romantic view of womanhood, and his early married years were his high point. When Maria died, the light went out of his life. We shall meet him throughout the story of Emily's life, a tolerant though excitable parent perhaps prone to temper.

From Maria the children learnt Methodism. They learnt that there was a world beyond this one, which God had created, and to which he wanted everyone to aspire. The eldest Brontë girl, Maria too, walked in exactly the way that both Father and Mother would have wished. The evangelical religion that both parents set before their children had its hard elements. Anne was faithful to them, and Charlotte sometimes so. Emily and Branwell dissented, but the whole notion that there is a transcendental dimension to life, learnt from the Christian religion in the first place, underlies all Emily wrote. Both parents were genuine unswerving believers in this dimension; neither the lives nor the books of any of the children can be understood without realizing this.

Both parents recognized the part of feeling in human life. Emily's life and works cannot be understood unless we realize that in addition to her sharp intelligence, she was possessed of a volatile range of emotions, much like her father. She did not find self-control easy, and sometimes abandoned her mind to these intense feelings, eventually finding outlets through artistic pursuits. Charlotte was not much less intense and variable.

Emily Jane Brontë was the fifth child in the family. She was born on 30 July 1818 in a pleasant stone house on Market Street at Thornton near Bradford. By this time her eldest sister, Maria, was five; Elizabeth was four, Charlotte not much more than two and Branwell just over a year. Mr Brontë and his wife loved children, and the new baby would soon be included in the routine walks round the parish which the older residents later remembered. The smaller children were carried and the eldest led by the hand, on these family rambles round the Thornton lanes. From his youth, walking had been as much of a pleasure as a duty to Mr Brontë. In this respect his family took after him.

Returning to the village, Patrick might make an inspection of the restoration work on the church, or he might lead the way back to the parsonage, and after settling the children with the young Garrs sisters, go into his study to continue his writing. He certainly thought of himself as an author. The composition of new material ran in his family, whether it was Irish poetry or his own simplified morality verse, on which both Burns and Wordsworth were influences. 1818 was the year of *The Maid of Killarney*, a fiction set in the South of Ireland. Among other things, it sought to show the happiness to be gained from living and dying as an Evangelical Christian. Mr Brontë's bardic talent had been harnessed to religion.

If the weather was fine the children would be safe playing in the village street not far from the parsonage, and on the rough closes of ground nearby.[5] Meanwhile Mr Brontë might leave his writing and take the path over the fields to the church. At this time he was very busy bringing the building and the worship up to date. The singers were brought down from the gallery to lead the hymn singing more effectively. Congregational singing is likely to have been loud and hearty in Thornton, and the small children, ushered into the parsonage pew on Sunday, would quickly pick up the words and rhythms of the hymns, which never left them throughout their lives. It is likely that Emily would be taken into church by the Garrs sisters and would show the first signs of having an acute musical ear.

One tale of Thornton has been omitted by many Brontë biographers. An old lady had heard that Mr Brontë had been seen shaving himself on a Sunday, against Sabbatarian prescription. When she asked about it, Mr Brontë apparently said, 'I should like you to keep what you say in your family, but I never shaved in all my life, or was ever shaved by anyone else. I have so little beard that a little clipping every three months is all that is necessary.'[6] This contradicts the evidence of people who saw Mr Brontë late in life and commented on the stubble on his chin.[7] It sounds rather like the kind of yarn the Irish Brontës pitched, with dead-pan faces, about ghosts in the glen. Like them, Mr Brontë must have been a leg-puller.

We have no exact record of when Emily started to walk. With so many elders to copy, she might well have been an early walker as she began to explore the inside of the parsonage. The front door would be open in summer, and we have seen the children playing in the street. In worse weather they might climb the stairs up from the kitchen to the maids' room and the large room which Ivy Holgate suggests may have been the night nursery. They are less likely to have played on the other staircase, which led to the principal bedrooms. Three stone steps led from the kitchen to the cobbled yard behind, which was surrounded by a high wall. This would make a good alternative playground to the road, but may have seemed rather shut in, even prison-like.

One of Mr Brontë's 'beautifying' touches to the old church was to add a bell turret. The place then became known as the 'Bell chapel', and the bell would be rung for Sunday service as a sign to the outlying farmers to begin their journey up to church. 'The sabbath bell' features in a poem of 1839; perhaps it was at Thornton that Emily first heard it so called. She had an extraordinarily retentive memory, by then just focusing.[8]

So much has been written about the Brontës as recluses, with some justification after 1825, that Mr Brontë's circle of friends may be forgotten. In Ulster, he showed an easy charm. At Thornton he soon made the acquaintance of Mr John Firth and his daughter Elizabeth.[9] Elizabeth, born in 1797, kept a diary, in which she recorded the frequent visits of the Brontë family to Kipping, the gracious house where she lived with her widowed father. She became godmother to Elizabeth Brontë. The diary provides documentary evidence for the

Brontë births and visits. During Emily's childhood the family constantly visited Kipping on a friendly basis. All the children spent the day of Anne's birth, 17 January 1820, at the house. If Emily would one day be 'reserved' and the others shy, this was not due to lack of social opportunity when they were very young. Mr and Mrs Brontë and their children were happy guests at Kipping. After his wife's death Mr Brontë proposed marriage to Elizabeth Firth, but was rejected.

With his family growing fast, Patrick was willing to take on a larger church and population. The controversy surrounding his appointment to the perpetual curacy of Haworth is well known and need not be chronicled again.[10]. The question was whether the parishioners had a right to choose their own clergyman, and it had nothing to do with Patrick himself. Once the villagers had been allowed to make their own choice, they accepted him. He was also acceptable to his fellow clergy in Bradford parish. Throughout his life he got on well with his colleagues, and his interminable correspondence with them and other public agencies shows that Emily was not brought up in a misanthropic household.

Elizabeth Firth reported that Mr Brontë was licensed to Haworth on 25 February 1820. There followed two months in which he seems to have been active at both churches, his old one at Thornton and the new one over the moors at Haworth. In April, the family belongings were moved on eight carts along the high tracks to their new home.[11] The family must surely have felt the move to be momentous. It was so: it is difficult to see how the literary talents of the Brontë children could have matured in the same way except in such a cut-off moorland village, with the churchyard at one side of the parsonage front garden, the lapwings and whinchats at the other, and homely Yorkshire talk surrounding them in the narrow village streets.

2

A 'Somewhat Eccentrick' Upbringing

The truth is, that happiness and misery have their origin within, depending comparatively little on outward circumstances. The mind is its own place.

– Patrick Brontë

Emily was to spend all but a few months of the next twenty years at Haworth parsonage. We need to familiarize ourselves with this beloved home of hers, but it will be no hardship. Even the casual visitor to Haworth can see how the family fitted their house like a glove. Part of the attraction of the Brontë story is their evocative four-square house, facing the gales from the high moors and brooding over the churchyard tombs below. Emily loved the house as much as any of the family. It provided a constant backdrop for her reading, writing and thinking. The views from the windows and the sounds heard inside and out are frequent in the poetry and contribute to *Wuthering Heights*. An exploration of the parsonage is a pleasant necessity.

Today the Brontë Society has made this easy. Great efforts have been made to restore the original building so that it corresponds as far as possible to what it was in the nineteenth century. Mrs Jocelyn Kellett's splendid book discusses the ways in which the house was altered during the Brontës' time there, and I shall be making many references to it.[1] Once Patrick had died, Mr Wade, his successor, was anxious to rebuild both church and parsonage. Parts of his additions have turned out to be valuable in providing extra accommodation for the museum, but they need to be thought away when when we try to visualize the Brontës in residence.

Charlotte too made alterations after her sisters died. Finding herself comfortably off in the early 1850s she decided to make the house more habitable for herself and her father, and ultimately for her husband, Mr Nicholls. Her changes were subtler than the later ones of Mr Wade but if we are to see the young Brontës in their childhood, these too have to be thought away.

If the Brontës entered the house by the front door on that far-off day in April 1820, they would see a wider hall than can be seen now. The wall on the right is the same, but that on the left was moved about eighteen inches into the hall in 1850. The new family, peering round the door into the hall in 1820 would not see the splendid archway, which fits the later measurements. Directly ahead of the children, the stairs occupied their present position. There was access below the half-landing to the cellar, where we shall find the beer being kept. There was also a small window, straight ahead, under the stairs, from which the back yard could be seen.

Once Mr Brontë had settled in, the room on the right of the hall became his study and remained so for the rest of his life. There are indications that this was the 'holy of holies' where Emily and the others would venture with respect. On the left of the hall was the dining room, later the scene of many imaginary adventures in childhood and some sadder times in adulthood. Emily ultimately died there. Behind the study was the kitchen. We shall find Emily baking in it in later years. On the other side, behind the dining room, was a store room, which was converted in the end for Mr Nicholls to use as a study. In 1820 it may not have been possible even to enter it from the hall. The door was probably outside, leading into the yard.

Possibly the Brontë family didn't enter their new home by the front door. They may have called the carts to a halt in the lane, near the old barn which was on the site of the present car park. They could then approach the back of the house, through a side gate, leading across a thin patch of garden (Mr Wade's extension covers this) and reach the house through the back kitchen.[2]

We know very little about the back premises at the parsonage, since no illustration taken from the rear has yet been found, and the rear was totally rebuilt by Wade. Old plans show that there was an extensive projection at the back, and old photographs prove that it had two storeys and at least one fireplace, the smoke from which escaped through an ugly tall fireclay chimney. On the ground floor was the back kitchen (to be distinguished from 'the kitchen'), where we find servants engaged in menial tasks. Above were probably the servants' bedrooms. The back kitchen was joined to the main kitchen by a passageway, apparently flagged, but little is known about it.[3]

We may guess that the Brontë children soon ran upstairs to see their bedrooms and stare out at the surrounding view. There were five rooms upstairs, but only the two over the dining room and Mr Brontë's study were without defects. It seems likely that Mr and Mrs Brontë would sleep either over the study or over the dining room, and in one of those rooms Mrs Brontë was soon to die. At the rear, the room over the kitchen would eventually become Branwell's. It seems likely that his view would be limited by the two-storey outbuildings. The room over the store had perhaps already undergone some conversion and at this time could apparently be approached only by an outside staircase of stone. Later Tabitha Aykroyd, the old servant, would sleep there.

The fifth room on the first floor was the little slip room which would become Emily's bedroom, after doing duty as a nursery when the children were young. However, it does not do to judge the space by what can be seen now. As in the case of the hall, this room was narrowed by eighteen inches in Charlotte's alterations of 1850. It is impossible to say when this slip room was created. At one time, even perhaps when the Brontës arrived, it may have been part of the landing.

All children love staring out of windows and Emily at any rate continued to enjoy this. The view to the east, from the front of the house, would then be unobscured by high trees. She could look across the churchyard to the church tower, which was not then as tall as it is now. The surroundings of the church were to be tidied and improved in 1824.[4] On the other side of Church Lane the schools would not be erected until 1832.[5] The Black Bull, however, would be visible, and the children would be able to get used during the following weeks to the view of the top of the village street, and the moorland over which they had come on their way from Thornton.

Both back rooms originally had views of the moors as far as Stanbury. We do not know whether the children could see these views because the height and precise location of the back premises is still doubtful. Later on Emily would become particularly fond of the west wind, which blew across these moors from Lancashire.

All water in the house had to be drawn from the pump. From an old plan we can guess there was one at the north end of the outhouses. There may have been another in the back kitchen, but this is uncertain.[6] For heat, the Brontës seem to have burned peat, just as Patrick had done in Ulster. This was stored in an outhouse across the yard backing on to the lane. Geese were later kept in 'the peat house', presumably this building. At the south-west corner of the garden stood the earth closet, which remained untouched in the Wade's alterations, but was taken down in the 1950s.[7]

We shall soon encounter the Brontë children engaged in boisterous games round the house. Detail is lacking, but it is worth remembering that they could run all the way round it without going through it. The evidence suggests that there was little attempt to do anything much with the gardens, even in the front. There were some fruit trees (currants, apparently), but no old-fashioned banks of hollyhocks and lupins. We may guess – there is no record – that the children would play on the outside staircase at the back. The cellar had a small window facing out just above ground level, looking towards the wall dividing the garden from the front lane: it seems likely that the cellar would play its part in the kind of imaginative games we shall soon hear of. It would do well as a prison, perhaps; but we have no definite proof of such use.

Haworth, though not a parish, was a large curacy.[8] The 'township' contained 10,540 acres, 'nearly half of it in uncultivated heaths and commons', as the *Yorkshire Directory* reported in 1848. It was more remote than Thornton and even today, though both are part of Bradford Metropolitan Borough, it has not been suburbanized in the same way. The 1823 *Yorkshire Directory* quotes the population in 1821 as 4,663, scattered over many hamlets, with the main nuclei at Stanbury, Near and Far Oxenhope, and Haworth village, then largely confined to the hillside beyond the river. Cloth manufacture was what it lived by. The 1823 *Directory* gives the most important woolstaplers as William Eccles, Joseph Sutcliffe, W. J. and J. Townend, Robert Pickles, Heaton and Sugden, and D. & W. Townend. Worsted manufacturers were the Feather brothers and James Greenwood. Among the names of the lesser tradesmen, some were to be important in the Brontë story: John Wood, plumber and glazier, John Greenwood, cabinet maker, and Abraham Wilkinson, who kept the Black Bull public house.

Haworth has been described so many times that it is superfluous to describe it again in detail. The sharp rise of the main street is most impressive and has proved too steep for motor vehicles at times. For horse-drawn carts it must have proved hard indeed, but we must assume that they frequently negotiated it all the same. It was a vital link between the moorland sheep-farms and the towns and cities. Beyond, the high moors stretched to Lancashire, providing a tract of open country that has changed little since Celtic times. Mr Brontë would see similarities between this and the Mourne mountains, and his children would want to liken it to the world of Walter Scott and the high fells of Wordsworth. Even in the twentieth century, adopted by the souvenir-sellers and supplied with a by-pass to help tourists to reach the top of the hill, Haworth is a workaday place with a rough edge to it. These surroundings were to suit the young Brontës admirably. Emily, even more than the others, fitted snugly into the landscape.

It is hard to tell how far Emily Brontë could have known her own mother. She died when the little girl was just over three.[9] In a smaller family, or if Emily had been the eldest, she would certainly have retained some memories of her. Charlotte claimed to remember her mother nursing Branwell on her lap, but no comment is recorded from Emily. A close relationship is possible, since the gap between Emily and Anne was longer than that between the other children, and possibly she had more opportunity to experience her mother than the other children had.

In any case, we cannot imagine Emily to have been a consistently neglected baby. All that we know of her two eldest sisters suggests that in their different ways they would be actively interested and involved in petting her. I shall suggest that the two eldest were rather more different from each other than is always recognized. Mr Brontë seems to have seen Maria as an intellectual, the successor to himself (although female) and repository of learning and religious fervour.[10] Elizabeth, less quick at learning, may have had more to do with the tiny tots. When Emily chose a pseudonym, she used 'Ellis'. Perhaps this was partly in deference to her Irish grandmother, 'Ayles', but it may also have been a tribute to her dead sister. We cannot know such things for certain; there were other Elizabeths in Emily's life, including her aunt. It is worth noting that as she moved through life Emily became more attached to Anne (who was like Elizabeth) than Charlotte (who had traits of Maria).

The next year, 1821, was to prove disastrous.[11] Mr Brontë had apparently spent a busy seven or eight months working himself into his new parish and getting to know the locals. He might have looked forward to a period of stability during which he could reform and enhance the church institutions, then settle his own family and return to the field of literary composition. But by the end of the year he was a widower, writing despondently to his old vicar at Dewsbury, John Buckworth, about the decline and death of his dear wife.

Mrs Gaskell got into a good deal of trouble about the way she reported the details of this year. Her informant was a woman who had been employed by Mr Brontë as nurse, and who apparently clashed with the two young servant girls. It seems that she encountered examples of the kind of thunderous temper in Mr Brontë that Emily illustrates in *Wuthering Heights*. As a result the nurse left, and many years later told Mrs Gaskell some stories that shocked Mr Brontë when he saw them in print, and which these days are generally discounted. It may seem unnecessary, in a life of Emily, to try to evaluate these reports, but against this there is some evidence that Emily was her father's favourite, whose character may have been very like his.

The disputed evidence reported to Mrs Gaskell by the dismissed nurse consisted of the following stories:

1 Mr Brontë had a fancy 'of not letting them have flesh-meat to eat . . . he thought that children should be

brought up simply and hardily: so they had nothing but potatoes for their dinner'.[12]

2 '. . . one day when the children had been out on the moors, and rain had come on, she thought their feet would be wet, and accordingly she rummaged out some coloured boots which had been given to them by a friend – the Mr Morgan, who married "Cousin Jane" . . . . These little pairs she ranged round the kitchen fire to warm; but, when the children came back, the boots were nowhere to be found; only a very strong odour of burnt leather was perceived. Mr Brontë had come in and seen them; they were too gay and luxurious for his children, and would foster a love of dress; so he had put them into the fire.'[13]

3 '. . . some one had given Mrs Brontë a silk gown . . . . She kept it treasured up in her drawers, which were generally locked. One day, however, while in the kitchen, she remembered that she had left the key in her drawer, and, hearing Mr Brontë up-stairs, she augured some ill to her dress, and, running up in haste, she found it cut into shreds.'[14]

4 'Once he got the hearth-rug, and, stuffing it up the grate, deliberately set it on fire, and remained in the room in spite of the stench, until it had smouldered and shrivelled away into uselessness.'[15]

5 'Another time he took some chairs, and sawed away at the backs till they were reduced to the condition of stools.'[16]

The nurse gave Mrs Gaskell some further information, which has not been disputed, and which will be dealt with later.

Writing in 1885, Leyland challenged these stories of Mr Brontë's eccentricity, basing his remarks on a conversation with Mr Brontë which took place on 8 July 1857, when Mr Brontë was eighty.[17] The old man then said clearly, 'Everything in that book which relates to my conduct to my family is either false or distorted.' He believed Mrs Gaskell had listened to village scandal, and had sought information from a discarded servant. He means the nurse, whose name does not seem to be discoverable.

Leyland challenged Mrs Gaskell's estimate of the character of the nurse, who had 'been detected in proceedings which caused Mr Brontë to dismiss her at once'. We cannot know what these 'proceedings' were but later servants were forbidden the cellar where the drink was kept. Leyland then says that the nurse had told these accounts of Mr Brontë's temper and conduct to 'a minister of the place'; it was in this way that Mrs Gaskell became acquainted with her.

The story about the silk gown was partially confirmed by Nancy Garrs, who gave it a totally different twist. She says of the dress that Mr Brontë disliked its enormous sleeves and one day, finding the opportunity, cut them off.

> The whole thing was a joke, which Mrs Brontë at once guessed at, and, going upstairs, she brought the dress down, saying to Nancy, 'Look what he has done; that falls to your share.' Nancy declares the other stories to be wholly unfounded [continues Leyland]. She speaks of Mr Brontë as a 'most affectionate husband; there was never a more affectionate father, never a kinder master . . . .'[18]

It must be said of the first of the nurse's stories that the young Brontës are later to be found cooking and eating meat of all kinds. However, this report comes from 1821. Mr Brontë himself had been reared on potatoes and herring, and he may perhaps in the early days have thought it a healthy and frugal diet. The two incidents involving pretty or fine clothes may be put down to an Evangelical dislike of adornment, the extreme of which is seen in Mr Brocklehurst's attitude in *Jane Eyre*. But the Brontë sisters never did dress fashionably, and they may quite well have picked up their Puritan attitude to dress from their father.[19]

On 30 July 1857, Patrick wrote with insight to Mrs Gaskell,

> I do not deny that I am somewhat eccentrick. Had I been numbered amongst the calm, sedate, concentric men of the world, I should not have been as I now am, and I should in all probability never have had such children as mine have been.[20]

In this he admits that he was *not* calm, *not* sedate. Cutting the arms off a silk dress, whether for a joke or not, seems consistent with the admission of eccentricity; and it appears perfectly possible that Mr Brontë could have burnt shoes or even mutilated chairs, without being any the less affectionate to his wife and children. His robust sense of humour and firm religious principles are part of his varied character, like his charm and warmth. Mrs Gaskell was also told of his habit of firing off pistols at random. He taught Emily to shoot, as we shall see, and she became adept.

The nurse also alleged that the children were 'spiritless' during this time: 'You would never have known there was a child in the house.' Of course, they were not spiritless, but, under the shadow of illness, they learnt to be quiet. Maria (aged seven) and Elizabeth (six) would lead the children hand-in-hand towards the moors (not actually across the moors, perhaps, as has sometimes been suggested). These two took 'thoughtful care' of the toddlers.[21]

We have firm evidence that at this time Maria would take the newspaper up to the 'children's study' (presumably the slip room) 'and be able to tell one everything when she came out; debates in parliament, and I don't know what all. She was as good as a mother to her sisters and brother . . . . There never were such good children.'[22] Maria, it seems, was a typical first child, identifying with her father, who had also been the eldest of a tribe. He too had learnt politics from his father and had quickly absorbed Hugh's moral and artistic precepts. Maria's mental and spiritual inheritance must have been abundant, and she was as emotionally intense as her parents.

The children, said the nurse, 'were good little creatures. Emily was the prettiest.'[23] This will not be the last time that witnesses emphasize Emily's prettiness, over and above that of the other girls. It will be important to establish that as a little girl, she was bright and attractive. This is certainly the impression given here.

Mrs Brontë declined steadily through 1821, after being taken ill on 29 January. Our source for the events of the rest of the year is Mr Brontë's letter to Buckworth.[24] He describes a 'gloomy day, a day of clouds and darkness', when three of the children (he does not say which three) were ill with scarlet fever. Next day the other three 'were in the same condition'. At this time, 'death seemed to have laid his hand on my dear wife . . . . She was cold and silent, and seemed hardly to notice what was passing around her.' This account may correspond to that of the nurse, quoted by Mrs Gaskell, to the effect that 'the mother was not very anxious to see her children, probably because the sight of them, knowing how soon they were to be left motherless, would have agitated her too much'. It is not quite supported by Nancy Garrs, who apparently told Mrs Chadwick that Mrs Brontë was interested in her children 'to the very last . . . though she could only see them at intervals, and one at a time, as it upset her'.

Like the nurse, Nancy Garrs stressed young Maria's care for the smaller children, though she did not give prominence to Elizabeth.[25] Her sister, Sarah, kept the girls quiet by teaching them needlework. Whether Emily, at three, was included in this is not clear, but Charlotte produced a chemise, which pleased her dying mother very much. All the children recovered 'at length' from the scarlet fever, but we may assume that April 1821 was an unhappy month for everyone until Elizabeth Branwell arrived from Penzance. She took over the reins, as a mature adult, from Maria, the Garrs sisters, and the nurse. Mr Brontë speaks of her as 'behaving as an affectionate mother' to his children.[26]

Mr Brontë did not hesitate to call in medical aid for his sick wife. This would be Emily's first acquaintance with doctors, and it seems probable that the waste of money and effort involved made an impression on her. Despite everything the doctor could do, Mrs Brontë became worse and worse. Her mind became disturbed; her husband put this down to diabolic intervention.[27] We cannot know whether Emily heard her mother raving (though Charlotte's most famous book hinges on a mad wife rampaging upstairs). We may well feel that this year of impending death could have had a considerable effect on a three-year-old. If the solitary interviews between the mother and her separate children upset her, we must suppose they would upset the children even more.

Mrs Brontë died on Saturday 15 September, 'calmly' according to her husband, and (as she apparently told the nurse) 'thankful that he never gave me an angry word'. She was buried a week later. Mr Brontë talks of the 'distressing prattle' of his children, reviving her memory hourly. She had passed on with 'humble confidence' in 'heaven, her eternal home', according to Patrick. He may well have used the phrase before the prattling children. To one child at least, later to write of Catherine that 'heaven was not my home', the arrangement may have appeared to be questionable.

3

Almost Swept Away

The house was perfectly still . . . I heard a deep, distant explosion . . . and I perceived a gentle tremor in the chamber in which I was standing, and in the glass of the window just before me.

– Patrick Brontë

It is hard to establish any facts in the next eighteen months of the lives of the Brontë children and in the life of Emily. There were soon to be attempts to send all but Anne to school. In the meantime, it seems that Mr Brontë taught them himself. Nancy Garrs is probably responsible for the report in Mrs Chadwick's book that they began to tell each other stories in bed as a way of remembering facts in geography and history.

> It was in these early days at Haworth that the children really began writing, for the father made a practice of telling them stories to illustrate a geography or history lesson, and they had to write it out the next morning. Consequently they thought it out in bed.[1]

A few years later Emily was sharing a bed with Charlotte. We have no idea what the bedtime arrangements were in 1822–3.

It seems likely that once Anne became a toddler the nurse was no longer needed. We have already seen that the cause of her departure may have been some kind of inefficiency or disgrace. This left the two girls, Nancy and Sarah Garrs, as sole servants living in. Nancy told Mrs Chadwick she would have taken more notice of the children if she had known they were later to be 'so much thought of'.[2] As it was, she seems to have given Mrs Chadwick some simple characterizations of her charges which will be worth examining. Elizabeth was 'gentle like the Branwells', Maria 'untidy', Charlotte 'most excitable and hot-tempered' and Emily had 'the eyes of a half-tamed creature and cared for nobody's opinion, only being happy with her animal pets'.[3]

We cannot be sure that these off-the-cuff phrases do originate from Nancy Garrs, but they sound rather like a servant's summary. The judgement on Charlotte is very strongly supported by records of old Haworth inhabitants; our main concern is Emily, but the evidential back-up found for this characterization of Charlotte (which certainly doesn't come from Mrs Gaskell) may give us confidence in accepting the others.[4] Emily, then, during the time of the Garrs servants, had 'half-tamed eyes'. Later we shall have other accounts of those eyes; at the moment we are seeing them in the face of a four-year-old, who, if the second part of the quotation is correct, is already proving wilful and attached to animals.

After the death of her sister, Elizabeth Branwell had returned to Cornwall. It was later said that she disliked Yorkshire, but it is noticeable that she paid a number of visits to Thornton before the move to Haworth, and once again returned in the final part of 1822.[5] She found the Garrs sisters the sole female guardians of five young girls. They were to remember her as a 'bit of a tyke' who wouldn't let them go down to the cellar to get their own ration of beer.

Apparently on the basis of this remark and an absence of warmth in Charlotte's comments about her, Elizabeth Branwell used to be considered harsh and cold, the possible origin of Aunt Reed. It was supposed she could have inculcated a joyless form of religion into the children, thus causing the revolt of Branwell and the withdrawal of Emily. It was said she believed in a form of Calvinism and might have been sharp to reprove the children's incipient sinfulness.

This may be so, but the Branwells were not Calvinists. As Wesleyans they would certainly not treat any type of sin lightly, but they did not believe in predestined damnation for anyone. Anne's later beliefs were an extension of Wesleyanism. If Aunt Elizabeth talked about Calvinism at all, it would be to condemn it.

More than twenty years ago Eanne Oram wrote a very detailed account of Elizabeth Branwell and her background, most carefully researched from every available source.[6] She points out that from the time when the aunt arrived at Haworth, her life was not her own. Her room, over the dining room, was used by the girls for sewing. Branwell read aloud to Charlotte in that room, and Anne slept there. We find Elizabeth Branwell impervious to the cheek of her nieces in the 1834 diary paper, and she is described by Branwell as 'the guide and director of all the happy days connected with my childhood'. That she was determined seems likely enough. Mrs Gaskell wrote:

> She . . . inspired them with sincere respect and not a little affection. They were, moreover, grateful to her for many habits she had enforced upon them, and which in time had become second nature: order, method, neatness in everything; a perfect knowledge of all kinds of household work; an exact punctuality, and obedience to the laws of time and place, of which no one but themselves, I have heard Charlotte say, could tell the value in after life; with their impulsive natures, it was positive repose to have learnt implicit obedience to external laws.[7]

Determined, methodical, punctual, then; but also tolerant, responsive and generous. 'A bit of a tyke' is going too far, and 'Calvinist' is baseless. Yet the amenability to discipline of Emily must be doubtful.

One enigmatic episode was reported by Mr Brontë to Mrs Gaskell as she probed Charlotte's childhood. Maria and Elizabeth had been sent, briefly, to Crofton Hall school at Wakefield, where once Mrs Mangnall had been headmistress. Their period there does not seem to have been a success and they had caught whooping cough. Some time during the early part of 1824, when they were back at Haworth, Mr Brontë found an old mask and put it on each of his children in turn. Every Brontë biographer has reported this episode and tried to extract some kind of sense from it. It remains as puzzling as ever.

> When my children were very young . . . thinking that they knew more than I had yet discovered, in order to

> make them speak with less timidity, I deemed that if they were put under a sort of cover I might gain my end; and happening to have a mask in the house, I told them all to stand and speak boldly from under the cover of the mask.[8]

So wrote Mr Brontë to Mrs Gaskell.

The project is unselfconsciously bizarre. It seems to be of a kind with the exploits of the Brontës of Ballynaskeagh, hooting to one another through the horn of an aurochs, or waving turnip lanterns in the dark to create an impression of ghosts in the glen. What kind of mask can it have been, and where had Mr Brontë got it? Did the six little Brontës stand side by side in the study, or did they wait outside the door for their turn? Did they see it as a joke, and bubble over with giggles, or was it all in deadly earnest, the strange whim of a father who loved warmly but was unpredictable and even liked to pretend to scare them?

Anne was asked a question about herself, Branwell about the differences between the sexes, Charlotte two questions about books, Elizabeth about the education of women and Maria about 'the best mode of spending time'. Emily was asked a direct question about Branwell. After thirty years the old man could remember what each was asked and how each replied: 'I may not have given precisely their words, but I have nearly done so, as they made a deep and lasting impression on my memory.' However, we should like to know how the questions for this half-humorous test were selected.[9]

In general, they seem appropriate to the child. Anne is asked a straightforward question directly about herself: 'What does a child like you most lack?' (I am paraphrasing). 'Age and experience,' answers Anne, without a trace of originality. Charlotte is asked a bookish question about 'the best book in the world'. She answers that it is the Bible. No surprise here, nor in her supplementary, 'The Book of Nature': these are Father's opinions dutifully echoed. Elizabeth, whom we shall meet as a calm, domestic little girl, and who is the only one at Cowan Bridge not intended to be a governess, is asked about women's education. She tells her father that the best education for a woman is 'That which will make her rule her house well'. Maria is the unworldly genius. She tells her father that the best mode of spending time is 'By laying it out in preparation for a happy eternity.' Branwell, the only boy, is asked to tell the difference between the intellects of men and women. 'By considering the differences in their bodies' he replies (in paraphrase). Considering Branwell's lack of success in comparison with the girls, this is an unperceptive reply, though it may give a clue to that lack of success.

But why was Emily asked a question not relating to herself, but to Branwell? 'I asked the next . . . what I had best do with her brother Branwell, who was sometimes a naughty boy.' 'Reason with him, and when he won't listen to reason, whip him,' answered the small Emily, rising six. Perhaps this is what Father did anyway, but is there a suggestion that Emily felt there might be more whipping of Branwell than actually happened? Several biographers have felt that Emily was jealous of Branwell; this reply may give a little support to that view.[10] Throughout his life Branwell was boastful and had rather an inflated sense of his own capacity. He will soon be trying to rule the roost in the Brontë nursery. Charlotte he will succeed in leading, but not Emily. On the other hand, the effect of having an older brother whom she could surpass if she wished seems to have made Emily contemptuous of most men of her own age and status: she shows respect only to her father and to M. Heger in Belgium, while she despises the curates.

The attitude Mr Brontë had taught to his children, which comes out so clearly in Charlotte's supplementary answer about 'the Book of Nature' was never more plainly shown than in the famous eruption of Crow Hill bog, and the religious use Mr Brontë made of it. 'His lightnings enlightened the world; the earth saw, and trembled', runs Psalm 97, verses 4–5. The Old Testament had a great deal of weight in those days, and Mr Brontë preached his sermon on that text. We need to understand what happened, how Mr Brontë saw it, and thus to deduce how the small Emily saw it, at the age of six.[11]

It was on 2 September 1824, with Maria, Elizabeth and Charlotte safe at school in Cowan Bridge that Mr Brontë sent the others, Branwell, Emily and Anne, across the moor ('the common') for an airing. They had all been ailing, perhaps with the after-effects of the scarlet fever or whooping cough. The day had been 'exceedingly fine', but the party was out a long time. Mr Brontë went to an upper window to look out for them. (The window of course faced away from the church, and must have avoided being hidden by the tall premises behind the kitchen.) Mr Brontë could see that the sky had gone dark. He heard 'the muttering of distant thunder, and saw the frequent flashing of the lightning'. The parsonage itself was very quiet as he stared out of the back window. Then he heard a 'deep and distant explosion' and the room seemed to tremble. The time was about 6 p.m.[12] Mr Brontë thought at the time that it was an earthquake. Though the moors had in fact been broken by an eruption, this was not an ordinary earthquake.[13]

The *Leeds Mercury* explained that the cause was probably the devastating effect of the huge volume of water pouring into the bog all at once, so that the 'mossy embankment' broke. (There had been rain for some days previous.) An area about 1,200 yards in circumference was 'excavated to a depth of from four to six yards', and a similar one, but not so large, lay below. A wide channel led from this cavity. 'Stones of an immense size and weight were hurried by the torrent more than a mile.' A great deal of 'earthy matter' was hustled down the side of the hill.

> This destructive torrent was confined within narrow bounds by the high glen through which it passed until it reached the hamlet of Ponden, where it expanded over some corn-fields, covering them to the depth of several feet; it also filled up the mill pond, choking up the water-course . . . putting an entire stop to the works. A stone bridge was also nearly swept away at this place, and several other bridges in its course were materially damaged . . . . The torrent was seen coming down the glen before it reached the hamlet by a person who gave the alarm, and thereby saved the lives of several children who would otherwise have been swept away.[14]

Emily and the others must have seen the liquefied moor coming down the hill towards them. Halliwell Sutcliffe later wrote, relying on the memories of the inhabitants of Ponden: 'Its solid, oncoming front was black and sticky . . . it seemed as if the whole moor top were turning over on its side and rolling downward.'[15] It is still not clear how Nancy Garrs protected her charges that afternoon. If they had been near the actual bog at the time, there would surely have been little hope for them. It seems likely that they were near Ponden, and they may have been the 'children' of the newspaper report. It is, in any case, difficult to see who else these children can have been, in an age when there were no scouts, guides or other youth organizations to be adventuring on the moor. From that point on, Ponden would surely seem numinous to Emily: frightening, yet exciting. Robin Skelton makes the assertion that all writers have had a childhood escape from sudden death, often by drowning.[16] This event was Emily Brontë's baptism. When the family arrived home, Mr Brontë treated the eruption as a sign from God, and the children's escape as a miracle.

Like the little Brontës, Robert Heaton of Ponden House was also out on that supernatural afternoon.[17] His territory was never to be the same again. Writing in 1879 J. Horsfall Turner records that at Ponden 'the ruin caused by the Crow Hill disruption may here be traced. A fish-pond stands on the site of a swamped meadow, and huge stones are scattered about.'[18]

There was one interesting consequence of the Crow Hill bog burst, apart from the likelihood that Emily's understanding of the godlike qualities of Nature was surely deepened. Our first knowledge of this related incident is in Scruton's *Thornton and the Brontës*. It will be necessary to quote the account in full, as I wish to suggest a new probability.

> One of Mr Inkersley's workmen, who lived to a good old age, remembered Mr Brontë calling at the printing office to correct the proofs of one of his printed sermons (issued in 1824), and of his being assisted by a little daughter, whom he believed to be Charlotte. It was much more likely, however, to have been Maria or Elizabeth, for Charlotte would then be only eight years old. While the young lady was correcting the proofs, her father was carrying on a vigorous conversation with Mr Inkersley on the politics of the day.[19]

If Scruton's date is correct, the little girl must certainly have been Emily. There is no record of any work of Mr Brontë's printed between 1818 and 1824. So Scruton's little proofreader must have been even more precocious than he thought: not eight or more, as Maria, Elizabeth and Charlotte (all away at school) would have been, but just turned six. In view of Emily's odd spelling and punctuation when she writes verse, we might wonder whether her proof-reading would be of much use, but on the other hand if we note the very positive response her reading would attract at Cowan Bridge, we may think she could read well enough in October 1824 to be able to understand and comment on this account of the eruption on the moors. Quite probably Mr Inkersley's printer would have been dazzled by the dramatic reading aloud that Emily could supply.

4

Maria Abused, Elizabeth Hurt

Papa lent me this book

– Maria Brontë, writing in an old geography book

'Knows . . . very little of Geography'

– Cowan Bridge superintendent, writing of Maria in the 'Entrance Book'

There was a time when my cheek burned
To give such scornful fiends the lie.

It has sometimes been said that Emily Brontë's experience of her first school, at Cowan Bridge, was much happier than that of her elder sisters. Winifred Gérin, for instance, calls the period 'happy isolation in the midst of the general misery'. But after this experience Emily hated schools: they made her physically sick. At Roe Head, later, she literally drooped: her face was bloodlessly pale, she became thin. These symptoms surely had reference to the Cowan Bridge experiences. There is a further point: it is often assumed that Jane Eyre is a character whose viewpoint is based on Charlotte; but thought may suggest that Emily's character and experience may have contributed to the fictional heroine.

The controversy over Cowan Bridge was the worst of the several which Mrs Gaskell stirred up by publishing her *Life of Charlotte Brontë*. Its repercussions have never quite been stilled. In this chapter we shall try to assemble as much information as possible about Cowan Bridge during the years 1824–5, and try to see the situation through the eyes of six-year-old Emily

Brontë. The reconstruction must be cautious, since Emily says nothing direct about the school. But we do have the impressions of two or three people who saw her there. We may be able to supplement these a little from *Jane Eyre*. Charlotte said to Mrs Gaskell that 'there was not a word in her account of the institution but what was true at the time she knew it'.[1] We shall start by testing these words against external evidence.

Cowan Bridge is situated in one of the most beautiful parts of England, where Yorkshire, Lancashire and Westmorland meet. It was and is an insignificant hamlet built round the fast-flowing river Leck. Behind the hamlet are fields and scattered copses of oak, holly, birch and hazel. Beyond these, the fells open out. A lane leads up from Cowan Bridge towards these fells, and to Leck chapel, rebuilt since the days of the Clergy Daughters' School. The hamlet, and Leck chapelry, are in the parish of Tunstall, Lancashire, the old parish church being two and a half miles away across country.[2]

Cowan Bridge itself takes its name from the old stone bridge which carries the Kendal–Leeds road across the river. It is two and a half miles from Kirkby Lonsdale, a pleasant market town which was prosperous and developing in the 1820s. The area round about is less harsh than Haworth, open to the west winds coming from the sea. The school site is certainly close to the river and might be damp, but the surroundings are pleasant, at least in summer.

It was in 1823 that William Carus Wilson, an evangelical clergyman whose family lived near Cowan Bridge, decided to found a school for the daughters of the clergy. The school was to be open to children one of whose parents was dead. He bought a row of cottages near the river, by the turnpike road, and spent much effort and money in adding to them so that they would be fit premises for the eighty or so girls he intended to take. The woodcut of the buildings which accompanied the advertisement has been reproduced many times and is familiar. Nevertheless a description may be useful.[3]

The original cottages, which still remain, faced the river on a north-west/south-east orientation. Mr Wilson added a large wing to accommodate a schoolroom on the ground floor and a dormitory above. A refectory occupied the north-west end. The woodcut shows a garden and verandah, exactly described in *Jane Eyre*. The verandah was to enable the girls to play outside in wet weather, and the gardens were to be allocated for them to grow their own vegetables.

Early records summarized by a headmistress of the school, Miss Williams, give many details of the fees, uniform, school regime, numbers and the like.[4] As we are trying to test Charlotte's claim to truth, we shall now compare these records with her account, so as to discover how far she was a reliable witness to detail, though she wrote more than twenty years later. We shall start with *Jane Eyre*, Chapter 5, as Jane arrives on a rainy evening on the coach from her home. It is worth noting that it was Emily, not Charlotte, who arrived at Cowan Bridge on a dark evening in early winter. It seems that Charlotte was brought to school by her father, while Emily may have come on the coach by herself. If so, this may be because she had seemed lively and independent, as – for example – in the matter of reading her father's proofs. However, Emily was six years and four months old when she went up to school, while Jane Eyre was ten.

Jane is led up a pebbly path from a door in the wall surrounding the school grounds and is soon taken into the building where there is a fire waiting. Here she is received by the superintendent, who asks her a few questions in a short catechism: 'how old I was, what was my name, whether I could read, write and sew a little . . .'. This bears an uncanny resemblance to the reality, for the records give brief details of the accomplishments of all the girls on arrival. So Emily was catechized on the evening of 25 November 1824, in front (we may hope) of a warm fire. We shall return in a while to the note made about her.

The school routine to which Jane Eyre awoke the next day was exactly the same as that which Emily Jane underwent at the end of November 1824. A bell woke the girls. Cowan Bridge records say this was at 6 a.m. There was a Bible reading preceded by prayers. Then came breakfast. Lessons lasted from 9 a.m. until noon. The next two hours were spent either in walking (school records) or playing (*Jane Eyre*); then dinner. There were three more hours of lessons from 2 p.m. till 5. Both sources agree that tea followed. There was an hour prep between 7 and 8 p.m.; it was the end of this period which Jane Eyre saw as she arrived. There is almost no discrepancy so far between the accounts of the novel and the records.

Jane Eyre seems to be describing the summer uniform. She mentions 'brown stuff frocks . . . and long holland pinafores'. The records say 'buff dresses of . . . "nankeen" . . . and brown holland pinafores'. When outside, according to Jane Eyre, the girls wore each a 'coarse straw bonnet, with strings of coloured calico'. The school source says they were 'white straw bonnets trimmed with green calico'. Jane says the school was 'a large building, half of which seemed grey and old, the other half quite new. The new part, containing the schoolroom and dormitory, was lit by mullioned and latticed windows . . .' We know that the part that seemed new *was* new, and the description fits the illustration precisely.

It is quite clear that Charlotte Brontë's memory of the buildings, routine and uniform at Cowan Bridge was almost photographic. In the final paragraph of Chapter 7, Jane says she could not have borne the punishment of 'standing on my natural feet in the middle of the room'. An old girl of the Clergy Daughters' School remembered her needlework mistress, Miss Shepton, threatening this as punishment for biting off a thread: 'If you do, you shall stand in the midst of the floor.'[5] We shall need to follow up Charlotte's rather more controversial memories or imaginings. Let us turn aside for a while to see what we can discover about Emily Brontë's attainments and reputation at Cowan Bridge.

Details of the catechizing sessions such as we found Jane Eyre experiencing were entered in the 'Entrance Book'.[6] The records for all four Brontë girls have been quoted in biographies on a number of occasions, but never accurately. Some points can be deduced from this book and from the 'Ledger' in which accounts with parents were kept. It may therefore be useful to quote parts of the Entrance Book verbatim. The book was ruled into columns. One heading reads 'For what educating'. Evidently, girls were asked what occupation they were preparing to follow in life. Maria, Charlotte and Emily all replied, if we are to trust the writing in the 'Entrance Book', that they were to be governesses. Perhaps significantly, the word 'governess' does not appear by Elizabeth's name.

Here are the entries for the four Brontës, omitting the repeated parental names and addresses, and duplicated dates of leaving. Punctuation is as in the Entrance Book.

Maria Brontë 10 1824 July 21st Vaccinated Chicken pox Scarlet Fever H.Cough [these appear under a heading 'Diseases had'] Reads tolerably – Writes pretty well – Ciphers a little – Works very badly Knows a little of Grammar very little of Geography and History. Has made some progress in reading French but knows nothing of the language grammatically

[On opposite page, as well as the word 'Governess']

Left school in ill health 14 Feby. died 6th May 1825. Her Father's account of her is 'She exhibited during her illness symptoms of a heart under divine influence.' – Decline.

Elizabeth Brontë 9 (ditto) Vaccinated Scarlet fever H Cough Reads little – Writes pretty well Ciphers none – Works very badly Knows nothing of Grammar, Geography, History or Accomplishments.
Left School in ill Health 31st May died 15th June 1825 died in decline

Charlotte Brontë 8 1824 Augst. 10th Vaccinated H. Cough Reads tolerably – Writes indifferently – Ciphers a little and works neatly. Knows nothing of Grammar, Geography, History or Accomplishments. Left School 1825 June 1st Governess Altogether clever of her age but knows nothing systematically

Emily Brontë 5¾ 1824 Novbr 25th H Cough Reads very prettily & Works a little
Left School June 1st 1825 Governess

The Brontës were not exceptional in evoking caustic comments on their attainments so far. Mary Eleanor Lowther, at eighteen, 'Reads vilely'; Charlotte Hayne (twenty-two) reads 'correctly but in a bad tone'; Lucy Howard 'Reads carelessly – Writes and Ciphers carelessly – Works pretty well – '; Elizabeth Hayes (six) 'Reads very well – Writes none – Ciphers none – Works a little'. Three years later Elizabeth was expelled.

A comparison between the notes made on the four Brontës is interesting. There are comments on the reading [aloud] of three of them. Maria reads 'tolerably', Elizabeth 'little' and Emily 'very prettily'. Of their needlework Maria and Elizabeth both work 'very badly', Charlotte 'neatly' and Emily 'a little'. Compared with Maria, Elizabeth reads 'little' instead of 'tolerably', writes 'pretty well', ciphers 'none' instead of 'a little', 'works' equally badly and knows no grammar, geography, history or French despite Mr Brontë's lessons and the bedtime rehearsals of them. Charlotte does better than Elizabeth in three areas (reading, ciphering, needlework) and is only beaten by her elder sister at writing. Under the column for 'For what educating', Elizabeth is the only Brontë child who does not have the word 'Governess' entered. Linking this evidence to her answer from under the mask, we see that Elizabeth is not regarded as an intellectual, and she contrasts markedly with both her elder and her younger sisters. She was perhaps avoiding competition with them; we shall have an example soon of her patience in suffering.

The comment on Emily's reading is interestingly positive: 'Reads very prettily'. Reading aloud demands a quick eye and ear and a good memory. The words have to be phrased carefully, and this compels the child to read ahead and remember what she has taken in. Reading aloud successfully argues a strong aural capacity. This Emily evidently had. Other children read 'vilely', 'indifferently', 'badly', 'miserably': Emily seems to be the best reader in the Entrance Book. Some other children read 'pretty well', but Emily's comment is exceptional. It looks as if there was some winsome quality in the little girl which immediately endeared her to the teacher who wrote the comment, either on the day she arrived or next day.

The superindendent of Cowan Bridge during the latter part of the Brontës' stay there was Anne Evans, subsequently Mrs Connor.[7] After describing an incident involving Elizabeth, which will be dealt with later, she told Mrs Gaskell that she had very slight recollections of the girls 'save that one, a darling child, under five years of age, was quite the pet nursling of the school'. This, of course, was Emily, and the report is quite surprising if we have expected to find her described as 'shy', 'reserved' or 'anti-social'. It seems that at six, Emily Brontë was pretty, talented, advanced in accomplishments, and generally popular.

Yet Cowan Bridge cannot have been a happy place for her; if it had been, surely subsequent forays into the world of school would have been eagerly awaited and wholeheartedly embraced. Charlotte later said she herself 'suffered to see my sisters perishing'.[8] All we know of Emily through her poetry suggests her sensitivity would be well aware of the harshness meted out to her sisters and she would feel sharply deprivations they suffered. A girl who had advised the whipping of her brother if he were to be naughty would not flinch from just punishment, but there is every suggestion in *Jane Eyre* that punishment at Cowan Bridge was not just. In particular, Maria, despite her untidiness, seems to have been patient and good, at any rate if Helen Burns is modelled on her. Emily must have witnessed unjust punishments of her eldest sister.

Mrs Gaskell managed to contact a lady who had been at Cowan Bridge at the same time as Maria and the others. She told some stories so hair-raising that Mrs Gaskell could only retell the mildest. This concerned a winter morning when Maria was ill and could not get out of bed. She had had a 'blister' applied, the aim of which was to relieve illness by getting rid of the mass of fluid, in this case on a wound in Maria's side. This seems not to have been working (one more failure on the part of the doctors for Emily to note). Other girls urged Maria to stay in bed, but she refused. As she began to dress and was putting on her black worsted stockings,

> Miss Scatcherd issued from her room, and, without asking a word of explanation from the sick and frightened girl, she took her by the arm, on the side to which the blister had been applied and by one vigorous movement whirled her out into the middle of the floor, abusing her all the time for dirty and untidy habits.[9]

This indignity was compounded by the girl being punished for lateness when she did arrive downstairs. Such episodes look more like sadism than discipline.

This incident is not mentioned in *Jane Eyre*, but the untidiness of Helen Burns is often stressed. We can reconstruct the scene that January morning, about the time when Anne, at home, might be having her fifth birthday. There is the large, ill-lit room, two hours before dawn, in which forty girls are assembled. Emily, Elizabeth Hayes and Martha Thompson are the youngest at between six and seven. Several 'girls' are really women at ages between nineteen and twenty-two. The Bible reading does not begin: a child is late. As Emily watches with those shifting eyes, she sees her sister Maria, already ill, hustled down the stairs and punished for lateness. In October

1839 Emily wrote 'There was a time when my cheek burned/ To give such scornful fiends the lie'. Was 'Miss Scatcherd' a scornful fiend, and did Emily blush? Might she possibly have used her charm to intervene on behalf of her sister? If she had done so, Mrs Gaskell's informant would surely have recorded this; so Emily stayed silent and watched.

On some later occasions Emily Brontë seems almost to have courted disaster and brought pain or trouble on herself. If the description of Maria as Helen Burns is at all accurate, she seems to have done the same. Her untidiness seems to have sprung from absent-mindedness; her thoughts were on higher things. She had been taught this at Haworth, but it would not be calculated to cool the temper of a teacher whose thoughts on a cold dark winter morning were not on higher things. Maria's stubborn spirit apparently led her to choose the path of saintly martyrdom. Emily's mind may have been divided as she watched the spectacle, seeing the situation grow bitter with the kind of cruelty exhibited years later in *Wuthering Heights*: shocked, pitying, yet curiously exalted.

Mrs Connor wrote to Mrs Gaskell that Elizabeth was also ill while at Cowan Bridge.

> The second, Elizabeth, is the only one of the family of whom I have a vivid recollection, from her meeting with a somewhat alarming accident, in consequence of which I had her for some time in my bed-room, not only for the sake of greater quiet, but that I might watch over her myself. Her head was severely cut, but she bore all the consequent suffering with exemplary patience, and by it won much upon my esteem.[10]

What caused this cut on the head? Why did Mrs Connor (Miss Evans) want to watch over Elizabeth herself? Was there someone else on the staff whom she couldn't trust? The great difference between the treatment of Maria and the treatment of Elizabeth raises the question of whether there were two contrasting regimes at Cowan Bridge; there is indeed a slight hint of this in *Jane Eyre* where Miss Temple clashes politely with Mr Brocklehurst.

Mr Nicholls, writing to the *Halifax Guardian* a letter printed on 18 July 1857, suggests that Miss Scatcherd is based on Miss Andrews, later Mrs Hill of Ohio, who 'combined the office of teacher with that of "superintendent of rooms", a situation, as far as I can learn, somewhat analagous to that of an upper housemaid'.[11] This was denied by his chief opponent in the long correspondence, but it is not certain that she was in a position to know at first hand. It seems possible that Miss Andrews might be in charge initially, until Miss Evans was appointed. The result might be a tussle of wills. This may be a little speculative, but it is interesting to note that the 'Entrance Book' and 'Ledger' are both a mixture of two hands, as if two people had joint charge, or perhaps rival charges. The Brontë entries are in one hand up to Charlotte's entrance on 10 August, but at Emily's entrance the hand changes. The first hand returns for an entry for Charlotte's clothes on 21 February and 'To Cash' on 23 September 1825. This handwriting change may be indicative, though it would be unwise to lay any stress on it.[12]

Having established Emily at Cowan Bridge, an attractive and apparently extrovert child, while at least one sister is being bullied, we may leave her childhood self for a while to look at her later poetry. A number of her poems refer to childhood incidents. One in particular was noted by Romer Wilson.[13] It mentions the age of six as a crucial time. This poem, 'Come hither, child', is much worked over in the manuscript, and dated 19 July 1839. A small fragment is on the same scrap of paper, reading

> *Alas that she would bid adieu*
> *To all the hopes her childhood knew*
> *Hushed his the harp.[sic]*

A second poem, possibly unfinished, is found on an undated scrap of paper. It begins,

> *It is not pride, it is not shame*
> *That makes her leave the gorgeous hall . . .*

It continues,

> *'Tis true she stands among the crowd*
> *An unmarked and an unloved child . . .*

The last stanza runs,

I saw her stand in the gallery long
Watching the little children there
As they were playing the pillars among
And bounding down the marble stair.[14]

Romer Wilson discusses 'Come hither, child' at length, relating it to her suggestion that Emily may have suffered a fit, which became the kernel of the 'red room' episode in *Jane Eyre*. The scene in the poem is a windy night of celebration, when the child is 'hardly six years old'. She has 'no one to love me there' and escapes from the room to a lonely place of sorrow. Her suicidal frame of mind is changed by the intervention of a mysterious musical note, apparently produced by an angel.

'It is not pride' seems to be on the same topic. In it the 'unmarked' (that is, 'unnoticed') child, stands lonely in the crowd until she glides out 'to the park' and lies down on the grass beneath a cedar tree. It is a wet and windy day, just as the wind is present in 'Come hither, child'. However, in 'It is not pride' there is no resolution of the child's unhappiness. A fragment beginning 'The inspiring music's thrilling sound' provides yet another example of the theme of desertion on a festal day. In this poem a young (?) female 'Forsaken by that Lady fair' glides through the revellers 'unheeding', while she covers her face so as not to allow it to be seen that she is on the point of tears. There are only three stanzas, in the last of which 'She hurries through the outer Hall/ And up the stairs through galleries dim . . .'. All three poems seem to be exploring a single nexus of feelings, which will recur in more sophisticated form.

First we have the festal scene. The 'hall' (all three poems) is full of revellers ('crowds' in two of the poems). Among them stands a girl, who is six years old in 'Come hither, child'. She is overcome with a feeling of rejection and alienation. In the two undated fragments, we are shown the tear 'quivering' or 'trembling'; in 'Come hither, child,' the escaping girl is going to 'sorrow'. We are specifically told that neither pride nor shame is the reason for her wish to escape, but the question 'What made her weep?', asked in one fragment, is not answered. However, earlier in that fragment a 'sudden fall' is mentioned, and in 'The inspiring music', we are told that she was *forsaken* by 'that Lady fair'. The scene then changes, and we watch the child either (a) gliding out of doors to the park, where she subsequently stands in a long gallery and watches children play 'the pillars among'; (b) gliding unheeded upstairs to some galleries which may be rather like the 'pillars' just mentioned; (c) in the dated, apparently completed 'Come hither, child,' finding a lonely room where the child prays for death.

Three pointers direct our search for the beginning of this group of poems to Cowan Bridge. Apart from this one period and the short time at Roe Head, Emily was never one in a crowd of children like those mentioned; in 'Come hither, child,' she specifically says the child is six; the pillars where the children are playing sound very like the pillars on the verandah facing the garden at the Clergy Daughters' School. The scene is changed by imagination and time, but not beyond recognition. The ladylike Miss Evans sounds like the 'Lady fair' of the 'inspiring music' fragment. All three suggest a sudden sorrow among festal crowds. Two suggest that the child has been 'deserted' and 'It is not pride' ascribes this to 'a sudden fall'. Of course, this is poetry, not direct factual autobiography. Poetry deals in feelings, not documentation. Nevertheless, the poet's feeling here is real, and may have been experienced at Cowan Bridge.

Two of the three poems leave the rejected child desolate and with tears in her eyes. As we explore more of Emily's poems we shall find many which she begins strongly, but loses the power to complete. These, apparently, she finds too painful or complex to struggle with. 'Come hither, child,' is much altered on the scrap of paper. Perhaps on this occasion she did feel she could wrestle a little more doggedly with the telling of the experience. We need to do the same, since it seems to be at the heart of Emily's understanding of what has sometimes been seen as a 'mystical' dimension, without which *Wuthering Heights* would have been impossible.

In 'Come hither, child,' ostensibly a Gondal poem because of its reference to 'Ula', Emily describes the desolation of a rejected six-year-old, who deliberately chooses to be where only 'heaven' could see her 'bend' (a difficult word here, but possibly suggesting the pliancy of a proud person humbled). The child prays for death. In the silence 'drear' she hears a musical note, later described as a 'seraph strain', which indicates that 'Gabriel' has come to take her to her father's home. The sound rose 'three times' then died and apparently was not heard again (text is uncertain).

Emily Brontë's feelings were extraordinarily acute. We shall find poems in which enormous power is invested in quite trivial events. The present three poems seem to be reflecting an occasion (I have suggested it may well be at Cowan Bridge) when Emily felt snubbed or rejected and 'prayed to die', but was consoled by an aural 'vision' of an angel. The aurality is interesting, but we might have been prepared for it in view of her pretty reading aloud. Romer Wilson thought the experience involved a 'fit'.[15] It may possibly be that Emily fainted, though we have no means of knowing. What we can postulate is that a rejection experience suffered by the 'pet nursling' set Emily on a path in which hurt inflicted by humans could be compensated by what she saw as superhuman communication. Such a 'gift' is also a 'pain', as Emily will later say. Meanwhile the experience has begun to divide her a little further from the cheerful crowd of girls in the 'hall'.

An hypothesis which goes beyond our evidence, but not far beyond, might run as follows. Emily Brontë, a 'child of the most ardent, loving, jealous and generous nature', was not personally unhappy at Cowan Bridge, being petted by both Miss Andrews and Miss Evans.[16] But she saw her eldest sister, her mother-substitute, Maria, tormented. She might have used her influence with Miss Evans to denounce Miss Andrews, but part of her enjoyed Maria's misery, whether because of latent jealousy or emotional excitement. Possibly some crisis arose in which Miss Evans became aware of Emily's complicity, or in which Emily fell from grace (this is, however, speculation). Hence 'It is not pride, it is not shame'; instead it was lack of loyalty, even treachery, a state of mind which is forever occurring in Emily's poetry, and which is, of course, the crux of *Wuthering Heights*, when Catherine chooses the world's approbation instead of what she really loves. The incidence of the word 'traitor' in the poems suggests that it is very emotive, and it may well have begun to be so at Cowan Bridge. At the very least, we have the suggestive contrast between Emily's high status as 'pet nursling' and deposed Maria's low one as degraded sloven.

Even if we consider that in *Jane Eyre* Charlotte exaggerated the ferocity of W. Carus Wilson (as Mr Brocklehurst) and the saintliness of Maria (as Helen Burns), there is some positive proof that the deprivations that the small Brontës underwent were not all imaginary. The eye-witness account of the treatment of Maria by Miss Andrews has already been mentioned. All sources seem to agree that there was a period when the catering at the school was very bad. A writer to the *Halifax Guardian* of 18 July 1857 mentioned food being inadequate in the years following the removal of the Brontës, though there was no dirt at the time.[17] Carus Wilson's son had already admitted to the same paper (on 28 May 1857) that the school managers had become anxious during the fever epidemic of spring 1825 and had brought in a doctor to check the food. He 'spoke rather scornfully of a baked rice pudding'. A contemporary of the Brontës was quoted by Charlotte's husband, Arthur Nicholls, writing on 3 June 1857.

> The housekeeper was very dirty with the cooking. I have frequently seen grease swimming on the milk and water we had for breakfast, in consequence of its having been boiled in a greasy copper, and I perfectly remember once being sent for a cup of tea for a teacher, who was ill in bed, and no spoon being at hand, the housekeeper stirred it with her finger, she being engaged in cutting up raw meat at the time.[18]

Mrs Connor's husband is quoted by Sarah Baldwin on 11 July 1857 to the effect that his wife used to allude 'to some unfortunate cook, who used at times to spoil the food, but . . . she was soon dismissed'. There seems to be no doubt that the Brontës were at Cowan Bridge during the time of this cook.

The older Brontë girls were certainly not strong, and it seems likely that Maria at any rate had not recovered from whooping cough when she went to school. Her stoicism covered up her discomfort, and, later, pain. The walks to Tunstall church on cold Sundays, related in *Jane Eyre*, cannot have done much good. These walks have been dismissed on two grounds. It has been said that the walk is in any case a pleasant one, and would not cause or exacerbate coughs and colds; and it has also been said that the children went to Leck chapel anyhow. The walk along the farm lanes can be pleasant in summer sun, but not when a cold winter wind is blowing. Leck chapel was apparently used by the younger children. We may assume that Emily went there, but Maria would have had to walk to Tunstall in the crocodile.[19]

Mrs Gaskell describes the shock with which Mr Brontë reacted on being told of Maria's illness and being summoned to collect her on St Valentine's day, 1825.[20] The 'low fever' epidemic may not have arrived by that time, and seems to have had nothing to do with the decline of the two Brontës. They were both victims of 'consumption'. The former pupil quoted in Mr Nicholls's letter considered that her harsh treatment at school was a factor in her illness:

> [I] suffered so severely from the treatment that I was never in the schoolroom during the last three months I was there, until about a week before I left, and was considered to be far gone in consumption. My mother (whose only child I was) was never informed of my illness . . . .

It seems likely that the lady quoted is Eliza Goodacre who left on 14 June 1825. Her three months would have been from the middle of March onwards. No children are recorded as leaving in March, but Isabella Whaley, who left 'in good health' on 2 April, died of typhus on 23 April.[21]

Mrs Gaskell describes her farewell given to Maria, travelling with her father on the Leeds coach, 'the girls crowding out into the road to follow her with their eyes over the bridge, past the cottages, and then "out of sight forever"'. Among the girls would be her three sisters, Elizabeth, Charlotte and Emily Jane. One can suppose they would be glad to have a visit from their father, despite the sad occasion; we know of only one other visit, earlier on, from the now-married Elizabeth Firth of Thornton. Mrs Gaskell's notion that Maria died 'a few days after her arrival home' is incorrect. Like Mary Chester, a girl who had left Cowan Bridge 'in ill health' the day before her, Maria lingered on for months.

Those left behind had the typhus epidemic to contend with. In addition to Isabella Whaley, one other girl (her sister) left in April, two (including Elizabeth) in May and seven in June. A girl who left on 1 March is recorded as dying on 29 April of 'decline', just like the Brontës. The typhus seems to have been exacerbated by some form of airborne virus leading to swift lung trouble. From February to June the school numbers declined from 51 to 43: these figures support the notion that the authorities had a great deal of disease to contend with that spring.

There is a mystery about the way in which Charlotte and Emily left the school. Mrs Gaskell heard that both went back to Cowan Bridge after the summer holidays. The records give 1 June as their last day, but the ledger shows that the account was not closed until 23 September. To complicate matters, Mrs Chadwick was told by a relative of Carus Wilson that the two Brontës had been taken on 31 May to Silverdale, where Mr Wilson had a residence at the Cove. We may possibly reconstruct events as follows.[22]

Maria died on 6 May (we shall return to the nature of her death and her last days in a while). Elizabeth must have been obviously ill by this time.[23] She was sent home on 31 May at the cost of 13 shillings. A Mrs Hardacre, said to be a school servant, went with her and apparently stayed overnight in Keighley. (The account may suggest that the school administration was in a muddle, since the bill for Emily's second half-year was entered a month too early, on 26 April instead of May. Emily was also charged 13 shillings for clothes on 31 May.) If Mr Wilson's relative is correct, he took the children to Silverdale with him on 31 May, presumably to remove them from the source of contamination at Cowan Bridge. We do not know if any other children went too.

Mr Brontë seems to have caught a coach the next day and collected the girls, so that they stayed at Silverdale only one night. Neither had really had time to appreciate the sea view and mild air of Silverdale, and Charlotte is generally considered to have first seen the sea at Bridlington years later. They arrived home to witness Elizabeth's last fortnight on earth, but Mr Brontë does not seem to have been in a hurry to close the school account. He was allowed abatement of fees for Maria and Elizabeth, and some money on their clothes, but Cowan Bridge appears to have ended by being in profit by £2. 14s. 2d. It does look as though even after the deaths of Maria and Elizabeth, the matter of return to school was left open. We do not know quite when the leaving date, 1 June, was written in the register.

Death, that struck when I was most confiding
In my certain Faith of Joy to be . . .

wrote Emily on 10 April 1845, twenty years later, and, as Catherine added in Lockwood's dream, 'It's twenty years . . . I've been a waif for twenty years'.[24] The Brontës were acutely interested in time and chronology, dating almost all their poems, celebrating birthdays with diary papers; the twenty-year ghost-life of Catherine is unlikely to be a coincidence. It seems likely that the death of Maria involved Emily in some feeling of guilt, as the death of a mother-figure is often seen by a small child as an occasion for guilt; I have suggested why this may possibly have been so for Emily. In 'Death, that struck when I was most confiding', the poet asks for a second death; as we have seen, there is some attraction in placing the beginning of this wish for death at the time of Cowan Bridge.

When Emily reached Haworth, there was no Maria. Elizabeth lay weakly in her bed upstairs, just as earlier their mother had lain. For some idea of what Elizabeth's funeral meant, we need to go to a poem of Branwell's, written in 1837, when there appears to have been some community of interest between him and Emily. Extracts from the poem, 'Caroline', are given in Winifred Gérin's *Branwell Brontë*.[25] She discusses the alternative interpretations for it, and argues convincingly against those who have thought the poem had no connection with the deaths of the eldest Brontës.

The viewpoint of the poem is that of a sister, Harriet, who may stand for Emily. We cannot insist on the literal truth of the incidents in it, nor can we separate the events at the two funerals, Maria's and Elizabeth's. The scene is transposed to a mansion, 'Woodchurch Hall'. One incident, though, that does have the stamp of veracity, is that of the child lifted by her mother to look at the dead face of her sister in the open coffin:

My mother lifted me to see
What might within that coffin be;
And, to this moment, I can feel
The voiceless gasp – the sickening chill –
With which I hid my whitened face
In the dear folds of her embrace;
For hardly dared I turn my head
Lest its wet eyes should view that bed.
'But, Harriet,' said my mother mild,
'Look at your *sister and my child*

'One moment, ere her form be hid
'For ever 'neath its coffin lid!'[26]

Harriet overcomes her reluctance and looks down at the dead girl. She is surprised to see her sister 'with flowers about her head', looking much as though she were still alive. Her 'too bright cheek' of the final consumptive days had now faded. 'Still did her lips the smile retain/Which parted them when hope was high'. Harriet tries to awaken her dead sister by touching her cheek. Then the coffin lid is pressed down and

I cared not whither I was borne:
I only felt that death had torn
My Caroline from me

The funeral procession moves through the churchyard and soon,

Down, down, they lowered her, sad and slow,
Into her narrow house below:
And deep, indeed, appeared to be
That one glimpse of eternity,
Where cut from life, corruption lay,
Where beauty soon should turn to clay.

These are, of course, Branwell's impressions. But Emily, almost seven, would have been through exactly the same agonizing day on 18 June 1825, and the ascription to 'Harriet' may be significant. The precise date within 1837 when this poem was written is not known, but there does seem to be some possibility of discussion between Emily and Branwell at that time.[27] It is impossible to overlook the effect on the surviving Brontës of the catastrophic death of those two sisters. A note in the Cowan Bridge register apparently refers to a lost letter of Mr Brontë. 'She exhibited during her illness many symptoms of a heart under divine influence', is recorded as his 'account' of her. If Emily saw herself as having complicity, even if only slightly, in the degradation and death of her eldest sister, this must affect her own self-regard. The poetic fragment told us that it was not pride or shame that forced the outcast away from the brightly lighted hall. Both these emotions will figure in Emily's story, and have perhaps been evident already. To them, we have to add a third chilling emotion, set to blight the ardent 'pet nursling': a lifelong struggle with guilt arising from treachery.

At first Cowan Bridge, despite the noisy crowds, had built up some confidence in Emily. But any gain must have been completely dashed by the disastrous end of the episode, a double death, striking 'when I was most confiding'.

5
Visions of Futurity

In the other island there was likewise a female who sat on an emerald throne. Her crown was formed of shamrocks. In her right hand she held a harp and her robes were of a crimson hue, as if they had been dyed in blood. She was as majestic as the other but in her countenance was something very sad and sorrowful, as if a terrible evil hung upon her.

– Charlotte Brontë, writing in 1829
(The 'terrible evil' was not British rule)

Just before Emily went to Cowan Bridge, Branwell had been given a box of toy soldiers.[1] They were the first of several, and were destined to be important in the literary lives of the Brontë sisters, as much as in that of their brother. It seems that Maria and Elizabeth had taken the lead in dramatizing episodes from history and geography that had to be learnt for the next morning. This tendency to dramatize would now focus partly on Branwell's soldiers and start a series of games that would last the four well into adulthood. After the deaths of the elder girls the games sometimes incorporated sudden deaths, though often the dead players were brought to life again.

The manner of playing was threefold. In the first place the soldiers could be handled by their keepers and act as little puppets. At this stage they were physically moved round the 'nursery' and perhaps other rooms in the house. To give life to these tiny men was exciting for the children, as it has been for many generations of children at all times. When the characters of the different soldiers had been developed, the four children could sometimes *be* them, acting for them without needing the physical puppet to be present. They acted other games too. Being quick readers and writers, they developed a third mode of playing with the soldiers: they wrote about their adventures. Once this habit had begun, the limitations of the toys were forgotten. They had their own lives and became transformed from soldiers in a box to characters in books, where they mixed on equal terms with the four children who had created them.

The development of these plays and stories was gradual. It has been explored by Dr Christine Alexander in much more detail than can be given here. If Emily wrote anything on her own about these plays, it has been lost, but her doings are sometimes reported by Charlotte, and we can see that her role was not passive. At this period, Emily and Charlotte seem to have been very close. We shall see Charlotte both as leader within the game and as governess. The latter role appears to have been resented by Emily, and this, with other factors, led to revolt. However, in 1826 such matters were far in the future. It was on 5 June of that year that Mr Brontë brought back yet another box of soldiers, this time after a clergy conference in Leeds.[2] For many years Mr Brontë seems to have been acutely interested in military matters; whether this is because he did *not* go out to help his brother at Ballynahinch, and thus lost an opportunity, we cannot tell. But his attempts to get Branwell and the girls interested in battles are interesting and had some success. This time, however, he also bought some less military toys for the girls: ninepins for Charlotte (but they turned later into little people), a toy village for Emily, and a dancing doll for Anne. Despite his eccentricity, Mr Brontë was acting as a dutiful and loving father.

There are two accounts of the reception of these soldiers, one by Branwell, one by Charlotte. Charlotte explains how Branwell came to the door of the bedroom on the morning of 6 June with the box in his hands.

> Emily and me jumped out of bed and I snacthed up one and exclaimed this is the Duke of Wellington it shall be mine . . . When I had said this Emily likewise took one and said it should be hers.[3]

The two conspiratorial sisters act together. Branwell puts up no resistance. Charlotte's memory here seems more accurate than that of Branwell. He writes,

> I carried them to Emily, Charlotte and Anne. They each took up a soldier, gave them names, which I consented to.[4]

As we have seen, Charlotte's was the Duke of Wellington. The other names were as interesting.

The two descriptions compared show Charlotte's sharp visualization and dramatic flair. The two girls (Emily is almost eight) jump out of bed, excited. Charlotte then 'snatches' up a soldier. Her account was written in 1829, by which time she was clearly leading the others in verbal description. By contrast Branwell is concerned to exert his authority over a nest of unruly girls; an effort in which he soon failed.

Now the other three soldiers are named:

> When Anne came down she took one also. Mine was the prettiest of the whole and perfect in every part Emily's was a Grave looking fellow we called him Gravey Anne's was a queer little thing very much like herself he was called waiting Boy Branwell chose Bonaparte.[5]

Branwell's account seems to suggest he has forgotten the original names, for he calls Emily's soldier 'Pare' and Anne's 'Trott', names which seem to have developed later. Charlotte does not say that 'Gravey' mirrored his owner's character, though Anne's soldier did reflect the 'queerness' of Anne. Two or three of these 'twelves' were still in existence in 1830.[6]

In classifying the plays in 1829 Charlotte calls this 'The Young Men's play'. She eventually wrote an account, dated 15 April 1829, of the voyage of 'The Twelve Adventurers' to Africa, where they became involved in wars with the local people, behaving much as colonialist soldiers were expected to behave at the time. This series of stories was destined to become the dominant series in the hearts of Charlotte and Branwell, but there was something in Emily which objected to following Charlotte's lead. Even while her elder sister was in control, Emily seems to have demanded her own way. In judging Emily's reaction, we need to recall Charlotte's earnest motherly and managing spirit.

When the next set of plays was added to the 'Young Men' a year later, Emily had to be different. By this time, the Brontës had evidently become familiar with *Aesop's Fables* and *The Arabian Nights*. They invented a large island 'inhabited' (says Charlotte) 'by people 6 miles high. The people we took out of Esop's fables.' The names of the chiefs were Hay Man (Charlotte's), Boaster (Branwell's), Hunter (Anne's) and Clown (Emily's). 'Our Cheif Men were 10 miles high except Emily's who was only 4.' The name Clown contradicts the 'Gravey' of the 'Young Men'. We shall see some further examples of high spirits in Emily which led to clowning. Her reaction here is interesting and exemplifies a trend which will become more noticeable.

That Emily needs to be different at all is interesting. One would think that the third child in the family might be quite happy for her elder brother and sister to make up the rules of the game, but she is not. In view of her own height in a few years' time, we may suppose that at nine she might be as tall as Charlotte at eleven. Height, evidently, is a sensitive point. One may almost guess at an argument preceding the decision here, which left Emily as the dissenter. Her modification seems to be in the direction of reality, toning down the exaggeration. Soon she tries to introduce into the communal games echoes of Yorkshire in place of Africa. Emily's tendency was to pull physical settings back towards commonsense knowledge, though emotions may move in the contrary direction.

This series of plays, named 'Our Fellows', seems mainly to have been controlled by Branwell, and it lasted only five months. Very soon it was superseded and merged in 'The Islanders'. Charlotte gave two accounts of the beginning of this play, the second of which appears in Mrs Gaskell's *Life*. It is worth quoting because of the vivid word picture given by the thirteen-year-old's sharp observation and memory (possibly modified by time, as she attempts to quote precise dialogue).

> The play of the Islanders was formed in December 1827 in the following manner. One night about the time when the cold sleet and dreary fogs of November are succeeded

> by the snow storms and high piercing night winds of confirmed winter, we were all sitting round the warm blazing kitchen fire having just concluded a quarrel with Tabby concerning the propriety of lighting a candle from which she came off victorious, no candle having been produced. a long pause succeeded which was at last broken by B saying, in a lazy manner, 'I don't know what to do.' This was re-echoed by E and A.
>
> T Wha ya may go t'bed.
> B: I'd rather do anything [than] that.
> & C: You're so glum tonight T. [? Well] suppose we had each an Island.
> B: If we had I would choose the Island of Man.
> C: And I would choose Isle of Wight.
> E: The Isle of Aran for me.
> A: And mine should be Guernsey.
> C: The Duke of Wellington should be my chief man.
> B: [? Heries] should be mine.
> E: Walter Scott should be mine.
> A: I should have Bentinck.
>
> Here our conversation was interrupted by [the], to us, dismal sound of the clock striking 7 and we were summoned off to bed. The next day we added several others to our list of names till we had got almost all the chief men in the kingdom.[7]

Thus, of all the possible heroes, Emily chooses Scott as her first man. She would often be found in a Scott-like dream landscape for many years to come.

Further characters were soon added to those chosen on the dark windy night in December. Emily adds Scott's relatives, Mr Lockhart (his son-in-law) and Johnny Lockhart (his grandson). During the following year the separate islands merged into 'Vision Island' which was so beautiful it might have been in fairyland. However, it was rather marred by having included in it from June 1828 the Palace School, the pupils of which were mostly young nobles, except for such men as Emily's Johnny Lockhart. In time, the school would be troublesome, and the pupils would revolt. Meanwhile – perhaps on the same night – (Charlotte says it was 1 December 1827) Charlotte and Emily invented some 'Bed plays'. 'Bed plays mean secret plays', Charlotte records. 'They are very nice ones. All our plays are very strange ones. Their nature I need not write on paper, for I think I shall always remember them.' So Charlotte (aged thirteen) and Emily (nine) shared secrets in a close-bound duo, warm in their snug nest while the piercing night winds of 'confirmed winter' raged outside.[8] They would certainly need to whisper if they were to keep the plays secret from the other children, and their father and aunt. In her adult years Emily did not readily go to sleep at night. We can see here that, as a child of nine, her active mind refused to rest.

On 13 February 1827 Mr Brontë had given Emily a Bible as a present.[9] Compared with Charlotte and Anne, she was to make little use of it. The dissident spirit of Emily has already been noted. Possibly Emily's 'affectionate father' had recognized, two years to the day after he had heard of Maria's illness, that his fourth daughter was not following in Maria's footsteps.[10] However, she was progressing with her stitching. She finished her first sampler on 22 April 1828, and it evidently passed her aunt's scrutiny despite the fact that in both the alphabets which it includes, in capitals and lower case, Emily shows her faintly dyslexic habit of reversing letter order. Both alphabets show V before U. (It was many years before Emily could learn the I before E rule.)[11]

She was also learning the piano. It is not clear which instrument this could have been, as the cottage piano currently on view in Mr Brontë's study was apparently bought in 1834.[12] However, piano music was being collected for Emily and later for Anne, from 1828 onward. She justified the time and money spent on lessons by eventually playing very well indeed. All the Brontës had a sharp musical ear. It is likely that Mr Brontë had played the violin as a child and teenager, like some of his brothers. Branwell took up the flute. Anne played the piano and sang. The first piece of music bought for Emily that I can discover is 'Morning Bells', a pleasant beginner's piece, acquired in March 1828; but she must have been learning the elements before this.[13] Emily's musical ear and sharp aural discrimination are important factors in her poetry and novel.

As time went on the four soldiers who had begun the 'Young Men's' play receded in favour of their sponsors, the four Brontës. They became the 'genii' in the manner of *The*

Arabian Nights, and were called Talli (or Taley), Branni (or Brany), Emmii and Anni (variously spelt).[14] In a map perhaps drawn in 1828 the four have carved up part of Africa, but it is interesting to note that Emily's part is allocated to 'Vittoria'. This may be evidence that Emily was already taking interest in Princess Victoria, whose accession and coronation she would follow closely in 1837–8.[15] Alternatively the two younger genii defended their soldiers with Pare (Parry) and Trott (Ross). The former had as prototype Sir Edward Parry, the Arctic explorer, and the latter Captain John Ross.

Charlotte supplies us with another vignette of Haworth parsonage in her systematized version of 'Tales of the Islanders' begun in March 1829. After mentioning a geography book lent to Maria by Mr Brontë, in which Maria had apparently written 'papa lent me this Book', she continues,

> I am in the kitchin of the parsonage house Haworth Taby the servent is washing up after Breakfast and Anne my youngest Sister (Maria was my eldest) is kneeling on a chair looking at some cakes whiche Tabby has been Baking for us. Emily is in the parlour brushing it papa and Branwell are gone to Keighly Aunt is up stairs in her Room and I am sitting by the table writing this in the kitchin.[16]

This is the first occasion on which we hear of Emily's capacity for domestic tasks. Did Emily resent brushing while Charlotte was writing a sort of diary? We shall see.

On the first day of the same month Emily had finished a better sampler, quoting both the Book of Proverbs and a psalm, perhaps from the Bible her father had given her. It is difficult to know whether to make judgements from the texts chosen. The Proverbs passage is chapter 30, verses 1–9, and the psalm quotation is from no. 145, 'The Lord is gracious, and full of compassion; slow to anger, and of great mercy: the Lord is good to all and his tender mercies are over all his works.'[17]

Next month Emily copied 'the whinchat' from a Bewick engraving. It has been reproduced a number of times and is dated 1 April 1829. It was to be followed next month by the ring-ousel, on 29 May.[18] For a girl just about to reach her eleventh birthday, they are well done, with accuracy and life.

Both are moorland birds: Emily draws no sparrows. We may take it that she is already walking on the moors with her elders, further, by now, than the family were able to go when Maria and Elizabeth led them: as far as the hills behind Ponden, where signs of the bog burst were still to be seen. It was about this time that Branwell certainly began to read the books in Ponden House library. It looks as if Emily, and perhaps the others, went with him. In late May also, Emily began to study a new musical task, the 'Sicilian Mariners' Hymn'.

In the early days, there seem to have been many attempts to ensure that they had a normal sociable childhood. This may have begun with Mrs Brontë, but after her death Aunt Branwell was not going to abandon the attempt. This September she took all the children to visit Cross-stone, near Todmorden, to see 'Uncle Fennell', who had been a guide, philosopher and friend to her during her Penzance childhood. Cross-stone was no great step from Haworth, but they would have to go by some form of conveyance along the moorland road to Hebden Bridge, where Branwell would later be employed on the railway. This expedition was not like the one to Cowan Bridge. Emily was going with her sisters and brother, and would be under the protection of her aunt and great-uncle. It would be a family occasion.

We do not know just when the family arrived at Mr Fennell's spacious parsonage. Charlotte wrote on 29 September to tell her father that they would soon be home.[19] The weather had been bad, so they had mainly stayed indoors. The girls had been sewing, and all the children had been taught their lessons by Mr Fennell every day. Branwell had been drawing 'from Nature', while Emily, Anne and Charlotte had all been copying pictures. These had been taken from a book of views of the Lake District, where Mr Fennell had recently been on a visit. All this seems to have been quietly enjoyable. The following Friday the Brontës came home, apparently in a gig, which was not large enough for Mr Fennell to come with them to visit Haworth. Thus ended a holiday that had been happy, despite the rain.

The year 1830 saw the culmination of the period of co-operation between the Brontë children in various forms of communal activity. The 'plays' had reached their most prolific under the direction of Charlotte and Branwell. It was in 1830 that Emily began to exert an influence which would help to divide the family, splitting them into two pairs. The evidence is that she became dissatisfied with the African emphasis of the stories, and was seeking ways of bringing the action back to the realistic moorland scene of Haworth and district.

The children were growing up. We have two records of mayhem created by the boisterous four at the parsonage which must be dated about now. There is the incident recorded by Leyland in which Tabby sent for help to her nephew's house. 'William,' she is alleged to have said, 'yah mun gooa up to Mr Brontë's, for aw'm sure yon childer's all gooin mad, an' aw darn't stop 'ith hause ony longer wi' em; an' aw'll stay here woll yah come back!' When the nephew reached the parsonage (Leyland goes on) 'the childer set up a great crack o' laughing, at the wonderful joke they had perpetrated on faithful Tabby'.[20]

The second concerns a certain Oak-Apple Day, 29 May, possibly from 1830, though it may be from the previous year or even 1828. Several versions have been given, but the first and probably most accurate seems to be from Erskine Stuart's *The Brontë Country*. It may be important and needs to be quoted exactly.

> A story of Emily, which has never yet seen the light of day, has come to our knowledge, and it gives one a lively impression of how the parsonage girls amused themselves when the father was from home, and helps to dispel the idea, which many people seem to possess, that the Brontës were little priggish blue-stockings who never engaged in a good romp. It was the 29th of May, the anniversary of the Restoration. Haworth parsonage was in a state of noisy rebellion, the father was from home, young feet ran lightly over the house, and the sound of boisterous laughter echoed everywhere. They were celebrating the day right royally, by representing King Charles in the oak. Emily was 'The Merry Monarch' and encouraged to escape from her pursuers by stepping out of a bedroom window into the branches of a fruit tree which grew up the front of the house. Unfortunately the bough broke, and she came to *terra firma*, luckily, however, unhurt. On the return of the father, he had the whole family on the carpet, but he could not by any amount of cajolery or threatening succeed in getting to

> the bottom of the affair. Emily, however, on her death bed confessed to her father.[21]

Mrs Chadwick gives a version of the story which differs as follows:

1 The fruit tree is said to be a cherry tree.
2 The tree was highly prized by their father, and 'one of the servants' blacked the broken end with soot.
3 Mr Brontë found this out, but could not discover the culprit.[22]

In view of this, there seems no justification for Winifred Gérin (who gives these two as her authorities) to write that, when he came home, 'Mr Brontë was given a full account of what had happened'. The source of the story may be William Wood, and it is not impossible that this occasion is the same as the previous one mentioned. The comment by Stuart that Emily confessed on her deathbed may seem odd, but we shall note a number of poems in which trees are used as metaphors; Anne and Charlotte are also found writing of trees symbolically; and Emily herself is likened to one by her sisters.[23] It is possible that this incident stamped itself firmly on Emily's mind, and that the image of a broken tree haunted her.

Meanwhile Emily continued to play a full part in Charlotte's various stories. She is one of the three 'Old Washerwomen of Strathfieldsaye' on 14 July 1830, when like her sisters she was 'seated on a green bank under a holly, knitting with the utmost rapidity' and talking all the time. This month Charlotte wrote the last volume of *Tales of the Islanders* and concluded it with

> *4 volume of the Plays of Islands*
> *That is Emily's Branwell's Ann's and my lands*
> *And now I bid a kind and glad good-bye*
> *To those who o'er my book cast indulgent eye.*[24]

The order in which her siblings is given may be significant. It must seem likely that she and Emily were still making up stories in bed, and thus Emily is most prominent.

Not long afterwards, in October 1830, a special feature was carried in *Young Men's Magazine*. It was called 'A Day at Parry's Palace'. 'Captain Parry', of course, was under the protection of Emily, who was in the process of changing him from an Arctic explorer to a Yorkshire yeoman. Parry's palace itself was

> a square building of stone surmounted by blue slates and some round stone pumpkins the garden around it was of moderate dimensions laid out in round oval or square flowerbeds rows of peas gooseberry bushes and black red and white currant trees Some few common Flowering shrubs & a grass plat to dry clothes on. All the convenient offices such as, wash-house, back kitchin stable & coal house were built in a line & backed by a row of trees.[25]

Emily, now married to Parry, helps to entertain the guest. The meal is followed by the appearance of 'Little Peter', Emily's son, who is wearing a dirty pinafore. Emily has to change the boy quickly.

When dinner arrived on the table, at twelve o'clock, it consisted of roast beef, Yorkshire pudding, mashed potatoes, apple pie and preserved cucumbers. 'Ross', Anne's hero, became sick an hour after dinner and death would have occurred had not 'the Genius Emily arrived. . . . She cured with an incantation and vanished.' There is plenty of evidence in the juvenilia of quarrelling between the children. They allow their characters to squabble roughly and taunt each other. This surely mirrors fierce arguments among the 'genii', of whom Emily may have been becoming rebellious and unwilling to allow the story to moulder in the tropics.[26]

Before we leave the early writings of Charlotte and Branwell, we should revisit a fragment that previous Brontë biographers have been coy about. It comes from *The Foundling*, written by Branwell between 31 May and 27 June 1833. Dr Alexander considers that it looks back to the days of the toy soldiers. The 'foundling' of the story arrives in Africa, where he finds the small men (perhaps based on the ninepins, Charlotte's present from Mr Brontë in 1826). These creatures speak a Yorkshire dialect and amuse 'themselves by singing the following exquisite stanzas':

> *Eamala is a gurt bellaring bull,*
> *Shoo swilled and swilled till she drank her full;*

Then shoo rolled abaat
Wi' a screeaam an' shaat
And aat of her pocket a knoife did pull.

An' wi' that knoife shoo'd a cutt her throit
If I hadn't gean her a strait waist-coit;
Then shoo flang and jumped
and girned and grumped,
But I didn't caare for her a doit.

A sooin shoo doffed her mantle of red
Shoo went an' shoo ligged her daan aent bed,
An'theare shoo slept
Till the haase wor swept
And all the goid liquor wor goan fro her head.

This verse is mentioned by Phillis Bentley in *The Brontës and their World*, but more often omitted by Emily's biographers.[27]

We may recall that in March 1829 Emily was 'in the parlour brushing it'. Perhaps this was a task Emily sometimes got tired of. The poem seems to tell of a day when she screamed and shouted in temper and perhaps even threatened to stab herself. No doubt there is a fictional element in the treatment of the event, but before we dismiss the whole matter we must recall the day when Tabby rushed down to William's house and begged him to go and calm the children. If the children could 'go mad' once, they could do so on various occasions. Perhaps sometimes Emily made bellowing noises like a 'gurt bull' and, like Hindley Earnshaw, made dangerous moves with knives. It looks as if Branwell may have had to wrap her up in a red coat; after extricating herself from this, she dashed up to the bedroom and sulked, or went to sleep, until the housework was done – which suggests that the housework may have been the cause of the quarrel.

Whether the 'drink' element of this set of verses is based on fact may be a matter for debate. We have heard that there was beer in the cellar. Later, Branwell became a drunkard; the Irish Brontës may have included a drinker or two, and one kept a public house; Mr Brontë had to defend himself against a charge of drinking; Anne was to portray drunken behaviour realistically and Emily dramatically. Certainly it will not do to dismiss this rough rhyme as irrelevant to the story of Emily Brontë. There will be other occasions on which we shall hear of violent bad temper, which may have been inherited from her father. The domestic work we have already met and will meet again frequently. There is plenty of evidence in the poetry that Emily found certain aspects of her own behaviour uncontrollable. A child of twelve in a rage is a shocked and divided child, who feels within a second personality. This child was going to grow up to be the creator of Heathcliff and Cathy and Edgar Linton. Such a novel is not achieved without stress.

It seems possible that a major quarrel caused the end of Emily's closeness to Charlotte. An account of this occurs in Branwell's *History of the Young Men* for 15 December 1830, a month before Charlotte went to Roe Head.[28] Part of the row was apparently conducted through the toy soldiers. After an altercation, Parry goes to rest, but Tracky 'came and unceremoniously sat upon him'. Parry jumped up and 'stamped upon' his enemy. But the chief genius Talli (Charlotte) came in and seized him to protect him,

> and the Ch – Gn – Emii took up her favourite Parry. But from this time forward a great hatred has subsisted between the two heroes, and also between Ross, or Trott as the King called him, and his monarch.

Anne, as might be expected, took Emily's part. It was the latest in a series of rebellions, and would lead in time to secession.

6

Bold, Beautiful and Bright

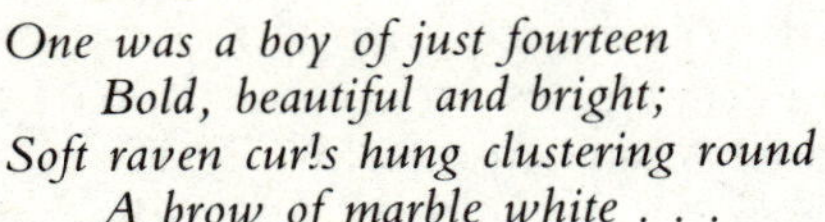

One was a boy of just fourteen
Bold, beautiful and bright;
Soft raven curls hung clustering round
A brow of marble white . . .

The other was a slender girl,
Blooming and young and fair.
The snowy neck was shaded with
The long bright sunny hair.

– Anne Brontë

Emily Brontë was twelve and a half when her elder sister left for Roe Head in January 1831 to continue her formal education.[1] Though this was not the end of the genii, Charlotte's absence clearly made a great deal of difference to the co-operative stories which had been written. Emily herself was growing and must have well overtaken Charlotte in height by now. There would be no more 'bed plays'. On the other hand, 'Annie' was becoming much more capable of sharing the inventions of her long-legged elder sister. At the age of eleven, she could walk a long way across moorland without tiring. Some Brontë historians believe that Gondal was begun at this time, and we shall examine probable ways in which this might happen.

Relations between Emily and Charlotte had been very close in childhood. Like Heathcliff and Catherine, they slept in the same bed and shared intimate secrets: 'Bed plays mean secret plays'. But here Emily stands on the brink of a great shift, which culminates in Charlotte's puzzled self-questioning after Emily's death, and her attempts to salve her conscience in print. The nature of their shared experience we can never know, but Emily's poems and novel are full of nightmares. We may well imagine that Charlotte had to comfort her highly strung sister on many occasions. Now the link was snapped, in part through quarrels, in part through circumstance. Charlotte began to acquire new interests, away from Haworth, and Emily made an alliance with Anne.

As a child on the verge of adolescence, Emily begins to discover herself. In the next seven years she will become introverted, self-divided and ill-at-ease with most other people. We have very little evidence by which to chart this process, and the poems in which she charts it for us do not begin until 1836. We shall try to do the best we can with the sparse data, and conclusions will be more than usually tentative. A neglected source is provided by the musical collection which Emily and Anne begin to build. But guesswork (which will always be acknowledged) may have to play a part.

It would be very useful to be able to determine exactly when Gondal was discovered. We have seen Emily trying to build Yorkshire into the African stories for some time. The clear inference is that when Charlotte went to school Emily took the opportunity to strike out with Anne and develop new plays. Romer Wilson points out that *Angora* may be a name developed from *Angria*, *Zalona* from *Zamorna*, and that *Zenobia*, who features in Anne's Gondal work, may be developed from Charlotte's *Zenobia* of 1829.[2] At one point Anne wrote some Gondal names into her *Grammar of General Geography*. These include Gondal itself, Gaaldine, Almedore, Elseraden, Ula, Zalona and Zedora; as Winifred Gérin says, some of them have an Arabic flavour, but there is nothing Arabic about the places themselves, which are a Pacific counterpart to the Atlantic Yorkshire.[3] Gondal's climate is Yorkshire climate, though Gaaldine's is tropical. We cannot date Anne's additions to the geography book.

It is hard to suppose that Emily and Anne wrote no 'plays' between October 1830 and November 1834, when 'the Gondals' will be found in Gaaldine. Either they invented Gondal soon after Charlotte left, or they tried to continue with her saga in parts of Angria where Charlotte and Branwell could not penetrate. But Charlotte returned from Roe Head in May 1832, and if Gondal had not been developed by then, the four children might have gone back to a common story. The concept of Gondal does seem to owe something to Angria. It looks as though it was a development, rather than a new conception. If Gondal had started as something new when Emily was sixteen, it should have been better organized, and the locations more appropriate. On balance, it looks as if it grew up at the time when Charlotte was away, in the years 1831–2, when Emily was about thirteen and Anne eleven.

Looking back on this time from the end of her adolescence, Emily notes in 1838, in 'Loud without the wind was roaring', that 'we' (that is, Anne and herself), rose at morning and made for 'the moors where the linnet was trilling/ Its song from the old granite stone'. In August 1839 in 'Fair sinks the summer evening now', she notes that 'this is just the joyous hour/ When we were wont to burst away . . . ' to 'go out to play'. And in the 1837 diary paper, written late in the afternoon, there is a discussion about whether the two girls will go out later on. We may understand from these accounts that the two of them were most likely to be found on the moors either early in the morning before domestic or educational work had begun, or late in the day. In these two poems and in the diary paper, Emily writes as though there was no adult constraint on when they went out, or where they went. It has been suggested that Branwell or Tabby would go with them, but Emily says they 'burst' away, which sounds a quite spontaneous process, beyond adult surveillance. They seem to have acted rather like the two 'Amazon' pirates in Arthur Ransome's *Swallows and Amazons* series, 'escaping' from the grown-up dungeon.[4]

In *Wuthering Heights* Heathcliff and Catherine have the same habit. Heathcliff tells Nelly how one night he and Cathy 'escaped from the wash-house to have a ramble at liberty'.[5] They race across the moor and through a bog, where Cathy loses her shoes, and she finishes the race barefoot. This is the night on which the two children discover Thrushcross Grange, and is the start of a division between them. It looks very much as though on one of their dusk rambles, Emily and Anne reached Ponden Hall after the lights were lit inside the windows, and amused themselves by peering in. There is no doubt that Ponden contributed one or two features to Thrushcross.

Ponden House (now called Ponden Hall) lies about two

miles across the moors in the Lancashire direction. A metalled road now leads from Haworth direct to the spot, which however has been changed by the building at the turn of the century of Ponden Reservoir. We shall need to reconstruct the scene as it was in the time of the Brontës. Though the road is an old road, it would not have been well surfaced, so that it would have been possible to walk quietly along it. The main road is not the only way to reach Ponden, and it seems probable that sometimes the girls would take a moorland path leading up to the site of the bog burst and then take the quick road home.[6] They may not have made directly for the house, at any rate not at first; there were plenty of other interesting things to see on the moors. But if they did end at Ponden, the evidence suggests that they could expect a welcome there.

Early critics were quick to infer a knowledge of Ponden House from the date which begins *Wuthering Heights*: 1801. This is the date prominent on the tablet over the front door of Ponden. The library at Thrushcross, in which Lockwood recuperates and Edgar lurks, is very like that at Ponden. From then on literary historians have set themselves the task of discovering how far the Brontës knew the house, and how much they made use of the library, which was splendid and well-stocked. The Heaton family, who owned the house, were traditional trustees of Haworth church. There are a number of short notes from Mr Brontë to heads of the Heaton household, bidding them to church or vestry meetings.[7] Later, a quarrel sprang up between the Heaton family and the old clergyman; it may even have been related to the publication of Emily's novel. But when the children were young, the families were on cordial terms. The following internal or circumstantial evidence suggests that they used the library.

1 The children were clearly influenced by Mungo Park's *Travels*, published in 1810, of which there was a copy at Ponden.[8]
2 Chateaubriand's *Travels in Greece and the Holy Land* was pirated by Branwell, who copied the title page in 1829. A copy was at Ponden.[9]
3 Winifred Gérin states that Voltaire's *Henriade*, translated by Charlotte in 1829, was in the library, though Tom Winnifrith has been unable to find it in the catalogue.[10]
4 It is considered that the rare word 'hermaphrodite' could

> only have been learnt by the young Brontës from Beaumont and Fletcher's play of that name; a copy was at Ponden.[11]

If we add to this the description of the library at Thrushcross Grange, there seems to be no doubt that the Brontë children were encouraged by Robert Heaton, the then head of the family, to borrow books fairly liberally, at least from about 1829. A secondary aim on the part of Emily and Anne when they set out across the moor may have been to borrow or return a book.

In 1831 the Heaton family consisted of Robert and Alice Heaton, who had been married ten years and had three children, all boys. These were Robert (born 4 May 1822), William (born 1 June 1825) and John (born 22 March 1827). The next child, a girl, died as an infant.[12] At the time when Emily and Anne seem to have taken to crossing the moor on their own, the eldest was nine. Winifred Gérin asserts that 'they became eventual playmates'.[13] There have been persistent attempts to prove some kind of romantic link between Emily and one of these boys. In view of their respective ages and the character of Emily, this seems unlikely, but the girls certainly must have met these boys; possibly Robert Heaton does duty for one of the iron-hearted Gondal lads. More interestingly, Mary Butterfield mentions that Robert Heaton (presumably the elder) is said to have planted a pear tree for Emily, which still flourishes in the garden of the house.[14] If so, this suggests that her winsome ways of Cowan Bridge days were not yet extinct.

Emily and Anne liked housekeepers, represented at the parsonage by Tabby and in their books by long-memoried retainers. Perhaps (but this is speculation) they may have been welcomed into the Ponden kitchen and been told two horrifying tales of the past. One concerned the seventeenth-century Henry Casson, who married a Heaton widow and ruled at Ponden for twenty years. After his death the true heir, Robert, had to buy back his own inheritance. I have suggested that Emily became interested in usurpers through her father's story of his own pseudo-grandfather, Welsh. If so, this might have made an impression on her, though it would be going too far to say that Casson *was* the origin of Heathcliff. We shall find yet another usurper story which must have been known to Emily later in this decade.

There had been a tragedy in the Heaton family not fifteen years before. The Robert Heaton who had rebuilt the house and put up the tablet over the new front door in 1801 had a daughter Elizabeth. She had formed an attachment to a Leeds grocer's boy, John Bakes, and had a child by him.[15] They were married at Haworth, Robert Heaton paying £200 to legitimize the baby. But John Bakes turned out to be a disastrous husband, who drank the profits while Elizabeth, far gone in consumption, ran the grocer's shop. She died at Ponden, after three years of marriage, in 1816. The small child she brought to the house, then about three, does not seem to have been heard of later. If it was a boy, and he was still alive and to be seen about the farm in a partly dependent condition, he might have made a model for Hareton. This is speculation, as is the idea that if he did exist, Emily might have formed a romantic attachment to him.

Emily is later to write about ruins, such as the 'old hall of Elbë' mentioned in a fragment. There was just such a neglected house at Ponden, called Ponden Old Hall. Confusingly, it was newer than the house itself, having been built in 1634 as an additional dwelling.[16] By renewing the older house (the one not built in 1634) in 1801, Robert Heaton had sealed the fate of this one. It will be seen that I am not encouraging the idea that Emily had any romantic reason for visiting Ponden. But some of the facets of the novel do seem to originate or strengthen there, and after its publication the family may have felt that Emily had betrayed them by raking up old scandals. This seems to confirm the view that she had been a welcome visitor and had been told the Ponden legends.

We know of very few people with whom Emily Brontë can be said to have been on close terms, even fewer who might have been described as her soul-mate. Since both the poems and the novel seem to cry out for an interpretation involving some such friendship at an impressionable age, we must search carefully for candidates for this honour. We cannot assume that if she was particularly friendly with one person at thirteen, this friendship continued for ever; but the 'ardent child' of Cowan Bridge would surely need some close tie at this stage of her life.

Yet any such person is hard to find. I have already

suggested that Maria and Elizabeth, in their different ways, fostered Emily's growth. Maria's ideas became unpalatable, but her enquiring mind is mirrored in Emily's. Elizabeth provided security, and we have seen evidence to suggest she was calm, more like Anne. The relationship between Emily and Charlotte fluctuates through their lives; it can be close, but is full of misunderstanding. It is sometimes said that Branwell and Emily formed a close attachment; but at this stage, Branwell was more an associate of Charlotte's. There will be times when Emily will talk to and enjoy the confidence of her father, whose character in some ways she shares. Her aunt, though not as repressive as she has been painted, does not seem to have been the same kind of person as her niece. But we do have overwhelming evidence that during this period (though not always) Emily and Anne were intimate. The nature and parameters of this association need examination. It will be important not to confuse the relationship between Anne and Emily as young women, which we shall explore in due time, with the childhood friendship we are now contemplating.

Ellen Nussey first met the two younger Brontës in summer 1833. She has a great deal to say about them, both about Emily's character and about the two together. We have two diary papers during the period under discussion, from 1834 and 1837. In 'Self-communion' Anne writes about her early friendship with Emily. There are passages in Emily's poems in which she deals with the same topic (one in 'The death of A. G. A.' is especially interesting). Some habits of the children continued beyond their childhood (for example, the habit of co-operating on Gondal, the habit of actually acting parts as they walked, of 'being' various characters). From these clues, we may construct a picture of the intimacy between Emily and Anne during 1831–7, until Emily departed for Law Hill.

Ellen Nussey, writing in her 1871 'Reminiscences', said, 'She and Anne were like twins – inseparable companions, and in the closest sympathy, which never had any interruption.'[17] In a letter to Clement Shorter, Ellen Nussey wrote: 'Anne and Emily were however very close friends, always together and in unison like dearly attached twins.'[18] Another of Ellen Nussey's comments stated that: 'She and gentle Anne were to be seen twined together as united statues of power and humility. They were to be seen with their arms lacing each other in their younger days whenever their occupations permitted their union.'[19]

By 1833, Emily had 'acquired a lithesome, graceful figure. She was the tallest person in the house, except her father.' We shall later follow Ellen Nussey on a walk with the twins and their brother and sister.[20]

Anne Brontë writes,

> *Oh, I have known a wondrous joy*
> *In early friendship's pure delight, –*
> *A genial bliss that could not cloy –*
> *My sun by day, my moon by night.*[21]

She can only be writing about her friendship with Emily. The next lines go on to discuss occasions when this close attachment was broken, but these causes of final dissension need not be examined yet.

In 'The death of A. G. A.' Emily writes, with more sophistication and caution, and admittedly in the persona of a wild princess called Angelica,

> *I've known a hundred kinds of love:*
> All *made the loved one rue; . . .*
> *Listen, I've known a burning heart*
> *To which my own was given;*
> *Nay, not in passion, do not start –*
> *Our love was love from heaven;*
> *At least, if heavenly love be born*
> *In the pure light of childhood's morn –*
> *Long ere the poison-tainted air*
> *From this world's plague-fen rises there . . .*
> *She was my all-sufficing light,*
> *My childhood's mate, my girlhood's guide,*
> *My only blessing, only pride.*[22]

This speech by Angelica to Douglas suggests that Emily is recalling a close childhood friendship. Taken together with Ellen Nussey's descriptions of Emily with Anne, the passage may be thought an indicator of the kind of relationship the two enjoyed. It is emphasized that this was not a 'passionate' friendship; this was a 'heavenly' love. 'My *soul* dwelt with her day and night', says Angelica. Just so did Catherine's soul dwell with Heathcliff.

Once again in this poem the betrayal theme is strong. Because of this Angelica enlists the help of Douglas to kill her old soul-mate. We may not be able to relate this precisely to the friendship between Emily and Anne, though perhaps the substitution of her sister for herself at Roe Head may have appeared a little in this light; the poem was written years later, in 1841. The use of this phrase 'a hundred kinds of love' (though hyperbolic) suggests that Emily had given the whole matter deep thought. This is worth remembering when we consider Catherine's famous speech to Nelly in *Wuthering Heights*. She claims to love Edgar in a different way from her love for Heathcliff. Sometimes this statement is glossed over, but it appears that Emily wants the reader to understand that Catherine, despite her flowery language, really 'loves' Edgar. Imagination has changed the roles rather: Heathcliff, the eternal rock, *is* Catherine, while Edgar is felt as outside and desired. But if we are right to emphasize the twin-like nature of the relationship between Emily and Anne, it is the Edgar-meek Anne whom Emily considers part of herself. The philosophy of the novel took years to grow; one of the factors which caused it to do so was surely the heartfelt intimacy between Emily and Anne Brontë.

There is very little hard evidence of Emily Brontë's life during 1831–2 when Charlotte had gone to school, but we are surely right to see the friendship between the two remaining sisters developing. The two girls certainly read books, probably aloud to each other as the rest of the family did. We have seen that Emily was interested in Scott, and we shall soon find evidence that she and Anne shared a liking for the work of Tom Moore, the Irish poet. In 1830 his *Life of Byron* was published. This was read by Emily, who is soon found copying the plates; it would be interesting because of its subject, who exercised a deep fascination on the Brontës and who seems to be one root of the Satanic elements in Heathcliff and Rochester. The whole circle of Romantic poets entered Emily's consciousness. Mr Brontë eventually bought a copy of the *Life of Byron*, though we do not know exactly when. Emily seems to have read the book thoroughly. Meanwhile, she may have had two other libraries to call upon, in addition to Ponden: Keighley Mechanics' Institute and a circulating library in the same town.[23]

In the *Life of Byron* Emily was able to see Aemilia Curran's engraving of Shelley. His name never occurs in her writing, but a series of poems written in late 1839 and early 1840 can hardly refer to anyone else. I shall discuss these poems in their context, but in 'It is too late to call thee now', she writes,

> *Yet, ever in my grateful breast*
> *Thy darling shade shall cherished be;*
> *For God alone doth know how blest*
> *My early years have been in thee!*

To what 'early years' is she referring? It seems most probable that she means the years we are now considering, from 1831 onwards, when Emily was thirteen and after. We may guess, but unfortunately can offer no sure proof, that the *Life of Byron* stirred Emily to read or re-read Shelley's poetry, the influence of which is deep in her own and in Anne's. Shelley's views on marriage, on the deity, on the soul, on love, are present at many points in *Wuthering Heights* and the later poetry. It may not be too much to suspect that at about thirteen she began to take him as a personal guide. The facts certainly fit such a hypothesis.

Anne's evident knowledge of 'Epipsychidion' suggests that she and Emily read the poem together, perhaps for the first time during this early teenage period.[24] It is full of platonic and romantic love, which the girls evidently felt quite proper to their present age. As Anne says in her 'Alexander and Zenobia' of 1 July 1837, of her two youthful figures reclining 'deep in a shady bower', 'One was a boy of just fourteen . . . '. Emily was 'just fourteen' in July 1832. In her poetry, she identifies sometimes with a female lover, sometimes with a male. Fourteen, according to Anne Brontë, is the proper age for romantic love.[25] It is also worth noting that critics who suppose that Emily allows Cathy to *reject* Edgar in favour of Heathcliff, or vice versa, have not read carefully enough. Cathy intends, in different ways, to love both; perhaps Emily obtained this idea from Shelley.

Our knowledge of the religious development of Emily Brontë is pitifully scant. If she was reading Shelley at this point in her life, she may have begun to be impatient with the Haworth church worship at about the same time. Whether she read much in the 'Blessed bible, book divine' about whom the parishioners sang in their special service on 22 July 1827, or followed the advice to 'Enquire, ye blooming youths, the way/ Which leads to Zion's hill' as exhorted before the sermon at the special Sunday School service on 14 August 1831, as the time went by Emily certainly did become disenchanted with the church. Older villagers remembered that she did not teach in the Sunday School, though the others did.

Her choice of music for the piano in 1832 is wholly secular, though later the children are found practising Handel's *Messiah*. Just before her thirteenth birthday she bought a piece called 'Purcell's Ground', and then 'Three original waltzes' by R. Andrew (3 October 1832) and 'Gems of the Opera', bought on 24 November. These show a developing musical capacity, but no link with the church music we might have expected. Patrick himself was concerned about the church choir, according to a letter of 6 June 1832, the complete interpretation of which is uncertain.[26] By this time it seems likely that Abraham Stansfield Sunderland, from Keighley, was giving lessons to Emily and Anne, and probably the others. We shall meet him in the 1834 diary paper. Very soon Patrick was trying to buy an organ for the church to give a fitting performance of *Messiah*. Emily, however, had already detached herself mentally from the proceedings.

When not being taught by Mr Sunderland, Emily and Anne were likely to find themselves under the tutelage of Charlotte, now returned from Roe Head.

> In the morning, from nine o'clock till half-past twelve, I instruct my Sisters and draw, then we walk till dinner, after dinner I sew till tea-time . . . . We are expecting company this afternoon and on Tuesday next we shall have all the Female teachers of the Sunday school to tea.[27]

So writes Charlotte to Ellen on 21 July 1832. One presumes that while Charlotte was sewing in the afternoon, Emily and Anne were half-way across the moors to Ponden. But Charlotte considers the entertainment of the Sunday School teachers to be a joint operation. Whether she would manage to summon Emily into the room at the same time as the teachers is dubious. Charlotte ends the letter in disappointment at not receiving a lock of Ellen's hair which had been promised. One needs to remember the sentimental aspect to female relationships at this time in trying to guess how Emily would treat Anne, or any other friends she might have.

There is a typical small dating problem about the expedition that the Brontës made with Ellen to Bolton Abbey. Wemyss

Reid considers that it took place in June 1833, basing his story on a manuscript written for him by Ellen.[28] This does not quite fit with a letter of Charlotte's written *after* the visit of Ellen to Haworth, in which details of the financial arrangements are still being argued.[29] But there can be no doubt that the expedition was a success and helped to foster the alliance between Ellen Nussey and the Brontës. Through it she became acquainted with Branwell and the two younger girls.

Bolton Abbey is a well-known beauty spot on the river Wharfe, about fourteen miles from Haworth. Winifred Gérin calculates that it would have taken the Haworth gig about two and a half hours to make the journey across Rombalds Moor and through the pretty village of Addingham. There are fine mature woods in the area, which is very different from Haworth or Keighley. Stepping stones lead across the river at a point where it is flanked by green meadows. The abbey ruins were certainly unlike anything the Brontës had seen before, romantic in the Gothic manner, and artistically superb. Many years later Anne took Emily to see York Minster, of which she had grown very fond. Until then, Emily would not have seen anything resembling this sight, unless it was the rather different cathedral in Brussels.

Wemyss Reid describes the bright morning scene outside the Devonshire Arms, where Ellen and her brothers wait for the Brontës to arrive.

> Their conveyance is no handsome carriage, but a rickety dog-cart, unmistakably betraying its neighbourhood to the carts and ploughs of some rural farmyard. The horse, freshly taken from the fields, is driven by a youth who, in spite of his countrified air, is no mere bumpkin. His shock of red hair hangs down in somewhat ragged locks behind his ears, for Branwell Brontë esteems himself a genius and a poet, and, following the fashion of the times, has that abhorrence of the barber's shears which genius is supposed to affect. But the lad's face is a handsome and striking one, full of Celtic fire and humour.[30]

Undoubtedly Bolton Abbey was a significant choice, and the visit was a real attempt on Ellen's part to further the relationship between the two families. It must surely have been her suggestion; she understood that her friend would be particularly attracted to the 'immemorial woods and vales of Bolton'.[31] The fast-flowing Wharfe was a larger version of the Ponden beck and other moorland streams. The abbey in dereliction could hardly fail to remind these connoisseurs of poetry of Wordsworth's Tintern and Scott's Melrose. The party seems to have been lucky with the weather, and it was no wonder that the day stayed in the memory for many years. At least two of Ellen's brothers appear to have been on the trip; thus Charlotte was introduced to Henry Nussey, who was later to propose marriage to her. As for Emily, we have not one word of her reaction. We may guess that she still considered herself enough of a child to skip across the stepping stones, while her encounter with the abbey ruins provides some material for later verse.

It was on 19 July 1833 that Ellen Nussey first came to Haworth to visit her friend. She remembered the visit all her life and gave various accounts of it to biographers. We shall examine some details from these accounts here. To Mrs Gaskell, who was mainly interested in Charlotte, Ellen wrote that 'Emily was a tall, long-armed girl, more fully grown than her elder sister; extremely reserved in manner.'[32]

In *Scribner's* (1871) Ellen said that

> Emily Brontë had by this time acquired a lithesome, graceful figure. She was the tallest person in the house, except her father. Her hair, which was naturally as beautiful as Charlotte's, was in the same unbecoming tight curl and frizz, and there was the same want of complexion. She had very beautiful eyes – kind, kindling eyes; but she did not often look at you; she was too reserved. Their colour might be said to be dark grey, at other times dark blue, they varied so. She talked very little.

This was the talkative, 'pretty nursling' of Cowan Bridge! Ellen then goes on to describe Emily's relationship with Anne, in a sentence already quoted. The same article dealt with their expedition on the moors, and this will be examined later.

Miss Robinson, describing Emily in 1833, again on Ellen's information, says,

> In 1833 Emily was nearly fifteen, a tall long-armed girl, full grown, elastic of tread; with a slight figure that looked queenly in her best dresses, but loose and boyish when she slouched over the moors, whistling to her dogs, and taking long strides over the rough earth. A tall, thin, loose-jointed girl – not ugly, but with irregular features and a pallid thick complexion. Her dark brown hair was naturally beautiful . . . in 1833 she wore it in an unbecoming tight curl and frizz. She had very beautiful eyes of *hazel colour* [my italics] . . . . She had an aquiline nose, a large expressive, prominent mouth. She talked little. No grace or style in dress belonged to Emily, but under her awkward clothes her natural movements had the lithe beauty of the wild creatures she loved.

This appears to be based partly on the *Scribner's* article, and in part on fresh material.[33]

In a letter to Shorter, Ellen wrote some details of Emily's behaviour without dates attached, so that we cannot be sure whether or not she is talking of this occasion. There are references to Emily's 'moral power'. Concerning her appearance, the letter mentions only her smile. ('One of her rare expressive looks was something to remember through life, there was such a depth of soul and feeling, and yet a shyness of revealing herself'.) Ellen's report of Emily's behaviour on the moors probably does belong here, and we shall consider it with the other accounts.

The most striking thing about these accounts is the confusion over the eye colour. This confusion is impossible to sort out; we shall have to conclude that her eyes were certainly not brown, but they were not a clear grey either. It looks as if they had a dash of yellow amidst the grey which caused Ellen to see them as hazel in some lights. Their expression struck Ellen, and we recall that as a child Emily's eyes were never still. Her complexion is also said to be pallid, despite her frequent excursions out of doors. In her adult life, she seems to have slept very little, and the pallor might sometimes be the result of tiredness. Her mouth is said to be prominent, and we shall notice this feature on Branwell's portrait when we come to it. The feature that was remembered by everyone later was Emily's height: her legs were longer than those of the rest of the family. Branwell and Charlotte were both short, and Anne not large. Emily was tall, like her father and some of his relatives.[34]

Emily showed no exuberance of spirit at home, it seems. She is said to talk little. But once out on the moors, her self-consciousness fell away. Once again, Ellen gave a number of versions of Emily's behaviour away from the house. The *Scribner's* version is the fullest, and we shall quote it entire, adding one or two items from that in *Charlotte Brontë and her Circle* which have been omitted from the earlier one.

> Emily had now begun to have the disposal of her own time [in 1833] . . . . In fine and suitable weather delightful rambles were made over the moors, and down into the glens and ravines that here and there broke the monotony of the moorland. The rugged bank and rippling brook were treasures of delight. Emily, Anne, and Branwell used to ford the streams, and sometimes placed stepping stones for the other two; there was always a lingering delight in these spots – every moss, every flower, every tint and form, were noted and enjoyed. Emily especially had a gleesome delight in these nooks of beauty, – her reserve for the time vanished. One long ramble made in these early days was far away over the moors to a spot familiar to Emily and Anne, which they called 'The Meeting of the Waters'. It was a small oasis of emerald green turf, broken here and there by small clear springs; a few large stones served as resting places; seated here, we were hidden from all the world, nothing appearing in view but miles and miles of heather, a glorious blue sky, and brightening sun. A fresh breeze wafted on us its exhilarating influence; we laughed and made mirth of each other, and settled we would call ourselves the quartette. Emily, half reclining on a slab of stone, played like a young child with the tadpoles in the water, making them swim about, and then fell to moralising on the strong and the weak, the brave and the cowardly, as she chased them with her hand.[35]

This passage constitutes one of our best sources for Emily as a teenager, and will bear a good deal of examination.

It looks as if two expeditions are being condensed into one. In the first, the four girls and Branwell are present; in the other, the four girls alone constitute 'the quartette'. That Emily and Anne spent time on the moor by themselves is shown when Ellen comes to discuss the green oasis which they know well. Neither Charlotte nor Branwell is included in this reference. The name of the oasis is 'The Meeting of the Waters' and there are various places which have been identified with it. In her *Haworth History Trail* Joanna Hutton suggests that it was at Ponden Waters before the making of the reservoir, though Sladen Valley has often been proposed. An actual meeting of two streams was at the east end of the present reservoir on low ground that has been flooded. Here the Ponden Clough beck met the more northerly stream in a small pool, calm enough for frogs to spawn.[36]

The name chosen by Emily and Anne is interesting. Here is evidence for their liking for the poems of Thomas Moore, the Irish lyricist, whose work influenced Anne's and who may not be totally absent from Emily's poems. He was one of the Shelley and Byron fraternity, whose *Life of Byron* we have already mentioned. But Anne at any rate, and (it seems) Emily too, enjoyed his verse for its own sake. Moore's poem, set to a classicized Irish tune called 'The Old Head of Dennis' begins

There is not in the wide world a valley so sweet
As the vale in whose bosom the bright waters meet;
Oh! the last rays of feeling from life must depart,
Ere the bloom of that valley shall fade from my heart.

Moore goes on to explain that it is not merely nature's spell which has made this place a special one, but that friends, 'the beloved of my bosom' were near. In fact, 'the best charms of Nature improve/ When we see them reflected in looks that we love'. The poem is likely to appeal to young teenagers, and we need to take Moore into account when considering the feeling life of Emily Brontë during this period.

The next part of the quotation is quite well known. Emily lies down on a rock and puts her hand into the water. There she starts to push the tadpoles about. Some would escape, some perhaps turn to confront the aggressor. Emily falls 'to moralising'. So little is heard of Emily off duty that her 'moralising' words (which are not even given) have been the subject of considerable comment. It is hard to see what to make of them, except to point out that Emily was not squeamish. She doesn't mind pushing tadpoles with her hands, but her 'moralising' has forever eluded us.

In her letter to Clement Shorter, Ellen, with little time to live, expanded somewhat on Emily's 'spirit of mischief' on the moors.

> She enjoyed leading Charlotte where she would not dare to go of her own free-will. Charlotte had a mortal dread of unknown animals, and it was Emily's pleasure to lead her into close vicinity, and then to tell her of how and of what she had done, laughing at her horror with great amusement.[37]

Just in this way the Irish Brontës frightened their neighbours with talk of headless horsemen, and Mr Brontë himself tried to petrify Ellen Nussey during breakfast by telling tales of the 1798 rebellion and perhaps of a dark sinister changeling who had usurped the family fortunes.[38]

What 'unknown animals' can Ellen mean? Bulls and cows, it must seem; but perhaps Charlotte disliked even tadpoles, in which case Emily's moralizing on cowardly and fearless animals might include moralizing on Charlotte. It was, after all, three years since the old alliance between Charlotte and Emily had broken up. Some years after this, Emily is writing about *not* despising the 'timid deer', and decides that as nature has made the deer, so is its character.[39] And Edgar 'possessed the power to depart [from Catherine] as much as a cat possesses the power to leave a mouse half killed'. The character of animals, and apparently of humans, is fixed. This seems a different view from that of Anne's hopeful heroine, Helen Huntingdon, who marries her Arthur in a vain effort to reform him: an impossible task, as Anne makes clear.

It is certainly pleasant to have this 'spirit of mischief' mentioned. The statuesque Emily, sphinx of modern literature, lacks it, as do Charlotte and her created Helen, who may be echoing Maria. Emily did have this impish delight in trouble-making, we are shown. It may be worth bearing this in mind as we follow her in her skirmishes with clergymen and schoolteachers. Looking back on this visit, Ellen felt sure that one root of *Wuthering Heights* was in Mr Brontë's ghoulish stories. They made one 'shiver and shrink from hearing; but they were full of grim humour and interest to Mr Brontë and his children'. These sessions terrified Ellen, who disliked Mr Brontë, apparently misreading his sense of humour and great talent for imaginative terror. Emily seems to have been thrilled by them and her face relaxed

> from its company rigour, while she stooped down to hand her porridge-bowl to the dog: she wore a strange expression, gratified, pleased, as though she had gained something which seemed to complete a picture in her mind.[40]

The picture Emily was building up was, we may suppose, her Irish-derived view of clan history, of death and the supernatural, and the personal force of the goblin who would become Heathcliff.[41]

Ellen also noted the Brontë enthusiasm for pets, again transmitted from Mr Brontë and perhaps his father before him. At that time the Brontë dog was Grasper, which Emily drew 'from life' in January 1834. He was an Irish terrier, and had been living in the parsonage since at least 1831. The dog was undoubtedly spoilt; both Emily and Anne are said to have fed him part of their own porridge at breakfast.[42] In his portrait, Grasper looks a sharp soul, cheerful and not quite as unmanageable as his successor, Keeper.

We have Ellen's word that there was not much drapery in the house at this time, and no curtains. Perhaps Emily made a point of mentioning curtains in 'Douglas's Ride', dated 11 July 1838, because they were new. They feature in a drawing by Charlotte, and Ellen seems to have been wrong in thinking there were no curtains at all until Charlotte became famous.[43] She stresses Mr Brontë's fear of fire, which is supposed to be one reason why the children always wore wool. This fear was a phobia gained in childhood, when at night the fire in the kiln room of the cottage at Imdel scorched the millers and farmers, as they listened to old Hugh Brunty's ballads and Irish myth. In the 1798 rebellion, soldiers apparently set light to the thatch of Patrick's house, whereupon old Hugh besought them in Irish Gaelic to put it out. Patrick would be able to see how speedily fire could threaten life. Emily had not witnessed this, and she may have disagreed about fire. Certainly in *Wuthering Heights* fires, though powerful, are welcome.

Throughout her life Emily gave the impression of being

well, except that she could overtax herself, and as Charlotte wrote to Dr Epps in 1848, 'Her temperament is highly nervous.'[44] But after Ellen went home, Emily developed erysipelas, a disease which is usually thought of as the result of a virus.

> Since you were here, Emily has been very ill; her ailment was Erysipelas in the arm, accompanied by severe bilious attacks, and great general debility: her arm was obliged to be cut to remove the noxious matter which had accumulated in the inflamed parts; it is now I am happy to say nearly healed, her health is in fact almost perfectly re-established: though the sickness continues to recur at intervals. Were I to tell you of the impression you have made on everyone here, you would accuse me of flattery. Papa and aunt are continually adducing you as an example for me to shape my actions and behaviour by, Emily and Anne say 'they never saw anyone they liked so much as Miss Nussey'.[45]

All in all, Ellen's visit had been a great success, and constituted another 'window on the world' for Emily and Anne. These two, as 'twins', are spoken of almost as if they are one person. This continues in 1834, when on 19 June Charlotte refers to them simply as 'sisters'. We have the strong impression that at this time the two younger Brontës had very much withdrawn into their own world of school-friends and a dimension outside Haworth.

A scrap of evidence concerning Emily's appearance at sixteen has been quoted in a number of books. In 'My Angria and the Angrians' Branwell (calling himself Patrick Benjamin Wiggins) describes his three sisters, 'sempstresses' of 'Howard'. Charlotte, a 'broad dumpy thing' does not come 'higher than my elbow'; Anne is 'nothing, absolutely nothing'; and Emily who is 'sixteen', is 'lean and scant, with a face about the size of a penny'.[46] As we know, Emily was also tall, a fact Branwell does not emphasize (it challenges him). Her thinness is interesting, and may be associated with her later failure at Roe Head. The brotherly feeling manifested by this description will also be noted.

The one document we have from Emily and her 'twin' in 1834 is the celebrated 'diary paper' of 24 November. There seems no doubt that this, the first of an erratic series, was based on an idea they found in Moore's *Life of Byron*, as was first noticed by John Hewish. It has already been suggested that this book became an important source for them. The diary paper has been described and illustrated in so many books on the Brontës that it seems unnecessary to reprint it in full.[47] It has a certain slapdash charm, like Charlotte's 1829 summary, in the parsonage kitchen where potatoes are supposed to be being peeled. Like Byron, the girls start off by describing their pets, but not in enough detail for us to be sure what kind of animals they were: doves, it is generally supposed. As well at these there is a pheasant maddeningly called Jasper (to become confused with Grasper). There is news about Sir Robert Peel standing for Leeds; and Aunt is shown to be less than wickedly repressive when she asks Anne 'Where are your feet, Anne?' 'On the floor, Aunt,' replies cheeky Anne. (We assume that the purpose of the question was to suggest that the lazy girl might use them to go and make the beds, mentioned just below.) No bolt from heaven strikes idle Annie, and still the girls have not done their piano practice.

All of a sudden we read 'The Gondals are discovering the interior of Gaaldine' and then, without punctuation, 'Sally mosley' (a live inhabitant of Haworth) 'is washing in the back kitchin'. The dates are in Emily's conventional hardwriting, and so is one line of text (but not the first). The rest is in Brontë small script. A possible blot in the margin has been turned into 'a bit of Lady Julets hair done by Anne'. (Lady Juliet is never heard of again.) Spelling is mediocre: 'phaesent', 'limted', 'ourselvs', 'derectly' are some examples. The girls say they 'want to go out to play'; they are sixteen and fourteen, enjoying an extended childhood. Yet, as we have seen, Anne will write of a boy-girl attachment involving someone of that age in 1837. 'The kitchin is in a very untidy state', writes Emily; just like the diary paper. Nevertheless this and its successors, of which there are five in all, give us almost all we ever have about herself directly from Emily's pen.

How exactly were the Gondals 'discovering the interior' of Gaaldine in the late morning of 24 November 1834? Not actively on their feet, evidently. Anne's were on the floor, but not moving. Not on paper either, since the girls had in front of them a scrap on which they were engaged in rivalling

Byron and describing the scene in the kitchen. They were peeling apples for a pudding and 'Aunts nuts and apples'. While this was going on, there could be no writing. What there could be was talking in pretended Gondal voices, and this is what we must imagine. One of the sisters may have been Lady Juliet. We may assume that the apples themselves were not seen concentratedly. The girls' vision was in Gaaldine, a hot country, and they must have chattered to themselves in the persons of the Gondal invaders as they peeled the apples. It is possible that later the whole scene could be recalled and written up, but this may not have happened. Gondal was at this time a living, changing world, the outlines of which could be erased and redrawn if necessary. Here we have 'oral Gondal', but if the sisters did succeed in getting out to play eventually, they might have gone out of the village and acted out the scene in a 'drama Gondal'. Probably the ideal place for such an enactment would be the moors round Ponden, where they could ford the becks near 'The Meeting of the Waters' and climb the scattered rocks which ten years before had been flung downhill in the wild eruption of Crow Hill bog.

7

What Happened at Roe Head?

Will the day be bright or cloudy?
Sweetly has its dawn begun;
But the heaven may shake with thunder
Ere the setting of the sun.

As two of my dear children are soon to be placed near you, I take the liberty of writing to you a few lines in order to request both you and Mr Franks to be so kind as to interpose with your advice and counsel to them in any case of necessity, and, if expedient, to write to Miss Branwell or me if our interference should be requisite. I will charge them strictly to attend to what you may advise, though it is not my intention to speak to them of this letter. They both have good abilities, and as far as I can judge their principles are good also, but they are very young, and unacquainted with the ways of this delusive and insnaring world; and though they will be placed under the superintendence of Miss Wooler, who will I doubt not do what she can for their good, yet I am well aware that neither they nor any other can ever, in this land of probation, be beyond the reach of temptation.[1]

Charlotte wrote to Ellen on 2 July 1835 to tell her that the cosy family atmosphere of the parsonage was to be broken up. Branwell was to go to the Royal Academy in London; Anne would stay at home; Charlotte would go to teach for Miss Wooler at her school at Roe Head, and Emily would go with her as a pupil. They would leave the day before Emily's birthday, on 29 July. The next day she would be seventeen.

We may have some idea of what Emily looked like at the time. The National Portrait Gallery's painting, which Branwell painted, may date from this year. The identification of the faces seems certain.[2] Its chief impression on us may be of a dreamy young girl, her hair quite dark and eyes a blue shade, but not bright blue; her dress green. She has pouting lips (one may guess she was unwilling to be painted) and a long nose. She seems much taller than Anne, who sits next to her. Her expression is watchful, almost wary.

Mr Brontë's letter is probably typical of those sent by anxious parents whose children are leaving home. After the tragedy of Cowan Bridge, it was to be expected that he should view with caution the placing of two children at a distance. Charlotte, of course, had been to Roe Head as a girl, and would only be going back to a familiar scene. But the interesting thing about Mr Brontë's letter is that he doesn't seem to doubt the physical safety of the girls: they will not catch tuberculosis this time. What he does seem to doubt is their moral fibre!

Was Emily showing signs of rebellion? Undoubtedly she would be a keen learner; what made Mr Brontë decide to take her away from the habit of indolent and unsystematic learning she had been following up to now? Perhaps the mild cheek of the 1834 diary paper had been exceeded by the tempersome Emily. She would surely take her part in sweeping and bedmaking as before, delaying and grumbling, if the past record is anything to go by. But perhaps she would not easily conform to rules laid down by her rather particular aunt, over whom she towered. When the sweeping was done, she would be over the moor to Ponden (we may plausibly guess), in a wild, unconventional way, leading her sweet sister astray. We recall Emily's reading: Scott and his extrovert heroines on the one hand, Shelley and his dangerous radicalism on the other. Emily gave up the discipline of the church; but then she must accept some other discipline, that of school. Of course, this is guesswork, but there is a tone of anxiety in Mr Brontë's letter which needs accounting for.

But 'liberty', as Charlotte later wrote, was something of which Emily flatly refused to be deprived. 'The change . . . from her own very noiseless, very secluded, but very unrestricted . . . life, to one of disciplined routine . . . was what she failed in enduring', wrote Charlotte.[3] This account of hers, written so much later, is the only external contemporary evidence we have about Roe Head's effect on Emily. She saw this kindly and well-tested school as a prison for seventeen-year-olds, and had many literary exemplars before her which told her that prisons were there to be escaped from. What happened in the prison, and how Emily escaped, we must try to suggest.

As a place, Roe Head was very acceptable. It was a pleasant, bow-fronted stone house, with tall sash windows. Anne made a drawing of it, showing its large front lawn and encircling trees. The gardens are surrounded by a stone wall, but the view beyond was easily seen from the upper windows of the house. It was a soft and leafy prospect, but it was not moorland.[4] 'My sister Emily loved the moors', wrote Charlotte in discussing her failure here. However green the country round Roe Head, it was tame and controlled, and did not correspond with Emily's personality. If the dells and becks round Ponden could become Gondal, Roe Head could not. Just three years later, when she went to Law Hill, there were places that reminded her of home, and she stayed for six months; at Roe Head, she lasted less than three.

It was not that the school was in alien surroundings. Maria and Elizabeth had actually been born nearby at Hartshead, and Emily might also have been interested in the legends of Robin Hood, whose supposed grave was a little way off, and an inn nearby was called after him. The three Miss Woolers who ran the school (a fourth had recently married) may well have been known to Mr Brontë from his curacy, and Charlotte had not been unhappy at school. Publicly she spoke well of Miss Margaret Wooler, though in one undated letter she writes rather scornfully of the sisters' pretensions to fine clothes.[5]

We have to guess at the regime at Roe Head and the atmosphere, as well as the personalities involved, from evidence which strictly relates to the next year or two, after Anne had replaced Emily. It should be remembered that Charlotte was a teacher and Emily (later Anne) a pupil. During Anne's time there was little mixing between the sisters. Charlotte hardly mentions her in her letters to Ellen, and clearly thought of herself as *in loco parentis*, not *sororis*. Thus it seems unlikely that Charlotte and Emily could share a bed, as Winifred Gérin suggests. She could not have 'unburdened her heart' to Charlotte even had she wished to.[6]

Charlotte formed no very high opinion of the girls who would be Emily's classmates. 'A. C. on one side of me, E. L. on the other . . . stupidity the atmosphere, school-books the employment, asses the society.' And later,

> I had been toiling for nearly half an hour with Miss Lister, Miss Marriott and Ellen Cook striving to teach them the distinction between an article and a substantive . . . . The thought came over me that I am to spend the best part of my life . . . forcibly suppressing my rage at the idleness the apathy . . . and most assinine stupidity of those fat-headed oafs.[7]

Emily must have found herself alone in a strange place, with 'oafs' surrounding her, and her sister cross and remote. Mr Brontë's fears for her moral welfare were quite mistaken, unless she felt like murder.

It is unlikely that Emily benefited from the academic side of the school any more than the social. There was some dusty ancient history (Plato not explored), Mangnall's 'Questions' as at the school Maria and Elizabeth had attended near Wakefield, grammar (as exemplified by Charlotte's toils with the article and substantive), Milton (traces of him do appear in Emily's verse, perhaps) and Shakespeare (perhaps the history plays in particular).[8] It is likely there was some calculation and that some attention was paid to needlework. In many of these fields Emily knew a good deal more than her mentors and was interested more vitally. Despite the well-meaning and kindly intentions of Miss Margaret Wooler, there was not much nourishment for Emily's soul here.

So 'every morning when she awoke the vision of home and the moors rushed on her', as Charlotte said.[9] There would be no time to think about these things, or write about Lady Juliet. Perhaps Emily wrote to Anne in letters which carefully sorted out the substantives and articles. We have no trace of any such letters. However well she herself had been treated years ago at Cowan Bridge, she knew that Brontës met death in such places. Nor could she repeat her childish success with the prison warders; she was far from a pretty nursling nowadays, being gawky and reserved, and (we might suspect) a rather sulky and unresponsive teenager. Throughout her life, Emily's imagination made mountains out of molehills; in no other August had Emily's life been confined. Now, when she was seventeen, must have seemed a little late to start, while the sun shone on the green meadows and valleys around.

Many years afterwards, in her Introduction to *Selections from Poems by Ellis Bell*, Charlotte, by then perhaps confused, apparently thought that the Law Hill poems, which we shall consider in their context, were written at Roe Head. In the belief that she was explaining them, she wrote,

> Nobody knew what ailed her but me – I knew only too well. In this struggle her health was quickly broken: her white face, attenuated form, and failing strength threatened rapid decline. I felt in my heart she would die, if she did not go home, and with this conviction obtained her recall.[10]

Clearly, physical symptoms were produced by Emily. She reproduced at least one of those suffered by Maria and Elizabeth at Cowan Bridge, the wasting away associated with tuberculosis. Possibly Emily thought she had the disease. More probably she was what we might now call anorexic; her body was refusing to sustain itself. Extreme mental misery brought physical misery, as it was to do before her eventual death. Her body had become an alien prison, but it was being alienated by her mind itself.

The result of this experience seems to have been to confirm Emily in the view that she was a deeply divided person. We might think she had succeeded in getting her own way in being brought back to Haworth. But any such success is not unmixed; if the subject's will had been stronger, he or she would have conquered the desire to escape: so a sophisticated thinker like Emily may have considered. So even her victory here constituted a defeat. We shall find poems in which she is perplexed by the muddle of desires found in herself.

To Charlotte the matter was simpler. She saw that Emily had 'failed in enduring' this 'change from her own home to a school' and played the rescuing parent.[11] One is grateful for a parent's intervention, though less so at seventeen. Still, Emily acquiesced, and was back at Haworth by late October, less than three months after setting out.

8

The Poetry of 'A. G. A.'

Why do I hate that lone green dell?
Buried in moors and mountains wild,
That is a spot I had loved too well
Had I but seen it when a child.

So Roe Head had been a disaster, deeply wounding, no doubt, to Emily's self-esteem. As though by telepathy, Branwell suffered a similar setback. He went to London, intending to enrol in the Royal Academy, but he either had a failure of nerve or lost his money. In any case, he returned to Haworth exactly as Emily had.[1] Branwell was different from Emily in being highly acceptable in a social context, but his social contexts were village or small town ones. London was another matter. This collapse set the tone for the rest of Branwell's life, and led him to desperation. He felt sick of painting, and began to see himself as a poet.

As for Emily, we now enter a period when there is little direct evidence for her life and development. We have to look back and forward in her work, to see if we can discern what is going on. We may also find her reflected dimly in the actions or work of her siblings, but the rest is guesswork.

When Branwell got back from London, Emily was the only sister at home. Up to this point there had apparently been no special link between the two. Some nineteenth-century commentators, hard put to find a reason for what they found unfeminine about *Wuthering Heights*, saw Branwell as a powerful Heathcliff-like figure, and imagined he had some kind of power over Emily. In reality, with all his talents, he was bombastic and easily deflated. Such scant evidence as we have suggests that she might help him if possible, but that there was little in common between their modes of thought.

Now, however, they might well share the feeling of failure. It is possible that poetry could have been discussed between them. By 7 December, Branwell decided to write to *Blackwood's* offering himself as a replacement for the recently dead James Hogg.[2] The tone of his letter seems very unlike Emily; it is difficult to think he consulted her. When Charlotte came back for Christmas (bringing Anne, who had already been at school as long as Emily, and was beginning to find it tolerable if not pleasant), she was writing poetry which looks very much like what Anne wrote three years later. 'We wove a web in childhood' looks as if it might be a co-operative venture, which later influenced Emily's Law Hill poems. It seems very likely that Charlotte showed her sister the poem, perhaps this Christmas.

What we do not know is whether Emily was writing poetry too. With Branwell beginning to think of a literary career, and Charlotte recording her memories in verse, it must seem likely that the Gondals began to express themselves in this medium. If so, their verse did not survive. The only extant work dating from Christmas 1835 is that of Charlotte and Branwell.

The first part of 1836 is not a great deal better. Anne went back to school with Charlotte, leaving Emily with Branwell again. He continued to write much the same kind of poetry as before, both Angrian and personal. All the Brontës mix some personal poetry with some fictional, but even the fictional includes some personal material. Branwell now submitted some of his poetry to *Blackwood's.* There is no evidence that this was with Emily's knowledge or help; we can scour the poems in vain for internal evidence. Meanwhile Charlotte, at Miss Wooler's, was searching her heart and blaming herself for insufficiently rigorous Christian principles. Emily and Branwell had both declined commitment to traditional religion.

The fact that Charlotte and Anne tried to cut short a visit to the Franks family at Huddersfield in June suggests that they were keen to get back to Emily at Haworth.[3] By about 24 or 25 June they were back home. It was during this summer holiday that the first known Gondal poem was written: 'Will the day be bright or cloudy', dated 12 July. It is known from a manuscript copied out in 1839, and may possibly have been tidied up at that time. It is a bare possibility that the subject of the poem is the birth of 'A. G. A.', the Gondal character who begins to occupy Emily's attention soon, and whose fictional career we shall be investigating.

When Charlotte and Anne went back to Roe Head, Charlotte corresponded with Branwell about their character Northangerland.[4] There is no suggestion that Emily was included in their planning. It would be interesting to know whether Emily and Anne also corresponded; we need to wait until mid-1837 before we have any clear knowledge of their relationship as late teenagers. Both wrote poems during December 1836, each with its reference to the stormy wind. But if Emily's date is correct, she wrote before Anne had returned. It is a strange coincidence that both should have poems dated December, in Emily's case after a lapse of five months. Anne's poem is clearly Gondal, being 'written' by a Lady Geralda, not otherwise known, but with a name interestingly similar to Emily's heroine. Emily's poem has no clear Gondal references, but is not purely a Haworth poem either. Our only other clue to Emily's occupation this winter is the purchase of some piano music: 'Favourite Waltzes'.

Branwell, it seems, now decided to work hard on poetry. He began half a year of composing and copying, mostly Angrian material. Though some of it bears a family likeness to Emily's work, there is no evidence of direct influence. It is just possible that the influence was the other way round. From this point until 1841, and with another small burst of interest in 1844, a major character in Emily's imagination was 'A. G. A.', a Gondal princess with dark hair and an imperious manner. From 'There shines the moon', begun in March 1837, we know that her first name was Augusta, and from 'To a wreath of snow', written in December 1837, we find that her third name was Almeda. We cannot positively say that Augusta was created in 1837, but on 10 March Branwell copied into his transcript book a poem called 'Augusta' written in 1834 and relating to a minor imaginary character called Augusta di Segovia.[5] It may be that Emily borrowed this minor Angrian character and Gondalized her. The actual date of the beginning of the first A. G. A. poem is given as 6 March 1837, though the first eight lines do not allude to Augusta, and could have been made up, according to Emily's practice, as a separate fragment, awaiting a Gondal story to be attached to. The name Augusta would have been familiar to Emily from

Byron's story, but I am inclined to think that she may have re-adopted it here after a conversation with Branwell.

Augusta grew to be a major Gondal figure. By Miss Ratchford she has been called 'Gondal's Queen', and at her greatest extremity she is thought of as accounting for the whole of Emily Brontë's poetic output.[6] It needs to be said at once that this theory cannot be sustained. There are seventeen poems in which Augusta is certainly a proponent, and more where she might be alluded to. But there seem to be other powerful Gondal princesses who might be her relations; in particular it has been thought that 'Rosina' could be another of her names. On the whole this seems dubious, and the attempt to make all Emily's work into Gondal work is even more difficult. Why this is so, we shall consider in detail when we reach the year 1844. But two or three references to 'Geraldine' are probably referring to A. G. A.'s second name.

By mid-1837, it may seem as though Augusta has become an obsession with Emily, a self-identification as strong as Charlotte's with Zamorna or Branwell's with Percy. The diary paper written on 26 June states that Emily is writing 'Agustus – Almedas life 1st vol – 4th page from the last'.[7] The doubtful spelling of this should not lead us to doubt that Augusta is the person meant. The volume in question may not have been extensive, but it was well advanced. This suggests considerable interest in the character, who must engage our interest too, as she is said to be the prototype of Catherine.

The last time we were able to discover much about Emily's creative fiction was in the old days of Parry's Palace, when she was co-operating with Charlotte. We saw then that Emily was becoming impatient with the lack of realism of the saga. Relations with Charlotte were declining before she went to Roe Head; a terminal quarrel has been suggested. Since then, Emily had changed greatly. We have found good reason for supposing that her reading had included Shelley's poems as well as more of Byron, and rare works from Ponden Hall. She had been able to form a very close alliance with Anne. Whether she was any nearer to controlling her impulsive nature is more doubtful. A poem which is undated, and which may have been written a little later begins,

All day I've toiled, but not with pain
In learning's golden mine . . .

and ends,

True to myself and true to all
May I be heedful still
And turn away from passion's call
And curb my own wild will.[8]

Emily's wild will issued in tempers like the 'roaring bull' episode, and the day when Parry 'stamped on' his enemy. The pacific Anne calmed these tempers, but found it hard not to be able to share her own favourite thoughts with Emily. That 'passion' for Emily could have had a sexual connotation we may well suppose, having regard to the lines quoted from 'The Death of A. G. A'.

One solution to the wild will and the call of passion, as well as the memory of the disastrous failure at Roe Head, was to project all these things on to a Gondal character. For this purpose A. G. A. was invented and developed. I have suggested that by late June she was becoming a prominent vehicle for Emily's self-expression, but not before a different attempt had been made to wrestle with her own self-organization. On 10 June we have a poem beginning 'The night of storms has passed'. It takes its rise, as so often, from real weather conditions.[9] There had been a storm overnight, with thunder. Emily adverts briefly to this, then proceeds to give details of a dream in which she 'stood by a marble tomb/ Where royal corpses lay'. A 'shadowy thing' appeared, and mesmerized her.

But still my eyes with maddening gaze
Were fixed upon its fearful face
And its were fixed on me.

The creature seemed 'close by, and yet far more far/ Than this world from the farthest star'. This space was 'the sea of death's eternity.

Worst of all, the ghost began to speak:

O bring not back again
The horror of that hour
When its lips opened and a sound
Awoke the stillness reigning round.

The ghost then issues a Gondal warning which seems hardly commensurate with the horror evinced at its trying to give its message. We need to remember Mr Brontë's breakfast stories, add a little of Frankenstein's monster, 'The Ancient Mariner' and 'Christabel', and the physical terror and paralysis suffered at Roe Head. Emily, now nearly nineteen, was realizing that her expression was blocked; she was gagged and bound.

One more poem needs to be considered here before we return to the diary paper. 'O God of heaven! the dream of horror' is dated 7 August 1837. The second part of the poem dissolves into some of Emily's least-felt Gondal pastiche, but it begins very seriously. For six stanzas she again discusses the horror of nightmare. The frightful dream 'is over now', she tells us. But it involved a 'sickened heart', an 'aching sense of utter woe', 'burning tears' and 'impatient rage'. The whirlwind of emotions touched on in this nightmare sequence is not fictitious. Claustrophobia stalks in the dream; even the non-Gondal part suggests a prison. We may think once more of the parsonage cellars: there was no firm evidence for their use in the children's early games, but it is tempting to infer it. Of course, Emily's spirit was experiencing metaphorical prison in aching reality. Anne was back at Roe Head, Branwell apparently drunken and beginning to lurch through his own lonely personality battles.[10] Nightmare had enveloped the 'darling child', who had now become a young woman without an escape route. Her heart cried out in intense horror at night, when no one was near.

There is not much hint of this in the celebrated 1837 diary paper, which shows an idyllic picture (drawn by Emily) of Anne and herself working on the Gondal story.[11] The time is 'past 4 o'Clock', and all the young Brontës are at home. The Charlotte/Branwell friendship is flourishing; Branwell is reading *Eugene Aram* (a book they all eventually read) to Charlotte while she sews. There is Angrian as well as Gondal news in the paper. Among the Gondals the 'Emperors and Empresses' of Gondal and Gaaldine are 'preparing to depart from Gaaldine to prepare for the coronation which will be on the 12th of July'. This was in imitation of Queen 'Vittiora' who 'ascended the throne this month'.

Most of the bottom part of the paper is taken up with Emily's drawing, which shows Anne writing her poem 'Alexandria and Zenobia' and the rear view of Emily herself sitting absorbed in her *Life of Augusta*. Littered on the table are 'the papers' which have been taken from 'the Tin Box', so labelled, and lying in front of Emily. Added below is a conversation, transcribed here with Emily's original spelling and punctuation:

> Aunt. come Emily Its past 4 o'clock /Emily, Yes Aunt
> Anne well/ do you intend to write in the evening
> Emily well what think you
> (we agreed to go out 1st to make sure if we get
> into a humor we may stay in

The last word is difficult to distinguish, and it is not too clear what these indecisive girls have finally agreed. But the whole scene is far from the nightmare of earlier in the year. It is hard to escape the view that despite her closeness to Anne, Emily was able to share only a fraction of her feeling; and certainly Anne was in the same position. They were no longer spiritually twins. The diary paper, despite its charm, seems very trivial for the product of a writer who was going to become a major English novelist.

There is no telling precisely where to locate the surprising visit of Uncle Hugh Brontë from County Down.[12] Later generations of Irish Brontës could only remember that it was dimly in the past, at a time when the girls had published nothing. True, there is a strange report that he paid a second visit, as late as 1848, when Branwell was dead. The Irish background of the Brontës, so influential to their early development, and as much (or more so) in the case of Emily as of Anne and Charlotte, has generally been glossed over. This would delight Charlotte, and as Emily made no direct reference to it, we may assume that she acquiesced in the silent conspiracy to forget the 'Brontë homeland' across the Irish Sea. For all that, it emerged as a deep interest in family history, both in Gondal and in *Wuthering Heights*. The eruption of Hugh on to the Yorkshire scene, and, probably in 1846, of James, must have left puzzles in the girls' minds which could not easily be solved.

In *The Brontës' Irish Background* I have tried to date Hugh's visit, but any attempt to do so must be tentative. Quite a probable date is 1837. The parsonage must have been thrown into confusion. Patrick did not dream of rejecting his brother, and in fact fêted him, drawing on old connections in the Hartshead area to allow him to introduce Hugh to Kirklees, where he tried on Robin Hood's helmet. There was a prophecy that anyone who did so would find his hair fall out. Hughey proved the prophecy true; but his hair grew again when he got back to Ballynaskeagh. Patrick also took him on a whirlwind tour of London, to see the queen. Hugh was not a visitor from outer space, only from County Down, and he had ordinary eyes, not those of a basilisk; yet his visit must have been disturbing to Emily, who might perhaps feel a strange kinship, but also a strange distance between herself and this cheery, unusual man.

Patrick gave his brothers a silver pencil case each on the occasion of this visit. Not a word of the whole matter escapes into the correspondence of Charlotte (unless Ellen destroyed this section). But we should note Patrick's attitude. He gives no prominence to his Irish relations, but he doesn't shrink from them. Patrick is always kind and dutiful, despite his firm views and his balancing of discretion with pugnacity. The existence of a large family of peasant brothers and sisters in Ireland, and the need to acknowledge his background, were reasons for Patrick's lack of progress in snobbish circles. One may perhaps see Irishness as Patrick's Heathcliff.

The early development of A. G. A. continued meanwhile. It is not much less trivial than the diary paper. On 19 August Emily writes (in the name of her Gondal princess) a poem of sadness and separation. Perhaps the real cause was the absence of Anne at Roe Head, but the poem emerges as one in which the princess misses the 'Lord of Elbë', Alexander. Anne had also written a poem about Alexander, mentioned in Emily's diary paper.[13] But Emily's poem is especially interesting in that its earlier versions show Alexander 'longing to be in sweet Elbë again', whereas the later version, from 1844, makes it clear that it has been decided that Alexander is dead. The Gondal story has evolved; it might change year by year. The live could be killed and the dead brought to life again.

In a poem dated only 'August 1837', 'A. G. A.' writes of her inability to speak her thoughts in poetry. Emily describes the 'solemn joy' at evening as she watches the summer day fade. But though 'Dreams have encircled me' from 'sunny childhood's careless time', she cannot put those visions into words. This poem shows the close identity between Emily

Brontë ('E. J. B.') and 'A. G. A.' at this time. The crux reached is typical of many poets; Emily identifies herself here with the tradition of Coleridge (for instance, in 'Kubla Khan') and many others. How far this identification is a conscious one, it is impossible to tell, but the poem is broken and despondent in the Coleridge manner: 'Strive no more; tis all in vain.'[14] We can understand her ecstasy at the 'smiling light' of the evening, and her doubt about her ability to express the ecstasy; the need for A. G. A. to intervene is less apparent.

On 7 September, Emily was copying, from a geometry book, diagrams which suggest she was following Shelley and others in seeing scientific and mathematical knowledge as related to philosophical understanding.[15] It is hard to see how she can have had direct knowledge of Plato, but this Greek understanding of mathematics as basic to knowledge is only one way in which she seems to be conversant with his ideas. In the nature of things, we rarely get a glimpse of Emily reading, though Ponden Hall library may still have been available to her. But Charlotte probably portrays her sister's concentration accurately in *Shirley*.

> After tea Shirley reads, and she is just about as tenacious of her book as she is lax of her needle. Her study is the rug, her seat a footstool. . . . The tawny and lion-like bulk of Tartar is ever stretched before her. . . . One hand of the mistress generally reposes on her serf's rude head, because if she takes it away he groans and is discontented. Shirley's mind is given to her book; she lifts not her eyes; she neither stirs nor speaks.[16]

This, of course, is Emily in adulthood. She is an intent and thoughtful reader.

If in August 'A. G. A.' is Emily unvarnished, as she seems to be, perhaps we should take autobiographically the poem 'Sleep brings no joy to me', written in November. 'The shadows of the dead/ My waking eyes may never see/ Surround my bed' surely takes us back to Maria and Elizabeth, the twin (and differing) poles of Emily's childhood. Just like Gondal characters, these two children were perpetually called back from the dead; in fact they returned of their own accord. In December, A. G. Almeda is in prison, but can see a wreath of snow through the bars. The prison motif continues to run through Emily's poetry. She will exploit it both as fact and metaphor. The fate of Emily (Emilia Viviani) in 'Epipsychidion' seems archetypal for her, and she sees the body as prison right through to *Wuthering Heights* and beyond. Such thoughts were strong at this time; as A. G. A. writes to A. S. in May 1838:

If thou hast sinned in this world of care
'Twas but the dust of thy drear abode –
Thy soul was pure when it entered here
And pure it will go again to God.[17]

In a beautiful short poem of 30 August 1838, Emily writes through A. G. A. of the strange feeling which causes the 'old guitar' to continue to play sad songs in memory of someone whom the player has forgotten.

It is as if the glassy brook
Should image still its willows fair
Though years ago the woodman's stroke
Laid low in dust their gleaming hair.[18]

It is impossible to say who, if it was any real person, floated into Emily's mind and provided the seed of this poem. It may have been Maria again, or Elizabeth. The sense of loss is strong, and the poem no less attractive because we cannot trace its origin. But still the intervention of A. G. A. seems unnecessary. Up to this point, at any rate, all we know of Augusta is that she is forlorn and frequently lamenting.

In May 1838 Charlotte suffered what amounted to a mild nervous collapse. She thought she could not ever return to teaching, and though she did eventually do so, it seems possible that Emily had decided to replace her for a while.[19] Mr Brontë, now sixty, could not live forever; when he went the girls would be penniless. They must learn to subdue their qualms and earn money. Some such consideration must have prompted Emily now to agree to go and teach for a Miss Patchett at Law Hill, near Halifax.

9

Law Hill and Halifax

What language can utter the feeling
That rose when, in exile afar,
On the brow of a lonely hill kneeling
I saw the brown heath growing there?

Charlotte avoided mentioning Law Hill in the Introduction to the 1850 Poem edition or the Biographical Memoir or Preface to the 1850 edition of *Wuthering Heights*. She seems to suggest that the poems written at Law Hill were composed at Roe Head. Because of this omission, it was a long time before literary historians could establish anything about Emily's time there; the chronology has only recently been confirmed.[1] There has also been a strange lack of interest in the school itself and the surroundings of Law Hill, despite increasing evidence that some of the geographical background of *Wuthering Heights* is from here. We shall need to assemble every scrap of material that can be gathered.

Mrs Gaskell, who was given incorrect dates by Ellen Nussey, does not reveal the name of the school 'at Halifax' where Emily taught.[2] She makes one other short mention of the episode, but shows no interest, or perhaps was 'warned off' by Charlotte. As with other matters concerning Emily, curiosity blossomed in the 1880s, when Miss Robinson and Mrs Chadwick undertook their research. The former's jaundiced view of Branwell stimulated Francis Leyland, a native of Halifax, to come to the aid of his memory, and Leyland was able to add a little about Emily at Law Hill. In the subsequent hundred years, progress was made by Thomas Keyworth, Charles Simpson and Hilda Marsden, who all contributed details about the Halifax landscape.[3] But rather remarkably, only one illustration of the Law Hill schoolroom has been published, in Raymond's *In the Steps of the Brontës*; the house itself has been featured more often.[4] It would be useful to quote the early writers, and to try to form a picture of the school and life there.

Miss Robinson does not give the name of the school and includes no details except to quote the letter of Charlotte, which we now know dates from 2 October 1838.[5] It speaks of Emily rising at 6 a.m., and not returning to bed until 'near eleven at night'; she has 'only one half hour of exercise between'. In a poem which we shall be considering, Emily herself writes of an 'hour', so it looks as though Charlotte is exaggerating the difficulties. The other detail included by Miss Robinson is the manner of Emily's departure:

> when spring came back, with its feverish weakness, with its beauty and memories, to that stern place of exile, she failed. Her health broke down, shattered by long-resisted homesickness. Weary and mortified at heart, Emily again went back to seek life and happiness on the wild moors of Haworth.[6]

Unfortunately, we don't know the source of this rather vague information.

Mrs Chadwick spent a good deal more effort on Law Hill and conveys a host of useful facts, which I shall extract. She quotes as source John Watkinson, then Chairman of the Council of the Brontë Society, whose wife was at the school, and whose memories will be dealt with later.[7] Mrs Chadwick gives a number of facts about Miss Elizabeth Patchett:

> . . . she was greatly respected and loved by her pupils. This is fully borne out by letters seen by the writer, all of which go to prove she was a kind schoolmistress . . . . Miss Elizabeth Patchett, according to one of her pupils still living, was a very beautiful woman, wearing her hair in curls. She was fond of teaching . . .
>
> Her relatives were naturally not pleased that Charlotte Brontë's letter to Miss Nussey should have been published by Mrs Gaskell. . . . The consequence was that

> the friends and relatives of the Patchetts refrained from discussing Emily Brontë for many years . . . .
>
> . . . it is evident that she was of a decided and practical turn of mind, and a person who knew how to carry out her duties as a schoolmistress.[8]

Concerning the curriculum, Mrs Chadwick says,

> The girls at the school were taught all the usual accomplishments, and horse-riding in addition: Miss Patchett is said to have been a very skilful horsewoman. . . . Emily Brontë pictures the elder Catherine in *Wuthering Heights* as a fearless rider.[9]

And of Emily's local knowledge while there she says,

> As the Patchetts were a very old Halifax family, it is possible that Emily Brontë would learn much of the district from Miss Patchett, who at the time was a handsome woman of forty-four . . . ; for the daily walks with the Head Mistress were a much-prized recreation, a former pupil told me.
>
> Unlike Cowan Bridge, the church was not far away and Emily was able to take her walks to the church and the moors with her pupils without any inconvenience, even in bad weather. There was a choice of walks, one leading down the valley to Brighouse . . .
>
> . . . one of the pupils allowed me to see a letter in which she mentions that Miss Patchett took some of the girls to Halifax to see the museum occasionally, and the stuffed birds and animals are mentioned in the letter as being of great interest.[10]

Law Hill stands at almost the highest point of the hill range to the east of Halifax. Built of the dark local stone, it seems forbidding and gaunt, rather a mockery of the elegant eighteenth-century style it was meant to represent. The house itself faces almost south, and has a garden in front with trees which (then as now) mask the house in summer. In latter years the front door was not used much, but perhaps in Miss Patchett's time it was.[11] To the west of the three-storey house is a cobbled yard where the younger children might play active games, rather like the corresponding paved area at Cowan Bridge. It is entered by an arch in a stone wall which links the house with the warehouse. This warehouse, where originally a wool business flourished, had been changed by the Patchett sisters into schoolrooms.

If we are to imagine Emily at her daily tasks, we need to visualize the school accommodation. The warehouse building had two storeys. Remains of an outside staircase leading from the yard to a high door seem to be visible in Raymond's illustration of the school, but Keyworth says the staircase was in the gable end, and points to a doorway already blocked up in his day.[12] These writers agree that the schoolroom was on the upper floor, but Mrs Chadwick writes, 'It was a long narrow building, divided into classrooms, and the pupils slept in the bedrooms overhead.' Mrs Chadwick's informant seems to have been Mrs Watkinson, and she should have known. Keyworth tried to discover, from an old inhabitant, where Emily had slept, but 'there is no special tradition to appropriate any special room to Emily'; the main building 'contained the sitting rooms and the dormitories'.[13]

It must be said that Mrs Chadwick's information about the use of the top floor of the old warehouse block seems more likely, and she says the pupils did not sleep 'at the farm', by which she seems to mean the house itself.[14] Emily was not a pupil. We just do not know whether at night she would have a bed near the children, or have a bedroom high in Law Hill house itself. In either place she is almost sure to have had a fine view of the distant prospects round Halifax. In either case, we should expect her room to be at the rear, since the Misses Patchett would have the main front bedrooms in the house itself, and the children would probably be placed near the stairs in the warehouse.

In her poem of 23 September, Emily seems to be looking out of a high window:

The evening sun was sinking down
On low green hills and clustered trees;
It was a scene as fair and lone
As ever felt the soothing breeze.

At this point she turns the poem into a meditation, apparently referring to her favourite bluebells. We never find out what was happening on the evening when the sun shone so finely. The poem is a typical Emily Brontë beginning, put aside to be turned perhaps into a Gondal narrative one day.

Law Hill was a working farm. The north part of the premises, at the back of the yard, contained a barn, hayloft, cowshed and stable.[15] The noise of cows and dogs would be all about Emily as she lay awake under the slates, or rose in the grey dawn of a late autumn morning. The close proximity of animals is very much a factor in *Wuthering Heights*. This experience was not gained at the parsonage, despite Keeper and other pets. Surely Emily first grew to know working animals at Law Hill. Parts of the farm buildings may still be seen, abutting rough fields behind.

Emily taught the younger children, it seems. Mrs Chadwick says that 'they soon forgot the time she spent with them, though there is no record that she was ever unkind'.[16] The young age of the girls may be the reason why Emily spent only half an hour in exercise with them, if we are to believe Charlotte's letter. On the other hand, Mrs Chadwick writes of daily walks with Miss Patchett for the children, and we must suppose that Emily would go along too, at least on many occasions. Visits to Brighouse and Halifax have already been mentioned, but we should dearly like to know where the other walks went. There is strong circumstantial evidence that Emily got to know the northern as well as the southern approaches to Southowram, but precise proof of the details of the walks has not been offered. In the north, Miss Patchett may have walked her pupils along the valley of the Red Beck to Shibden, or up the steep tracks of the rough hillside where there was a chunky stone-cased house called High Sunderland. Both these would be exciting places to visit, though both very different. In 1838, Shibden was in process of being rebuilt by its enterprising and very lively owner Miss Anne Lister.[17] High Sunderland was beginning a long decline from which it was delivered by demolition more than a hundred years later. There seems to be no doubt that it could clearly be seen from the top windows at Law Hill, and that from there Emily absorbed the distant, romantic view of the old windswept yeoman house.[18]

Early commentators on the Brontës did not doubt that the location of Emily's *Wuthering Heights* was to be found in the moorland area beyond Haworth. So little had Emily ever been away from the parsonage that it seemed common sense to assume that the novel had been set there. It was Thomas Keyworth, already mentioned, who first suggested a strong Halifax influence. He was followed in 1907 by J. Craven, who proposed that Ponden Hall was the original of Thrushcross Grange.[19] But in *Brontë Society Transactions* No. 34, T. W. Hanson, a Halifax historian, noted similarities between Wuthering Heights and High Sunderland, believing that Emily saw the drawings of the hall in John Horner's *Buildings in the Town and Parish of Halifax*, published in 1835, to which Miss Patchett subscribed, and whose copy would therefore be a prominent new exhibit in her library when Emily arrived in 1838.[20] In *Brontë Society Transactions* No. 67 Hilda Marsden meticulously showed that Emily's knowledge of High Sunderland went deeper than could be accounted for by a mere acquaintance with the engravings.[21] Miss Marsden went beyond this, and produced a detailed circumstantial case for Emily's being thoroughly familiar with a number of landmarks in the Shibden valley and district, some of which are almost unique. I find Hilda Marsden's closely reasoned argument entirely convincing except in a few minor points, and propose to adopt it as the basis of the following pages.

High Sunderland was demolished in 1950, after years of neglect and decay. It was in a very poor state when Ernest Raymond saw it in the 1940s. Hanson saw it when it was in rather better shape, and was not quite as convinced as Hilda Marsden that it formed the basis for the building at Wuthering Heights. He preferred the view that the gateways only contributed to the house in the novel. But undoubtedly the position of High Sunderland is similar to that of Wuthering Heights. Let us follow Lockwood on his first visit.

'Pure, bracing ventilation they must have up there at all times', he says. The 'north wind, blowing over the edge' has caused fir trees to slant, and some gaunt thorns are stretching their arms one way only. 'Happily, the architect had foresight to build it strong: the narrow windows are set deeply in the wall, and the corners defended with large jutting stones.' So Wuthering Heights, like High Sunderland, faces south, and is below the brow of a hill over which the north wind hustles.

'Before passing the threshold,' says Lockwood, 'I paused to admire a quantity of grotesque carving lavished over the front, and especially about the principal door, above which, among a wilderness of griffins, and shameless little boys, I detected the date "1500" and the name "Hareton Earnshaw".'[22] He goes on to say that he would have requested a short history of the place from Heathcliff if he hadn't appeared so surly. There would have been nothing about such farms as 'Top Withens', near Haworth, which would have made one enquire about their history.

We turn now to Horner's engravings, and photographs of High Sunderland taken before its demolition. There are two decorated entrances to the hall, one gateway leading straight into the 'house', that is, the large hall where much of the living in such houses went on. The 'jutting stones' are visible in Horner's pictures and in views of the south face taken just before demolition. They are buttresses, actually built of eleven courses of stones.

The yard gateway has a sculptured head as a keystone, five smaller heads along the entablature, a coat of arms and two birds which could be griffins: all this on the house front side. On the yard side, Horner shows another head as keystone, several more heads along the entablature, some animals including (apparently) lions, two shields, and a huge statue of a naked giant. The house door seems to have a sun above it, and two twisted naked male figures, not perhaps 'little boys'. Both doorways have writing over them, though neither contains a date. Even in Horner's drawings, the stone appears to be cracked and old.

Like the windows, the front door is set 'deeply into the wall'. There is an entrance porch which appears to be about nine feet deep. High Sunderland's windows *were* deep-set, as well they might be, for the house had been a timber-framed one, enclosed in stone in the seventeenth century. Each window is divided by stout mullions, so that each appears 'narrow'. There can really be no doubt that Wuthering Heights from the outside is High Sunderland hall, with the date, and the name of Hareton Earnshaw added over the gateway, which represents the two High Sunderland gates rolled into one. The scene is completed by Nelly's remark that Joseph is closing the gate 'as if we lived in an ancient castle'. High Sunderland, with its castellations and pinnacles, looked very much like a castle.

It is doubtful whether the three-dimensional feel of

Wuthering Heights could have come from a study of Horner's drawings alone. There are many similarities between the plan of the farm and High Sunderland. Once through the decorated main door, Lockwood finds himself in the 'house', the regular name for the living room in yeoman farmhouses of the time. Wuthering Heights, however, turns out to be a bit bigger than the average farmhouse. 'I believe at Wuthering Heights, the kitchen is forced to retreat altogether into another quarter', says Lockwood. At High Sunderland the kitchen was reached by turning right (east) out of the housebody (see plan of High Sunderland, page 285). When a large bough falls across the 'east chimney' in the gale at the Heights, the collapse sends debris into the kitchen fire.[23] We can see on Horner's drawing which chimney is meant. Whether Emily could have learnt that this was the kitchen chimney without going there in person, or at least talking to someone who knew the inside of High Sunderland, is doubtful. It looks as if she visited the hall sometime during the winter of 1838–9, as well as staring at the castle-like building from a high window at Law Hill.

The land and house at High Sunderland were owned by William Priestley, founder of the Halifax Quarterly Choral Society, and regular soloist. He is certain to have known Elizabeth Patchett, but he did not live at High Sunderland himself, according to the 1841 census. By this time (and surely two years earlier) the hall was tenanted by a farming family named Wood, who seem to have occupied the main house, with eight other small tenements carved out of it, one for the labourer Joseph Grey, and most of the rest occupied by weavers. We may dismiss the idea that Emily Brontë could have been formally entertained at High Sunderland, but the picture of an old house with a 'history', but now in decline, is sustained by the state of High Sunderland around 1840. Like Wuthering Heights, it is the second most imposing building in the township (Northowram), Shibden (Thrushcross) being the best, but has fallen on hard times.

Like Wuthering Heights, Thrushcross Grange has no place on the moors behind Haworth, except for the features culled from Ponden Hall. Throughout, it is regarded as a gentleman's residence. It has a large park surrounding it, and this was a green park, though wild. This was not, then, the kind of country where Ponden is situated.[24] The view from the parlour (upstairs, as at Shibden) shows Edgar and Catherine a beautiful misty vale with a beck running down it. The house is surrounded by trees, like Shibden. It is apparently visible from Wuthering Heights, though not from the house itself. The description and location correspond well with the details of Shibden Hall, in the valley to the north of Southowram. Thrushcross park is contiguous with the estate of the Heights, and Gimmerton is too far off for Heathcliff to wish to live there. Gimmerton seems to be based on Southowram.

There are still more similarities between the Southowram area and the moors near Wuthering Heights. Keyworth suggested that Gimmerton chapel, in decay, is to be equated with a disused church at Southowram, Chapel-le-Breer.[25] The precise state of the building in 1838 is unknown, but a new church had been built in 1823, nearer the village. The Law Hill party went to this church, St Anne's, on Sundays. The older building had been near 'Sough Pastures', and sure enough at one point Emily refers to 'the chapel of Gimmerden Sough'.[26] The abandoned chapel seems to have retained a place in her memory; it may have been on the school walk to Brighouse. (It was, of course, an Anglican 'chapel' like Haworth and Thornton.)

Emily Brontë included another interesting feature of local landscape in her book. At the road junction near Shibden where a lane to High Sunderland leaves the old Wakefield Road there is or was an old sandstone pillar built into the wall. It is perhaps intended as a mile post rather than a direction post. In *Wuthering Heights* Nelly describes it as 'a stone where the highway branches off on to the moor at your left hand; a rough sandstone pillar, with the letters W. H. cut on its north side, on the east, G., and on the south-west, T. G. It serves as a guide post to the Grange, the Heights, and village'.[27] Emily has her points of the compass right if she is describing the Northowram/Southowram area, as well as Wuthering Heights. Miss Marsden reports that the real inscriptions were, 'Wakefield 15 miles' and 'Northowram and Bradford'.[28] Nelly dwells long on this 'weather-worn block', which Hilda Marsden calls 'perished and black with age'. However, even this may not exhaust the sources of Emily's background colour. A few yards from Law Hill on the opposite side of the road near Withen Fields is another old direction pillar of stone, erected in 1750, with directions to Leeds, Wakefield and Halifax.[29] This is still in place, and was marked on the earliest six-inch Ordnance Survey map, where it is called a 'guide post'. We may note Withen Fields as a source of the novel's name, combined perhaps with the 'Withens' near Ponden.

Only in one respect does Emily seem to depart radically from the geography of Shibden and district as she imagined it to be in the late eighteenth century. Her distances are too great. Though Thrushcross can be seen from Wuthering Heights (as Shibden can be seen from High Sunderland), they are said to be four miles apart.[30] Heathcliff tells Nelly that he and Catherine, as children out for a 'ramble' at liberty, 'ran from the top of the heights to the park without stopping'. If the park was two miles from gate to house, as is elsewhere said, then the teenagers ran two miles non-stop. Catherine was beaten 'because she was barefoot'. Whereas covering large distances would have presented no difficulty for Catherine and Heathcliff, sustained running might have done. Emily's report of the distance between Wuthering Heights and Thrushcross needs scaling down. As the crow flies, it is about two and half miles from Haworth to Ponden, a distance frequently 'rambled' by Emily, but her imagination seems to expand this to four miles when she transfers the rambling to North Halifax.

The Shibden valley wove itself into Emily's mind, as she looked across from the high point at Law Hill. Unique and romantic, the castellated farm at High Sunderland brooded there, remote and windswept under its northern hill. Emily accentuates the remoteness: 'two or three miles was the ordinary distance between cottage and cottage', says Nelly to Lockwood. This must be exaggeration: it would be untrue even of the wild moors beyond Stanbury.[31]

The sparseness of poetry during the first part of the autumn suggests that Emily was much occupied with teaching. We may speculate that the sociable Miss Patchett would occupy some of Emily's spare time with welcoming conversation, and it seems that it was not until October that she was moved to write verse, or had time to do so, after the initial poem about the 'low green hills' already mentioned. Two 'Songs' by 'Julius Brenzaida' are dated 17 October. Julius is generally thought to be a prototype for Heathcliff: it is interesting that the major 'hero' of *Wuthering Heights* is being formed at the same time as the setting for the novel is discovered.

In both these poems Julius addresses 'Geraldine', who is

presumably identical with A. G. A. The second of the two has the words 'Love's Farewell' pencilled in at the top. They may be in Emily's own hand, though some features may suggest Charlotte. In any case, this putative title cannot be earlier than 1844, and may date from the 1846 selection and revision.[32] How far these poems can be made to reveal Emily's state of mind at the time is dubious. In the first Emily refers to 'Autumn's mild returning' and makes Julius plead with Geraldine to come to him in the moonlight. It is a poem of yearning in separation, a frequent theme with Emily. In the second poem Julius accuses Geraldine of treachery; both poems will be considered again when we come to look at the way in which the novel developed from Gondal. Evidently, Gondal was helping Emily to console herself for the loss of Haworth.

A possibly completed poem ascribed to A. G. A. and two undated fragments which follow in one of the little manuscripts appear to be the next poetic attempts. All three may have a reference to the actual situation at Law Hill. The first poem, 'Where were ye all?' is a poem of seeking in crowds. As the poet, or A. G. A., looks, she sees 'an eye that shone like thine'. Always very conscious of eyes, Emily may have been looking at the crowded schoolroom, or the poem may have been suggested by a journey to Halifax or Southowram church. The eye's owner is male, and the man's voice, though 'never heard before' was reminiscent of 'years gone by'. Emily frequently turned very slight external experiences into literature; this may be an example of this process.

The first of the two fragments appears to have been written on a night of full moon, possibly 2 November. 'I paused on the threshold' seems to have been jotted down after Emily had finished either a walk or a supervisory visit to the children's dormitory. As she stands on the threshold, the poet turns and looks at the full moon, and hears the wind, which 'murmured past with a wild eerie sound'. She then turns and enters 'my dark prison-house', surely Law Hill. It seems that she must have kept a sheaf of scraps of paper, or a notebook, on which to write as the mood took her. In this case, it looks as if the lines must have been scribbled down by the light of a dip or candle, and the inspiration ran out after six of them. We shall often find Emily awake at night, writing beginnings of poems which are never completed.

Either that day or more probably one of the next few, the second fragment was written. It consists of four lines:

O come with me, thus ran the song;
The moon is bright in Autumn's sky,
And thou hast toiled and laboured long
With aching head and weary eye.

However, the best production of the week was written on Thursday 1 November, and it may indeed have preceded the former two fragments. (This depends on how seriously we take the phrase 'full moon' in 'I paused on the threshold'; the moon may have been almost full, or beginning to wane.) Once again the theme is Gondal; the poem has often been quoted because of its resemblance to some themes in *Wuthering Heights*. Headed 'F. de Samara to A. G. A.' it begins, 'Light up thy halls! 'Tis closing day:' and it will have been begun in the time following tea, when perhaps the pupils were at preparation. If they were, possibly the supervising teacher could write her own work as she watched them.

The poem's weather is firmly based on the real weather at the time.

I'm drear and lone and far away –
Cold blows on my breast the northwind's bitter sigh,
And oh, my couch is bleak beneath the rainy sky!

Greenwich records describe heavy rain early in the day; there were showers and hail in Yorkshire and there was a strong wind, though it was a west, not a north, wind.[33] The 'exile' theme is strong; but the poem now moves to Gondal, where Samara is considering suicide. Later, however, he returns to the fact of exile, seeing the wind as the connection between himself and his home:

I shall not tread again the deep glens where it rose –
I feel it on my face – 'Where, wild blast, dost thou roam?
What do we, Wanderer, here, so far away from home?'

The poem ends with a message to the wind, which it is to take back to A. G. A. in Gondal. Fernando says that A. G. A. will suffer her own pangs when he is gone. But these are frenzied thoughts: '*Life* bows to my control but *Love* I cannot kill!' He may kill himself, but he expects to feel the same love for A. G. A. afterwards as before. It is this view of love as well as life after death which has caused the poem to be related to the novel.

By now the incidence of poetry composition is much more frequent than when Emily was at home. Despite the difficulties, she managed to find time to write. There may have been many stimuli besides the school walks to places which Emily had never seen before. The cultivated Miss Patchett may have taken the literary magazines, and there Emily might see, in *Fraser's* for June 1838, a long article on the poet Shelley.[34] I have argued at length in *Brontë Facts and Brontë Problems* and elsewhere that the similarity between her thought and his was not accidental. A series of poems written between now and 1840 seem to refer to the Romantic poet directly, and allude to events in his life. Later poems reflect his thought, and at second hand Anne also adopts some Shelleyan views.

On 5 November 1838 Emily Brontë wrote a poem which she later copied into her non-Gondal manuscript book, when she sorted and copied her poems in the early months of 1844. The poem begins, 'O Dream, where art thou now?' and relates the waning for Emily of a fair, bright vision. She has now become disillusioned with this image (though the evidence is that she later readopted it). Natural beauties like the sun-beam and storm, the full moon and solemn night were once 'entwined with thee'; but now Emily Brontë links them with 'weary pain'. The vision she is lamenting seems likely to be that of a translated Shelley, revivified through an encounter with his poems, possibly through the *Fraser's* article. It is impossible to argue the case in full here; I have not yet encountered a better hypothesis, but the theory seems incapable of definite proof.

The poem 'O Dream' is typical in revealing a mood which though intense, will not last. While such feelings are on her, Emily will give herself over to them wholly, in the present instance dwelling upon the shattering of her dream. This immediacy in Emily is one of the secrets of *Wuthering Heights*, because she has the capacity to feel intensely on every page, in every mood of every character, even if they are contradictory.

To the mood of the moment, she is totally given up. The urgency of these moods will not be denied. We may recall the so-called slanderous stories about Mr Brontë hacking the backs off chairs in a fury. In Emily's case, the mood will emerge in writing, but it is essentially the same force. However, as we shall see in subsequent poems, once the mood is snapped, the poem cannot be finished, and will be put aside or completed on another day, coldly and often with a Gondal incident.

Four major poems of November and December will be dealt with later. For the moment, we may turn to examine the other evidence concerning Emily's stay at Law Hill. For example, some of the names for *Wuthering Heights* seem to have been picked up in the Halifax area. The house itself is partly *High* Sunderland, partly *Withen* Fields (Emily's etymology was at fault here, since 'Withen' = willow trees). Thomas Keyworth was told that a Mrs Earnshaw had been a servant at Law Hill, but he may have misheard, since according to the 1841 census it was Sarah *Robertshaw* who lived in one of the Law Hill tenements. *Lockwood* is the name of a place near Huddersfield, sometimes mentioned in the *Halifax Guardian*. If Thrushcross Grange is Shibden Hall, we may note the road junction at the rear of Shibden, called *Stump Cross*. Catherine's name is partly developed from the Gondal Geraldine, but may also reflect the patch of woodland a little higher up the Shibden valley called *Catherine Slack*. The name of the only male servant at Law Hill farm, aged 55 in the 1841 Census, was *Joseph* Tollis.[35]

Mrs Chadwick managed to speak with several old pupils of the school who said that Emily was not unpopular,

> though she could not easily associate with others, and her work was hard because she had not the faculty of doing it quickly. Unlike Charlotte, she was not good at needlework, and like her elder sister Maria, though clever in her own unique way, she was untidy and fond of day-dreaming.[36]

We have already suspected Emily of day-dreaming, and writing her thoughts down in verse, while supervising the prep at the school. Her untidiness is borne out by aspects of her manuscripts. It is interesting that she is thought to be a slow worker, and the point needs bearing in mind when we come to consider how long *Wuthering Heights* took to write.

One pupil who remembered Emily Brontë as her teacher was Laura Ellen Robinson, then aged eight.[37] She later became Mrs Watkinson, and was approached by Mrs Chadwick, to whom she talked about her memories and showed letters written at the time. The letters have not been traced; however, the grown-up Laura remembered that she had heard Emily Brontë say that the house-dog, to which she was devoted, 'was dearer to her than they were'. Emily's friendships with animals throughout her life were very intense and often noticed. At Law Hill she would have opportunities to make friends with horses, since Miss Elizabeth Patchett was a rider, and almost certainly included riding as an extra on her curriculum.

One should not take the comparison of house-dog and children too seriously. Real dislike of her pupils would surely have been visited by unpopularity. Leyland found another witness (unfortunately we do not know who) to say that 'she was not at all of an unkindly nature; on the contrary, her disposition was generous and considerate to those with whom she was on familiar terms.'[38] The remark about the house-dog could well have been an example of Emily's humour which misfired. Leyland does note Emily's 'extreme reserve with strangers', however; but it may be supposed that this would not operate strongly with small children, any more than with animals.

Four poems written in the last weeks of 1838 mark a stage in Emily's poetic development. All are personal poems, and were later copied into the A manuscript. They are: 'Loud without the wind was roaring', 'A little while', 'How still, how happy', and 'The Bluebell'. All touch on the poet's thoughts as she contemplates her exile in Law Hill, and we may, with care, use them as a biographical source.

The date of 'Loud without the wind was roaring' is unlikely to be 11 November, the date of the copy manuscript. The earlier fragment, E 12, which gives the first ten lines, is headed 'November' only. I should be inclined to put the date during the third week in the month, when there was a period of high winds. In reflective mood, Emily recalls her childhood when 'we' (Anne and herself, we may suppose) rose at dawn to run across the moors near Haworth. In the next stanza she recalls her delight when 'in exile afar' (that is, in Halifax), she finds a patch of brown heath while kneeling 'On the brow of a lonely hill'. The heath laments that 'the grim walls enfold me'; whether this heather patch was on Beacon Hill or nearer High Sunderland one cannot be sure. Emily seems to be suggesting that industrialization is harming the heather, but this does not quite fit with the idea of a 'lonely' hill.

'A little while' is one of Emily's best known early poems, often quoted because of its reference to 'a little and a lone green lane' in stanza eight. The poem does give some idea of how she felt during her period of teaching. The Law Hill girls are the 'noisy crowd', and, as in the fragment already discussed, the school is likened to a dungeon: 'I hear my dungeon bars recoil'. Whether literally or not, the rest period is described as an 'hour of rest' in the final stanza. Charlotte's letter of 2 October mentioned *half* an hour, but if these poems were written during rest periods, they seem more like a full hour's work than half an hour's. 'A little while' discusses two options for Emily's imagination. She may visit either Haworth ('a spot 'mid barren hills', of which she says that the 'hearth of home' is 'longed for') or Gondal, which she calls 'another clime, another sky'. It is in Gondal that the lone green lane is to be found; but this shows how close the geography of Gondal had come to be to that of Yorkshire.

The third poem in the group indicates a change of mind about the virtues of stillness. 'How still, how happy!' are words that would hardly go together at one time. We have seen Emily as a child full of energy and boisterous behaviour, moods which accord with breezy weather, and interestingly, 'the plash of the surge'. This reference to the sea may suggest that after all Emily did see it at Silverdale when she stayed at The Cove as a six-year-old. (However, as so often, she may be describing an emotional attachment to a phantom, an imaginary sea.) This third poem is very oral in tone; the poet addresses a companion: 'Come, sit down on this sunny stone/ . . . But sit – for we are all alone.' As we are examining the poems from a biographical point of view, it is worth asking whether the person addressed is real or imaginary. Did Emily form any habit of wandering by herself across the hills near Halifax? Alternatively, is there any evidence that she formed any close attachments there, as has been suggested by one or two writers? In the latter case, she might be addressing that friend in the present poem.[39]

Certain features of the poem may be checked, if the date is correct. The day was fine, according to Shackleton, the Keighley meteorologist. When Emily says 'my heart loves December's smile', she is referring to a pleasant winter's day, with the sun shining so as to provide the 'sunny stone' in stanza four. This, however, is inconsistent with the 'blue ice' in the final stanza, and temperatures of 43 degrees rule out any ice: that was imaginary. The poem could have been composed in the open air: there is plenty of evidence to suggest that Emily wrote in the open air when at home. However, 7 December was a Friday and it is by no means clear how she could have had time to do this.

Undoubtedly the Law Hill period was a time of growth for Emily Brontë, which is why such a writer as Romer Wilson says 'Something very desperate must have befallen Emily in soul or body in 1838.'[40] We have seen that in early November she laments the departure of a dream-figure, whom I consider may be Shelley. The dream-figure did not actually depart, but his influence was renewed in the two subsequent years. It is possible that he may have been in Emily's mind on the walk to the 'sunny stone'. Possibly, she was imagining Anne. It took little to stir Emily's emotions, her hate and affection, and it is hard to believe that she felt nothing at all for her charges, despite the 'house-dog' taunt. She may possibly have written the poem on a school walk (this might explain the Friday dating), and if so one of the little girls may have been addressed in the poem.

It seems certain that Emily was still at Law Hill on 18 December, when she wrote a poem about the bluebell, comparing its sweetness to the wild, sad spell in the heather, or the fragrance of the violet. The ice she describes in this poem could have been real ice; the day temperature reached only 29 degrees.[41] Once again we have mention of a 'wall' which the sunlight catches as the dusk comes on. Like the 'grim walls' that enfolded the heath in the earlier poem, this may be part of the wall of the house or schoolroom at Law Hill. We may speculate on the possibility that Emily is writing of a wall at High Sunderland, but it seems likely that at dusk she would need to be in the near vicinity of Law Hill. She hankers in the poem for 'the fields of home'; and she would certainly see them soon, as there were only three or four days to the Christmas break.

It is worth noting that Emily survived the term at Law Hill, and that in late January she would go back there. Though the school is a 'dungeon' and 'my dark prison-house', and though she was frequently dreaming of Haworth and had apparently given a very sombre picture of her exile to Charlotte in her early letter, she loved the house-dog and did not hate the children to the point where she became unpopular. We shall see that a few years later she was able to form a relationship with a pupil in Belgium, and we may think that despite her shyness, Emily could be pleasant to the people she took to. It seems that the evidence points to an attachment to the locale of the grotesque house, High Sunderland, on the opposite hill. She had heard or would soon hear the odd story of how Law Hill itself came to be built. She had a library to browse in without going across the moors to Ponden. She had possibly been to concerts in Halifax, or visited the museum. Frustrated and taxed as she was by this exposure to the semi-public life of a teacher, perhaps conscious of her unconventionality, Emily Brontë was learning and was not totally unhappy. The physical sickness of Roe Head had not returned.

Emily had shown little concern with Gondal during the last weeks of the autumn term at Halifax. But once home, where she met Charlotte, just returned for good from Miss Wooler's school at Dewsbury Moor, she was able to give her dream world more attention. She tore some notebook pages into four (the ruled lines on some of the pieces suggest that they had been brought back from Law Hill) and began to copy out her poems to date, apparently arranging them by subject. She made use of Brontë small script, but she began very neatly, with carefully formed letters and adequate space between the lines. We may consider it likely that this activity took up the first part of January, and that not much of the Gondal prose narrative was composed at this time. Original poetic composition was almost non-existent.[42]

However, on 12 January 1839 she responded, as so often, to a change in the weather by writing a Gondal poem celebrating the relaxation of frosty conditions after two very cold days. That day the temperature shot up to 50 degrees[43] and, as Emily wrote, 'chained the snow-swollen streams no more'. This poem describes the darkness at evening, and from the reference to the streams we can guess that on Saturday 12 January Emily – perhaps with Anne – walked across to the

Sladen or Ponden Clough beck. The poem concerns a rider who wanders on the moor, having set his horse loose. Horses do occasionally appear in Emily's poems, and we may recall that she had recently been brought into close contact with them at Miss Patchett's. There is also a Coleridgean feel to the poem, in which a female moorland spirit whose 'wavy hair on her shoulders bare . . . shone like soft clouds round the moon' describes how she guards the animals on the hillside. There is no similar poem in Emily's output. Here Emily seems to identify with the 'spirit', and we may perhaps hazard a more than usually contented view of herself. She copied the poem on to one of the quarter sheets she was then using, making few alterations.

It seems likely that the composition of this poem interrupted the copying, but by the time the holiday was ended, so far as we can tell, fourteen sides of the quarter sheets had been covered. The collection consisted of personal poems from 1837 and 1838, with some Gondal pieces, mostly relating to A. G. A. On the next side, No. 15, Emily wrote the number 2 and began to copy an undated poem beginning, 'It was night and on the mountains'. The poem ran to four stanzas and may have been a fresh composition. The piece of paper was then put away and we shall hear no more of it until 21 August. It looks as if the number 2 at the head means she is moving to a fresh topic; these tiny headings are paralleled elsewhere.

Both Leyland and Miss Robinson state that Emily was at Law Hill for six months, so we may suppose that she returned about the third week in January in cloudy weather during which the thermometer was seldom above freezing point. This term may have been a harder one, for no poetry was written. We have only Miss Robinson's word for the suggestion that Emily once again declined: 'when spring came back, with its feverish weakness, with its beauty and memories . . . her health broke down, shattered by long-resisted homesickness'. It is hard to discover who was Miss Robinson's informant, and the evidence must be treated with some caution. But the absence of poetry, compared with the abundant crop in November–December, and the spate of copying in January, may support her account. Alternatively, we might wonder whether this gap in poetic output does not signal time spent on fiction, possibly an early attempt to compose *Wuthering Heights*.

In addition to becoming acquainted with High Sunderland and Chapel-le-Breer, it has been suggested that Emily also encountered two other elements of the novel at this time. The first concerns a certain John Walsh, who had been buried nearby at Coldwell Hill in 1823. If we have been correct in thinking that Emily knew the story of the Welsh, or Walsh, who had usurped the patrimony of the Prunty family (or so it was said), then she might have been interested to hear of the malevolence of another Walsh.[44] This man was said to speak so coarsely that the vicar of Halifax would run out of his way to avoid him. He was buried, not in consecrated ground, but in one of his own fields 'as far away from his wife as possible'. Miss Patchett would have known of this unpleasant man, of whom there is objective evidence in the undated Southowram survey in Halifax library.[45]

Better known and almost certain to have been relayed to Emily Brontë was the story of how Law Hill came to be built. A few years older than Haworth parsonage, it had been standing for about sixty-seven years when Emily first saw it. Though built in eighteenth-century style, no one could call it gracious to look at, and it may not be surprising that an early rumour suggested that it might be the original for Wuthering Heights. However, it was the builder of Law Hill who reproduced the 'Welsh' legend, and may have provided Emily with the emotional link which had caused her to remain at Law Hill for a while and to remember the area long after she had left. Law Hill had been built by a usurper, similar to Welsh Prunty.

The usurper's name was Jack Sharp, and he had been the adopted child of John Walker of Walterclough, a hall which stood about a mile from Law Hill, down in the valley.[46] A wool merchant, Walker had replaced his own son by Sharp, who was a child of his sister-in-law. As in the legend of Welsh, Jack Sharp had outpaced the real son and soon had the old man under his thumb. For a long time there was no resistance to this alienation of the house and lands, and it was the second generation which provided it in the end. At this Jack took whatever he could from his old home of Waterclough and built himself a new house on top of the hill overlooking it: so Law Hill came to be built. (In one other respect it echoed the Prunty or Brunty story; it was called 'Mount Pleasant', the same name as the lime kilns where

Patrick's father had worked in County Louth.)[47] Sharp lived riotously and was finally ruined in the American War of Independence. His worsted warehouse, across the yard from the house, became neglected and was finally turned into a schoolhouse. One can easily imagine that Elizabeth Patchett told this story as an explanation to Emily of why there was such an extensive range of buildings ready for the lively schoolgirls who first came there about 1825.

We now return to the dream character whose ruthlessness dispossessed rightful heirs; he is formulated in the poems as Julius Brenzaida and will eventually become Heathcliff. This dream (perhaps merging at times with the Shelley dream) develops strongly after Halifax. The names of the criminal will change, but some of his character is crystallizing here in the vicinity of High Sunderland, Shibden and Law Hill. Her Law Hill 'exile' deeply affected Emily Brontë and it is natural to ask whether she found some deep personal attachment there which formed the basis of her understanding of Catherine and Heathcliff.

Absolutely no definitive answer can be given to this question. It might be worth remarking that some authors who have held this view were unaware of the precise date of the Law Hill episode, and so ascribed poems to that period which were in fact written at Haworth, before Emily set out.[48] Law Hill affected Emily, without doubt. She may well have been on friendly terms with Elizabeth Patchett, the handsome horse-riding headmistress. It is quite possible that Emily would have wished to recreate the positive side of Cowan Bridge, a protective love from Miss Evans. (With this we might connect the 'motherly protection' aspect of the Gondal poem already mentioned.) Circumstantial evidence seems to suggest that Miss Patchett told her yarns and took her on walks. Miss Patchett's neighbour, Anne Lister of Shibden, returned from a continental journey in November 1838. She is alleged to have been a lesbian; quite certainly she was a forceful lady of great intellect and energy, as appears from her diaries.[49] However, there is no mention in them of any contact with Miss Patchett during November 1838–March 1839, unless in the strange coded passages frequently found in the diary.

There was probably one other teacher of Emily's age at Law Hill. The 1841 census shows two under-teachers, one of whom will presumably be Emily's replacement. Their names were Charlotte Hartley and Jane Aspden; a possible echo of the latter's name may be in the poem 'Aspin Castle' of 1842, but the link is a slim one. Someone may have been with Emily on the day she wrote 'How still, how happy!', as has already been suggested. But we need to be very cautious: Emily's imagination was exceedingly active. The oldest pupil listed in the 1841 census was fifteen. We have seen that Emily was not unpopular among her pupils, who were the younger children, but it is hard to see her becoming the soul-mate of any, and then claiming to prefer the house-dog.

To conclude that Emily found and was robbed of a lover at Law Hill would be very rash indeed. We shall, in fact, later find a poem in which she denies all experience of actual love affairs. However, Emily listened and observed acutely. The impressions she received at Law Hill may have included emotional cross-currents as well as romantic and mysterious stories from the past, and the odd brooding presence of dilapidated High Sunderland Hall. The lack of poetry in early 1839 is suggestive, and we may at least consider the possibility that the early steps in creating her novel may have been undertaken at this time.

10

A Serious Poet

Perhaps this is the destined hour
When hell shall lose its fatal power
And heaven itself shall bend above
To hail the soul redeemed by love.

The year 1839 was one in which Emily Brontë climbed out of despondency towards self-acceptance. Even after returning from Law Hill, she could not shake off her low spirits, despite the bright spring days. In April, she lost the company of Anne, who went to Blake Hall, not far from Roe Head, to be governess in the Ingham family, some of whose traits she portrayed in *Agnes Grey*. Emily laments Anne's departure in a poem beginning, 'From our evening fireside now', accurate on weather details, which abruptly switches to Gondal when inspiration runs out. At this point, Anne, her sister, becomes 'Arthur, brother'.[1]

By May, she was still sad, looking without joy on the newly blooming flowers. In 'May flowers are opening' she makes reference to 'The glad eyes around me' and says

If heaven would rain on me
That future storm of care
So their fond hearts were free
I'd be content to bear.

The eyes 'Must weep as mine have done'. How have Emily's eyes wept? Despite its non-Gondal start we cannot be sure the poem has no fictional reference, though the deliberate signature below, 'E. J. Brontë', suggests not. One might have thought that Emily has wept no more than Charlotte, breaking down at Miss Wooler's in mid-1838, or Branwell, failing to enter the Royal Academy in 1835. It is possible that Emily is not thinking of her brother and sister, since the setting for the poem is by a moorland stream ('The sun is gladly shining/The stream sings merrily'). Possibly she is writing at Ponden, near 'the Meeting of the Waters', and can see the Heaton youngsters, the eldest of whom is now seventeen. This is, of course, pure speculation, but both Branwell and Charlotte had done their share of weeping and could hardly be seen as young innocents following Emily's tragic footsteps.

About this time, Emily decided on further copying of poems. This time she decided to write in conventional handwriting, and to use a full-size though not impressive notebook. It has become known as the C manuscript. Considerably mutilated, as poems copied in 1844 were torn out or crossed through, it is still our only authority for some of her early work. This all seems to be part of the increased self-confidence which stems from Law Hill despite its drawbacks. We may feel that indirectly Miss Patchett had encouraged her assistant teacher to take a more serious view of art.

In June a nostalgic poem was begun, called 'The hours of day have glided by', and lamenting the absence of 'a sound/We know shall ne'er be heard again . . . *Their* feet shall never waken more/The echoes in the galleries wide . . .' In 1844 this poem was tidied up and integrated into the Gondal story, which was then being systematized. Now, it surely must have been composed out of anguish for the two sisters so much missed at Haworth.

Before turning to some external factors, we might examine one more poem of the summer of 1839, though it anticipates a little. Written on 12 August, it was never revised or recopied, and presents a splendid example of Emily's poetic struggle and processes. She begins with an enquiry from a bystander. 'How long will you remain? The midnight hour/Has tolled its last note from that minster tower. The bystander must be Charlotte, and the scene is the parsonage parlour. The 'minster' is the church, and the clock the original eighteenth-century one, parts of which still survived in store in the 1930s.[2] It is a drowsy scene, with the lamp burning low, the fire out. Emily is trying to write, but her 'cold hands hardly hold the useless pen'. However, she is furious at the idea of being asked to leave her work and meditation. 'No: let me linger, leave me, let me be . . .' She asks not to be torn away from her 'blissful dream, that never comes with day'. The earlier version, erased, perhaps mentions the word 'ghost'; it is a vision 'dear though false'. Does this scene help us to understand Emily's reputed mysticism?

Her own word, often used, and to be developed, is 'vision'. It seems highly likely that from childhood (we noted the importance of 'Come hither, child', which was written in July of this year) Emily's strong imagination had put into pictures her overwhelming feeling that the dead were near her. In early years, this meant her sisters, though we have found some suggestions that later she saw a dead poet whom I have identified as Shelley, and whose full effect is still to be explored. The intensity of this vision transported her, so that the everyday world of Haworth was left behind. It is hard to accept that this vision was one of the Gondal world, whose unrealistic and shadowy characters seem to lack the power, though clearly there were times when Gondal did satisfy her creative needs.

The ghost ministered to Emily, communing with her and strengthening her lonely mind. At the moment, Anne was in Mirfield, and at the end of the month Emily would write another nostalgic poem regretting absence and the departure of her family. Just possibly she sometimes saw Anne as a vision, but it seems more likely that the creatures of her mind, taking their origin from dead people who once lived, seemed more real to her. The poem's questioner next asks whether the poet can really find pleasure in the shadowy room: 'Besides, your face has not a sign of joy/ And more than tearful sorrow fills your eye . . .' Emily's expressive eyes have more than once been mentioned. We can imagine Charlotte, later to reproach herself for misunderstanding her sister, watching her now in puzzlement, as the intensity of her absorption in the world of vision became apparent in her expression.

The poem soon modulates to Gondal, bringing in 'children's merry voices', woods and a river. It is not signed by a Gondal character, and we are not certain who this matronly (or fatherly) character might be. It is almost certain that Emily didn't know either. All the evidence suggests that she often made up Gondal poems in her own persona, then found a Gondal character to whom they might apply; or else she began them as personal poems and turned them to Gondal when her inspiration ran out. In this poem Emily speaks of the 'woe-worn mind' which mourns at night, so that hearts 'throb in pain' during the darkness. Day gives back the joy of living and the mourner receives 'shadowy gleams of infancy' to cheer him. We shall find poems which state the opposite, that day is too painful and night soothes. The truth is that Emily's sensitive disposition was now so far wounded that there was no safe time at which dreadful memories might not return.

The look of this manuscript provides strong evidence of the identity of poetic content with the poet's real non-fictional state. Round its edge are various 'doodles', suggesting a dreamy state of mind. At the top of the page is what looks like a feather, and on the right a decorated cross. Misty lines follow the poem's lines. The most interesting drawing is that of a winged snake, about opposite the description of the 'vision'. It has a snake's head but no tongue, and wings like a pterodactyl issuing from its body. It descends in whirls down the left-hand margin. These doodles bear a remarkable similarity to the drawings Shelley drew in his notebooks, which of course Emily had certainly not seen or heard of.[3] At the end of the poem she has written in a dreamy way 'Regive' (from line 35 of the poem) and repeated it several times across the page. There is finally a doodle made later, consisting of two sloppy concentric circles, the ends neatly joined together. Both the snake and the circles might have caused a Jungian to see evidence of the 'worm Ouroboros', which Shelley drew. Its significance is 'Eternity' because it has no end or beginning. It is hard to see where Emily could have encountered such a concept, but just possibly she might have met it at Ponden.

It is evident that at this time Emily and Charlotte were happy together, though Emily's protesting rhetoric shows she felt her sister did not understand her. This spiritual separation irked Charlotte and seems to be responsible for her questing guilt at Emily's death. On her side, though Emily regretted separation, she seems not to have taken great steps towards others, expecting them to seek her out rather than the reverse. If Emily was driven into lonely visions and the world of Gondal, it was of her own choice, sometimes perhaps almost a conscious one.

In July 1839 Branwell took a trip with Hartley Merrall and other friends to Liverpool, intended to set him back on his feet after his vicissitudes following the Royal Academy failure.[4] He had been working as a portrait painter in Bradford (though Emily did not visit him in mid-1838, as is sometimes stated). But he was not single-minded, preferring to become involved with as racy a set as he could find, though not untalented in his chosen trade. It might be valuable here to write a little more about Emily's relations with her wayward brother, to whom she is often thought to be close.

It must be said that, as in their childhood, there is little evidence to suggest any special relationship between the two at this time. The main reasons why this has been supposed appear to be:

1 That Emily copied 'The Wanderer', a long poem of Branwell's, on the supposed visit to Bradford in July 1838.

   But the copy is in Branwell's own handwriting, and this was misidentified by early Brontë editors.[5]

2 That Emily's poem, 'Shed no tears o'er that tomb', and perhaps also 'The soft unclouded blue of air', both written in 1839, refer to Branwell.

   But the 'iron man' of the later poem is very unlike Branwell. Branwell was not made of iron, but something much more malleable. The Gondal character who is the subject of 'The soft unclouded blue of air' is a forerunner of Heathcliff perhaps, but we have known for a long time that Heathcliff is in no way developed from Branwell. Branwell was soft-hearted, sentimental, imaginative, weak-willed, of insignificant stature: he was almost the antithesis of Heathcliff. It might be better to see the Gondal 'iron man' as a component of Emily's own self, the part which had refused to intervene with the Cowan Bridge staff on behalf of Maria, possibly.

   The man over whose tomb we must not shed tears is most likely to be Shelley.[6] He is probably not a Gondal figure, but has been a voyager, now destined for Hell. More will be said about this obsessional subject of Emily Brontë's poetry shortly.

3 That Branwell somehow aided Emily in the writing of *Wuthering Heights*, which was now beginning to be written.

> We have seen that a sketch of the novel might possibly have been begun in 1838–9. But the introduction of Branwell into the supposed conditions of its writing stems from subjective Victorian views of Emily. Quite simply, it seemed hard to believe that it could have had a female author, and readers looked round for a male collaborator. But the *Wuthering Heights* themes first surfaced in Gondal, and Gondal was shared with Anne, not Branwell.

We have already considered whether Emily and Branwell could have been close in childhood, and decided not. Prior to 1830 her collaborator was Charlotte, and after 1830 Anne. It is not difficult to see why Emily preferred Anne. Anne had patience to balance Emily's incautious enthusiasms. She was kinder and more malleable than the other two (so long as she saw no moral objection to Emily's thought or behaviour). Unless we consider that Lockwood may be in part derived from Branwell, Emily's brother does not figure in her work, though in Anne's Feargus and Lord Lowborough, both from *Wildfell Hall*, he probably does. (In Chapter 13 I shall mention one small touch of Branwell which did reach Emily's novel.)[7] It seems most likely that at the present time, Branwell was rapidly alienating himself from his sisters' goodwill. Both Anne and Emily must have known by now that they had more capacity for work and better artistic judgement than he had. Whenever the 'gun group' portrait was painted (it may have been in 1839), we can hardly imagine either Anne or Emily wanting to be in the room long with the pheasant corpses shown lying on the table. Branwell continued to love shooting: this can hardly have endeared him to his nature-loving family.[8]

More extraordinary, some biographers have written as though the vaguely incestuous tone suggested in *Wuthering Heights* by the ambiguous relationship between Heathcliff and Catherine could have mirrored something in the relations between Emily and Branwell. We shall return to the Heathcliff/Catherine relationship later. To compare what we know of Branwell with Heathcliff is to show how different the two are. Of course Emily would have said that she 'loved' her brother in a vague, undifferentiated way; but in general, he typified some of the worst faults of men to her, and she did not generally get on well with men, whether they were curates or M. Heger, the Belgian schoolmaster. Perhaps she liked her created men better, though even her image of Shelley in the poems we shall soon explore is 'weak and vain', while Lockwood, Edgar, Joseph and Hindley all have major faults for the reader to disapprove. There seem to have been two exceptions to this blight on men: Mr Brontë himself, and the new curate of 1839, William Weightman.

As Ellen Nussey told Clement Shorter, among the curates, 'Mr Weightman was her only exception for any conventional courtesy.'[9] William Weightman first arrived at Haworth in August, signing the register for the first time on the 19th. He had come from Appleby, via Durham, where he had obtained a Licentiate in Theology, not an MA as his memorial states. The evidence suggests that we must put down young William as a plausible rogue, very attractive to girls and likely to be forgiven for his lapses.[10] Branwell got on well with him, and he worked his way into the confidence of Aunt Elizabeth. Patrick approved of him too, delivering a heartfelt sermon at his untimely death in 1842. He was clearly an outgoing man who pleased everyone, though he liked to shoot game and was not averse to a drink. His personal charm must have broken through Emily's defences, but we are not to read into this situation the idea that her heart was engaged, as Anne's undoubtedly was.

Even so, Emily was more than courteous. According to Miss Robinson, whose informant was Ellen Nussey, Weightman always called in on the girls when he left Mr Brontë's study.[11] Miss Branwell would come downstairs, and the curate would be asked to join them all in a cup of tea. Doubtless she thought there was safety in numbers, and 'none enjoyed the fun more than quiet Emily . . . "her countenance glimmering as it always did when she enjoyed herself"' (these last are Ellen's own words).[12] It was at this time that Emily acquired the nickname of 'The Major', though the precise reason is not clear. It seems likely that Charlotte is alluding to this in calling Shirley 'Captain Keeldar'. The assumption has always been made that Emily's martial presence was involved in protecting Charlotte (and possibly Anne) from Weightman's unwanted attentions. it seems more likely that in his company she let slip her guard – we have heard from Ellen of her glimmering countenance – and genuinely tried to be friendly. In doing so, she might be inclined to organize, set goals for a walk and so on. With her extra height, and her long legs, she might have given a military impression without there being any intention to guard her sisters. Emily seems to have been 'bossy' by nature: this should not lead us to exaggerate, in the twentieth century, the impression of 'masculinity' she sometimes gave to nineteenth-century observers.

The arrival of Mr Weightman did not prevent Emily from pursuing the Gondal game. Whether she wrote to Anne about it we do not know, but from 21 August, two days after Weightman's first signature in the register, dates an exceptionally interesting fragment in Emily's handwriting. It was the subject of an article in *Brontë Society Transactions* in 1962, but some advance can be made in its interpretation.[13] The list appears on manuscript D 8, the odd sheet in the group of scraps which Emily was using this year. She began copying poems about A. G. A. on to them in January, as we saw. Becoming dissatisfied with these small transcripts, she began a full-scale transcript book on her return from Law Hill (manuscript C), but continued to use up the scraps for new poems until 1844 at least. We have seen one such poem in a state of development during the night of 12 August. Though the scrap called D 8 was packed and taken to Belgium in 1842, the writing style of the Gondal list we are about to consider is that of 1839, and there can be no real doubt that it was written on 21 August of that year. It is incomplete, but unique and precious. It is the only fragment relating to Emily's Gondal prose that has ever been found, despite suggestions to the contrary by various writers.

The first column gives the names of the Gondal characters. Ronald Stwart (i.e. Stewart) seems to be married to Regina. He is twenty-eight, she twenty-four. Their birthdays are given, together with a complete list of physical characteristics. Ronald has brown hair and grey eyes, English nose, red and white complexion, and is six feet tall, while his wife is five feet seven inches, has dark brown hair, grey eyes, a Greek nose, and fair (?) complexion. The next pair are perhaps related to Ronald; possibly Marcellus is his brother. He is only twenty-one, and has light brown hair, grey eyes, a Roman nose, fair complexion, and apparently lives in a castle. His wife Flora is younger and five inches shorter than her husband at five feet six inches; she is only seventeen. Not all the columns of information can be understood. The letter after the characters' birthdate may perhaps be the initial of the town of their birth (E could stand for Exina perhaps), but the number seven at the end, and the part-filled last two columns, give too few data to be interpreted.[14]

The list is fascinating in several ways. We see Emily's acute interest in physical appearance. Hair colour, eye colour, height, are important to her. These Gondal people are romantic characters, out of Scott; two at any rate live in a castle. Their physical attributes are striking. They do not have 'mousy' hair, but attractive colours like chestnut. They seem to flout normal couplings of hair and eyes, their dark brown hair going with light eyes (this combination does occur in Ireland). They appear much taller than average, the three young women being five feet six or five feet seven inches. Emily seems to have been about this height.[15] These characters are not a fair cross-section of humanity: they are as young and as striking as the characters in *Wuthering Heights*.

All these Gondal people *are* Emily Brontë, and illustrate her attitude to characterization, so different from Anne's. Like them, Emily is taller than average; like them, she has dark hair but light eyes; the eldest is only seven years older than Emily, the youngest four years younger. Four out of five have summer birthdays, like Emily. Emily did not live in a castle, but even her non-Gondal verse is often couched in terms which suggest that she often thought of her home that way. High Sunderland looked like a castle, and Wuthering Heights is at one point compared to one. When we remember that this list was made for her own eyes and was unlikely to be seen by anyone else, we must marvel at the secretive nature of its information. She writes nothing in full, even the name Stewart being shortened. Just so did Patrick write the initial 'B' in his notebook, occasionally expanding it to Br–te. By this period of her life, Emily was increasingly living inside herself.

However, the list does show some sharp interest in character, even though it is subjective. We can well imagine that Emily might have begun planning *Wuthering Heights* in this way, by deciding on Catherine's appearance, and by pairing off the marriageable youngsters. It is interesting too, that these characters are not the same as those who appear in the poems, obsessed as they are at this time with the story of A. G. A. It seems likely that the Gondal poetry is very unrepresentative of the whole saga; possibly only those in A. G. A.'s circle would break into verse. The same is true of Anne's Gondal lists, which do not mention her poetic characters.[16]

Late in August, Charlotte went away on holiday with Ellen. With Anne still at Blake Hall, Emily was the only sister at Haworth.[17] On 30 August she wrote an unusually frank poem of loneliness. After a damp day the sky cleared towards evening and the sun shone on the church tower. 'And this is just the joyous hour/When we were wont to burst away,' Emily writes. But today there is 'No merry footstep on the stair/No laugh – no heart-awaking tone.' Emily missed her sisters badly, and wandered that evening in the garden, thinking she might hear the sound of their feet approaching. At this point she wondered whether the others had gone for good, and would no more provide those 'sun-blinks through the mists of care'. She consoled herself with the reflection that in the end there would be a 'more divine return', apparently alluding to Eternity, when the sisters would be together for ever.

When Anne came back she was quickly captivated by William Weightman, and was writing about him by 1 January 1840.[18] Emily's poems at this time are very reflective and emotional, suggesting that she caught the echo of Anne's involvement. We must now examine carefully the poems of nostalgic or romanticized yearning which she produced. We shall then move on to note current developments in the character of A. G. A., who seems to have started life as quite a gentle princess, but who will now become harsher.[19]

The romantic poems under consideration are as follows:

'Shed no tears o'er that tomb', dated 26 July 1839 (C 11)
'The wind, I hear it sighing', 29 October 1839 (A 14)
'There should be no despair for you', undated (A 16)
'Well, some may hate, and some may scorn', 14 November 1839 (A 17)
'That wind I used to hear it swelling', 28 November 1839 (D 13)
'Far, far away is mirth withdrawn', March 1840 (A 18)
'It is too late to call thee now', April 1840 (A 13)

A 15, which would complete the set of A poems from 13–18, is 'Love and Friendship' and cannot be dated, though it looks as if it might fit in somewhere here. It should be noted that both in A manuscript and elsewhere, Emily often tries to group her poems by subject, and it would be reasonable to suppose that these form a group. 'Shed no tears' was not recopied; we shall see why not. 'That wind' may have been felt to be incomplete, and it was also left.

It is important to note that none of these poems is a Gondal poem. If A 13–18 had been Gondal poems they would have been copied into the B manuscript; Emily is very careful to divide her work, as we shall see when we reach the year 1844. 'That wind' is rather slight. It was written on a day when the wind seems to have picked up later on, and by nightfall was bringing sleety rain: hence Emily is reminded of 'winter nights' in line 5, though November could be described as late autumn. C 11 is harder to pin down. We saw Emily begin to copy C manuscript earlier during the year. Many of the poems in it *are* Gondal poems, but it is not labelled or confined to them. It would not be unreasonable to leave the poem on one side till the others have been considered, and then see whether or not it coheres with them.

In 'Well, some may hate and some may scorn' Emily writes of a man ('his', line 23) who may be hated or scorned. His hopes were ruined, his fame blighted. So she begins, but soon changes her stance, through considering 'one word' in connection with him. He was vain, weak, false, proud, and has nothing to do with her. But these turned out too to be untrue thoughts: the timid deer is not despicable, and we do not mock the wolf or leveret for their respective weaknesses. Emily ends the poem by begging Heaven to give the spirit of the man rest. In 'Far, far away' she lies awake 'three long hours before the morn' and seeks the company of 'thou shade'. The man she calls to her bedside ('He', line 33) is 'deserted' and his corpse lies 'cold', 'mingled with a foreign mould'. His name was blighted, tarnished by shame. His 'phantom face' is 'dark with woe'. It is a time of overwhelming fear, a 'night of grief' but Emily must 'cling closely to thy side'. It seems that this man must expect a terrible doom when dead; but God will not actually torture him because 'Man cannot read the Almighty mind'. In the final stanza she wakes from her dream and says, '*He* rests, and I endure the woe/That left his spirit long ago.'

In 'It is too late to call thee now,' Emily wonders whether it is too late to call 'Thy darling shade' and decides it is so.

> *Yet ever in my grateful breast*
> *Thy darling shade shall cherished be;*
> *For God alone doth know how blest*
> *My early years have been in thee!*

Again, in the undated poems, 'There should be no despair for you' (whose relevance to the present series is suggested by Emily's placing of it when she copied the poems in 1844), she asks rhetorically whether the 'best-beloved of years' are not near her heart forever. These 'best beloved' would include Maria and Elizabeth and possibly other dead souls, but in view of the placing we may well prefer the subject of the whole group as a predominant influence.

In 'The wind I hear it sighing' Emily hears a strong wind howl round the house. It is not '*That* wind' but only '*The* wind'. In fact, it was a north-easter. Now 'Old feelings' gather about Emily's heart, like vultures. Though once kind, they are now cheerless. If only she could be rid of her past woe, she would give her up past pleasures; then and only then might she find her soul 'another love'.

What, then, is the subject which Emily, as poet, is dealing with? In A 13, A 17 and A 18 she seems to be talking of the same lonely and misunderstood person, for whom she feels. She clings closely to him. He is not a Gondal fiction; he is not Branwell, who will not die for nine years. This man, on the other hand, is dead 'long ago', but is not a dead sister. All this we may say with certainty. But we may go further: this man angered God, in the eyes of the world. He could be expected to bring down the wrath of the heavens after death. Emily admits he could be considered shameful, despite his clearly seen 'phantom face' whose tears she condones. He might even be considered vain or proud, and her soul will not be totally subject to him. One alarming word is associated with him and gives her pause. He died overseas and was buried there.

Of course this vision is romanticized and mixed with feelings derived from the love felt for the dead sisters. But it must be stressed again that this man is not a Gondal fiction. It is hard to find a candidate for this identity more appropriate than Shelley, whose thought permeates Emily's and who called himself an atheist. We have seen that she and Anne read 'Epipsychidion', in which the surprising addresses to 'Emily' refer to Aemilia Viviani. To Emily Brontë, however, they may have sounded like direct addresses from the land of the dead, in which she believed implicitly. Now we see her calling on 'thou shade' to come to her room. It seems impossible to prove that this was Shelley, but if not, then who was it? Who else can be suggested who flouted convention and religion, who shared Emily's views, and did so 'long ago' before Emily was out of the nursery? It must be a person whose picture Emily had seen (hence the 'phantom face') and whose writings she could read.

In 'Shed no tears' we find the opposite view starkly stated, the view that the man is damned; and we discover one or two more corroborative details. The man over whose tomb we are enjoined not to weep seems to have died in a storm, like that raging on 26 July 1839. But 'His bark will strive no more/Across the waters of despair/To reach that glorious shore'. Like the Brontës, Shelley lived his own legend. The constant 'boat' metaphor of his poems concludes with his own death in a boat which he determined to take out on a day of doubtful weather. He sought Eternity like Emily; he was willing to look for it through death. If Emily considered herself to be in Shelley's tradition, this may explain her reaction to death when she faced it in 1848. This poem is interesting for the way in which the poet works herself up into a fury of self-hate, in hating her idol.

That wrath will never spare,
Will never pity know,
Will mock its victim's maddened prayer,
Will triumph in his woe.

Even Emily may have thought this too violent, for she did not recopy it.

The boat ready to sail with Emily and Shelley (as she may have read 'Epipsychidion') capsized and will bring eternal revenge. The boat was perhaps one of the 'rare and real delights' mentioned in 'That wind' as being known in Emily's early years. Its reality, however, seemed more appropriate to adolescence than young womanhood, and from now on we shall find Emily often more dubious about the reality of her imaginative experiences. It should not be forgotten that this group of poems is being written just before and for some time after her twenty-first birthday, a time when she may well have felt the need for assessment and a change of course. This might be accentuated by Anne's part-concealed attachment to a living man. The woman who made up the Gondals and set them in pairs must have wondered whether she would herself ever find 'another love' and so become part of such a pair, or whether her imaginary link with a ghost could prove a hindrance to any such relationship.

Meanwhile, A. G. A. becomes savage. In a poem attributed to F. de Samara, Emily accuses her princess of every sort of falsehood and cruelty.[20] Evidently she has cast him into the 'Gaaldine prison caves'. 'Thy sun is near meridian height', begins Samara, echoing a Shelleyan line.[21] A. G. A. is a 'false friend' and 'treacherous guide' whose heart can be satiated with pride. He invites her to come in person and gloat over the raving madness of her dying victim. Yet once the two were in love, and had embraced near Elderno's lake in the summer moonlight. Samara speculates on her method of repaying this love, but concludes with the thought that if there is any God whose 'arm is strong' her spirit will be tortured in hell.

This change in the character of A. G. A. is odd, and may possibly correspond with a change in the dominant self-image of Emily herself. It is not a great deal different from 'Shed no tears' in which the writer seems to take a delight in the everlasting torment of the disgraced hero, and this is a non-Gondal poem. In these poems we have examples of the anti-Emily, flouting Maria's calm doctrines of heaven (at any rate if Helen's thoughts in *Jane Eyre* really represent Maria's). In several poems she writes of the bitterness experienced in waking from her vision; perhaps she actually blames the vision, and imbues it with the qualities of a torturer. A. G. A. seems to be Samara's vision of love, but is a sadistic lover, imprisoning her beloved in repayment for her own treacherous attachment to him. Emily made one attempt to reinstate A. G. A., in a poem begun on 6 May 1840, but broken off (we do not know exactly at which point).[22] This failing, she decided to kill her. We shall see that she would not die, and insisted on resurfacing as Catherine.

Meanwhile the new curate sent valentines to all the girls, including Ellen who was staying at Haworth just then. Anne took hers seriously, and was disinclined to go to her new post at Thorp Green, but she tore herself away.[23] Ellen's had a verse beginning 'Fair Ellen, fair Ellen', but whose were those addressed 'Away, fond love' and 'Soul divine'? As only three of the first lines were recalled by Charlotte in her letter of 17 March 1840, we cannot be sure to which sister each valentine belonged. 'Soul divine' sounds like Emily, but it may not have been. Later that month all of them, including Ellen, went with Weightman to a Classical lecture he was giving to the Keighley Mechanics' Institute. As Winifred Gérin points out, Mrs Gaskell avoids mentioning him in her biography, thus underlining the seriousness with which his attentions were viewed, especially by Anne, and even somewhat by Charlotte; but surely not at all by Emily. Yet even she, as we have seen, caught the slightly flirtatious atmosphere of the parsonage that spring, and turned it into a quest for her own lost affection.

In the absence of Anne, Emily became less attached to Gondal. The same was even more true of Anne herself. But we lose track of both the sisters in the second half of 1840, and it is not until the middle of the following year that there is any more documentary evidence. It was, by now, time for the next of the four-year diary papers. This one is Emily's least known, and it seems best to transcribe it direct from Shorter's copy in *Charlotte Brontë and her Circle*.[24] In some ways it is little more grown-up than its predecessor, though Emily makes a good attempt to produce a wider vocabulary. She begins with a statement of its aim, but this is contradicted lower down when she starts to discuss the school project, and suggests that she and Anne will look at the diary paper in July. The paper, in that case, is not clearly to be opened 'when Anne is 25 years old'. The following transcription reproduces Emily's spelling and punctuation, and where possible, I have tried to record her changes of mind.

A Paper to be opened
when Anne is
25 years old
[Sketch] or my next birthday after – [Sketch]
if
– all be well –

Emily Jane Brontë July the 30*th* 1841 –

It is Friday evening – near 9 o'clock ~~a~~ wild rainy weather I am seated in the dining room alone having just concluded tidying our desk-boxes – writing this document – Papa is in the parlour Aunt up stairs in her room – she has ~~just~~ been reading Blackwood's Magazine to papa – Victoria and Adelaide are ensconsed in the peat-house – Keeper is in the kitchen – Hero in his cage – We are all stout and hear~~tiy~~ as I hope is the case with Charlotte, Branwell, and Anne, of whom the first is at John White Esq[re] upper royd House, Rawden The second is at Luddenden foot and the third is I believe ~~Sc~~ at Scarborough – enditing perhaps a paper corresponding to this –

~~There~~ A scheme is at present in agitation for setting us up in a school of our own as yet nothing is determined but I hope and trust it may go on and prosper and answer our highest expectations – this day 4 years I wonder whether we shall still be dragging on in our present condition or established to our hearts content Time will show –

I guess that at the time appointed for the opening of this paper – we (ie) Charlotte, Anne and I – shall ~~will~~ be all merrily seated in our own sitting-room in some pleasant shall ~~p~~—— and flourishing seminary having just gathered in for the midsummer holydays our debts will be paid off and we shall have c~~h~~ash in hand to a considerable amount – Papa Aunt and Branwell will either have been ~~,~~ or be coming – to visit us – it will be a fine warm [sum]mers evening – very different from this bleak look-out [and(?)] Anne and I will perchance slip out into the garden [for] a few (?) minutes to peruse our papers and – I hope either this or something better will be the case –

The Gondalians (+++) are at present in a~~n~~ threatening state but there is no open rupture as yet – all the princes and princesses of the Royal royaltys are at the palace of Instruction – I have a good many books on hand – but I am sorry to say that – as usual I make small progress with any – however I have just made a new regularity paper! and I mean verb sap – to do great things – and now I close sending from far an ex-[hor]tation of Courage . . . . courage! to exiled and harassed Anne

wishing she was here EB(?)

Shorter read the illegible word between the repeated 'courage' as 'boys', and as he had the original, he may be correct.

This diary paper raises more questions than it solves. Why is it so vague as to timing? It is to be opened 'when Anne is 25 years old' or when Emily is 27. The idea of the four-year gap is interesting, and seems to have been put into practice. But considering that both sisters have reputations for careful dating in their novels, the vagueness is strange. It is hard to tell how the clause 'If all be well' relates. Is it only the second part, indicating that the diary paper would be opened on Anne's birthday, or 'If all be well' on Emily's? It may be thought that this is a fruitless question, but it is interesting that there is a discrepancy between the accurate Emily, aware of time, and an apparently ambiguous intention here. One way to reconcile the contradiction would be to suppose that Emily was romantically making provision for some memorial of herself in case she should die before her sister. This raises the question why she thought that might be a possibility, when it has always been thought that Anne was the one with indifferent health.

However one reads the tone of the opening, Emily then spends some effort speculating on the school proposal, which became important to the family and was the cause of the two elder sisters' travelling to Belgium. At the moment they are 'dragging on' but she hopes the school 'or something better' will have come to fruition in four years' time. There is no question of Branwell being involved in the school plan, though he will be expected to visit. Charlotte is included, but she will be entertaining the visitors while Emily and Anne slip out into the summery garden to unseal the four-year-old diary papers. The twinship between dreamy Emily and her compliant sister is still firm in Emily's eyes.

Others have noted Emily's keenness to improve herself. She has a good many books on hand, but isn't succeeding in reading them (or writing them?) This underlines the curious streak of indolence in Emily which prevented her from getting on with the housework in the earlier diary paper, and seems to contradict the speedy feel of *Wuthering Heights*. Sometimes, as we have seen, this indolence seems to spill over into trance, and a poem may begin. Practical tasks such as brushing the parlour or feeding the animals may be done without breaking the trance. We shall see Emily extending her capacities for this.

What does Emily mean by saying the Gondalians are in a 'threatening' state? Who will cause and who will suffer the 'rupture'? The 'palace of instruction' seems to be a prison, and I have already suggested that it may descend from the prisons of the children's early plays. The princes and princesses are in prison, so how can there be 'no open rupture'? Does this phrase conceal a split between Emily and Anne? Or are the rebel Gondals going to divide into mutually antagonistic groups of freedom-fighters?

From a literary point of view this paper can be said to be an advance on that of 1837. There is a better vocabulary, but the 'mechanics' of English are still deplorable. It is not, in fact, until they encounter the demands of printers that the Brontës take any care over punctuation and capitalization. Here, capitals are used for proper names, but the beginning of a new sentence may be indicated neither by a capital nor a preceding full stop. But Emily does use a capital T for 'Time', as she does at intervals in her poem manuscripts.

One very interesting point is that Emily records that she has tidied 'our' desk-boxes. These were the boxes, used as desks, which could be carried out into the garden or even on to the moors to write. Emily's survived her death and, when opened, contained an enigmatic note from her publisher. It is surprising that Emily has tidied not only her own box but Anne's too. Anne, then, could have no secret writing that Emily could not see. (In fact, however, she wrote quite different kinds of poems at Thorp Green, of which Emily had no immediate sight.) Emily's action shows the kind of community that Emily assumed existed between her and Anne. Ellen had called them twins, and Emily was still working on that basis. But whether Anne could have tidied Emily's desk with impunity is another matter. In 1845, Emily will go into a rage because Charlotte reads her poems. In the novel, Catherine and Heathcliff shared things, and Heathcliff alleges they would never quarrel over who had the lap-dog and who hadn't.[25] It looks as though Emily's notion of shared childhood interests lasted at least until she was twenty-three.

Gradually the idea that the three sisters should open a school led Charlotte to consider that they should go abroad to perfect their languages. She was proposing this to Aunt Elizabeth by 29 September 1841, and had already decided that Emily, not Anne, would come with her.[26] She had also decided that

Brussels was the place to go, having heard about it from Mary Taylor, though some consideration was given to alternatives. How Emily first received the suggestion we cannot know. On the face of it, living in Brussels would be even less attractive than Roe Head or Halifax. We know very little about her feelings this autumn, except that she drew a coloured picture of a hawk on 27 October. It has sometimes been identified with Hero, but he is a creature we know little of. It is a lively painting, but, like the bird pictures of 1829, closely based on Bewick.[27] As though trying half to conceal who really drew it, Emily writes at the top, 'By E. J. B.të –', even though presumably no one but herself would be looking at it. Hero, if it is he, sits rather disconsolately on a broken branch. Within a year we shall find Emily making a rather more portentous drawing, not simply of a broken branch, but of a totally broken mature tree.

The last we hear of Emily in 1841 is when Charlotte writes to her from Upperwood, where there is more governessing to do. 'You are not to suppose that this note . . . [has] any information on the subject we both have considerably at heart . . . . Belgium is a long way off, and people are everywhere hard to spur up to a proper speed.'[28] 'Spurring up' people was Charlotte's role in life, it seems; and Emily, being the nearest and dearest, was the most likely to get in the way of the process.

11

Brussels

O Innocence, that cannot live
With heart-wrung anguish long –
Dear childhood's Innocence, forgive
For I have done thee wrong!

There is no real evidence that Emily wanted to go to Brussels. She may well have felt it was necessary in order to improve the sisters' chances of running a succesful seminary. But she does not seem to have lent any great effort to profiting socially from her stay there. We shall see that she was disliked by some of her fellow pupils, and got on badly with M. Heger, the visiting teacher who played a large part in Charlotte's liking for Belgium and tested her conscience. Emily proved a surly companion on walks and made no attempt, so far as we know, to return after Aunt Elizabeth's death. We may find a note of misanthropy in her written exercises. But she did form one strong attachment there at least, and M. Heger applauded her for her strong intellect. Despite this, it seems that Emily's reclusive and anti-social character was now fixed.

During the eight months in Brussels, Emily wrote one complete poem and started two more. There is not the faintest sign of a reference to Belgium in them. The first is Gondal and the other two seem English. Belgium appears to leave no trace on *Wuthering Heights*: it is as if Emily Brontë blotted the episode from her consciousness, like so much else. Did Brussels play any part at all in the development of her art? Perhaps the answer lies in the philosophical speculation which M. Heger seems to have encouraged in setting essay topics.

Emily's essays done in Brussels provide almost the only justification for dealing with this period in any detail.

As with Cowan Bridge, a great deal of the routine of the Pensionnat Heger has been reconstructed from Charlotte's fiction, in this case *Villette* and *The Professor*. But Charlotte remembered best the period she spent there alone when she returned without Emily in 1843. I shall try to avoid giving detail which only occurs in Charlotte's work, and attempt to rely mainly on external sources from Mrs Gaskell onwards. She talked to Mrs Jenkins, the wife of the British chaplain, who met the Brontës, including Patrick, after their long journey from England.[1] Mrs Gaskell was also in time to see the pensionnat for herself, before major alterations to Brussels changed the whole area. Mrs Jenkins told her that the Brontës' visits to her caused 'more pain than pleasure' to the girls.[2] 'Emily hardly uttered more than a monosyllable.' Charlotte also found communication difficult, and 'had a habit of gradually wheeling round in her chair, so as almost to conceal her face from the person to whom she was speaking'.[3]

Mrs Jenkins would know none of this as she introduced the girls to the Hegers on Tuesday 15 February. At this point Mary Taylor, Charlotte's old school friend, who was going to join her sister Martha at a school at Koekelberg nearby, left them: soon Charlotte and Emily were alone in a foreign country, surrounded by people speaking French, almost all of whom were Catholics.[4] Charlotte's first full extant letter to Ellen is dated three months later, but the tone suggests that it actually is the first, except for a composite letter in which Mary and Martha Taylor also wrote. 'We are completely isolated in the midst of numbers', Charlotte wrote.[5] Despite this, both she and Emily have been in good health and have been able to work well. M. Heger had given them a few private lessons, but these have 'already excited much spite and jealousy in the school'.

Mrs Gaskell records that the visiting lecturer, whom Charlotte was already describing as sometimes borrowing the 'lineaments of an insane tomcat, sometimes that of a delirious hyena' considered Emily's genius even higher than that of Charlotte's. He thus echoed the prevailing view at Haworth. One wonders sometimes if Emily's persona was not partly formed in response to the prevalent view of remote and lofty genius.

> Emily had a head for logic, and a capability of argument, unusual in a man, and rare indeed in a woman . . . . Impairing the force of this gift, was her stubborn tenacity of will, which rendered her obtuse to all reasoning where her own wishes, or her own sense of right, was concerned. 'She should have been a man – a great navigator,' said M. Heger in speaking of her. 'Her powerful reason would have deduced new spheres of discovery from the knowledge of the old; and her strong, imperious will would never have been daunted by opposition or difficulty; never have given way but with life.' And yet, moreover, her faculty of imagination was such that, if she had written a history, her view of scenes and characters would have been so vivid, and so powerfully expressed, and supported by such a show of argument, that it would have dominated over the reader, whatever might have been his previous opinions, or his cooler perceptions of its truth. But she appeared egotistical and exacting compared to Charlotte, who was always unselfish (this is M. Heger's testimony); and in the anxiety of the elder to make her younger sister contented, she allowed her to exercise a kind of unconscious tyranny over her.[6]

Though given after M. Heger knew of Emily's fame, this is shrewd, throwing light on the retreat from Roe Head. Emily's French devoirs support M. Heger's comments. On paper, at any rate, Emily could argue. There may be some implications too that she argued with her rhetoric teacher face to face, despite Mrs Jenkins's comments about her monosyllabic speech. M. Heger was a thoughtful opponent, whom Emily might see as meriting reasoned refutation. The 'unconscious tyranny' we have seen developing through displays of temper so strong that Charlotte feared Emily would go mad. M. Heger is the first of Emily's teachers since Cowan Bridge to venture any comment about her. Miss Evans saw a pretty Emily, whose winsome but determined small-girl ways got her what she wanted. As a teenager and adult Emily became more stubborn and got her way by force.

But in M. Heger she had met her match. Emily (who 'works like a horse') and he 'don't draw well together at all', remarks Charlotte to Ellen.[7] Later, in the introduction to

'Selections from Poems by Ellis and Acton Bell' Charlotte said her sister 'again seemed sinking, but this time she rallied through the mere force of resolution'.[8] There was no choice for Emily this time: Anne was too far away to be sent for as substitute, and she had no option but to make the best of the Brussels sojourn.

Seven of Emily's French devoirs are given in Winifred Gérin's *Emily Brontë* and an eighth has been purchased since by the Brontë Society. They are almost all signed 'Emily J. Brontë' and are written in ordinary handwriting, not the Brontë small script of the bulk of the poems. They are, then, intended from the first to be read by non-Brontë eyes. As such they must give us clues to Emily's thought which would be very valuable in view of the loss of all the Gondal prose; as we shall see, they do have some similarities to Gondal.

However, the problem of interpretation cannot be glossed over, even if it seems finicky to argue over it. We need to return to Mrs Gaskell to see what the purpose of these devoirs was, and how freely Emily believed she could write.[9] M. Heger told her that he had proposed to read to the Brontës extracts from some French masters, then analyse them, and finally suggest that they should follow these French models in expressing their own thoughts. 'After explaining his plan to them', writes Mrs Gaskell, he awaited their reply.

> Emily spoke first; and said she saw no good to be derived from it; and that, by adopting it, they should lose all originality of thought and expression. She would have entered into an argument on the subject, but for this, M. Heger had no time.

More evidence of Emily's interest in being much more than monosyllabic with her tutor!

It is interesting to see Emily reacting so strongly to this plan. Evidently, she presented M. Heger with a formidable opponent, not afraid to stick to her guns. The actual point she makes is equally interesting. M. Heger is using an eighteenth-century approach, involving the perfection of style; Emily opposes the Romantic notion of 'originality'. We should be careful not to read too much into her refusal, however; there is plenty of evidence in the poem manuscripts to show that Emily is deeply concerned with the verbal style of her poems, and that they are not artless or spontaneous productions. The actual devoirs themselves are strongly influenced by French exemplars, despite Emily's protest. But nevertheless, we should hold on to this, the one recorded opinion of Emily Brontë on the topic of form and meaning in literature.

M. Heger seems to have brushed Emily's objection aside. He told Mrs Gaskell he had been teaching them for about four months (but it may have been longer), when he chose to read them Victor Hugo's portrait of Mirabeau, concentrating on what he called '*la charpente*' of the passage. He then gave Mrs Gaskell two pieces of work which he said had been done as a result. One was Charlotte's '*Portrait de Pierre l'Hermite*', dated 31 July 1842, the other Emily's '*Portrait: Le Roi Harold avant le Bataille de Hastings*', dated June 1842. The slight discrepancy in dates may give us a moment's pause, but in the absence of more detail we may proceed on the assumption that Emily's devoir really was the result of the same process.[10]

She begins by saying that Harold is easily described by his '*figure et son maintien*'. He is parading at some distance from the camp, on a hill from which he can look down on his army. He recalls that the '*usurpateurs*' are encamping on his ground and using his woods for fuel. Then he thinks of his own men, '*aussi fidèles que braves*', and cannot imagine defeat. This thought transforms Harold. He is no longer a king but a hero. Emily pictures him in peacetime, a captive in his own palace, deceived by flattery, lost in a labyrinth of folly and vice. What a change is produced now, as he finds himself bereft of his palace, his ministers and courtesans! '*Quelle difference*!' For the purposes of this exercise, Emily considers his courage free from rashness, his pride from arrogance; only Death can bring him low. At this ironic point she breaks off.

We may note the Shelleyan view of the court as a place where kings are corrupted. A similar view may have filtered down to Emily from her Irish grandfather, if we are to believe William Wright's account of old Hugh Brunty's republicanism.[11] Harold only becomes himself when he leaves the court, climbs up the hill and is overcome with anger at his enemy's depredations. Anger makes him heroic, and we begin to admire him. Emily refrains from emphasizing that Death will be his master, leaving M. Heger (and subsequent readers) to note the contrast between the proud king before the battle, and the miserable result. There is a little hint here of the terseness of *Wuthering Heights* and we realize that Emily Brontë is a writer who will expect her readers to infer their own conclusions. Though later on we may consider that Anne is attacking her sister for the sin of pride, there are often hints that Emily knows that pride comes before a fall.

During the previous month Emily had written for M. Heger a devoir entitled '*Le Chat*'. In it she likens cats to humans. Cats use guile. They hide their '*misanthropie*' under a veil of softness. They do not snatch their food, but rub themselves against their master, and put out paws as soft as down. Once they attain what they want, they abandon this show and revert to cruelty. In cats, we call this behaviour hypocrisy; in humans, politeness. Anyone who complains about the way in which cats play with their victims before killing them should remember fox-hunting. However, cats are really perceptive; they know how little our favours are worth. In any case, their wickedness derives from Adam: cats were not naughty in Paradise.

It is likely that M. Heger would be brought up sharp by this remarkable essay. In it Emily manages to suggest that if cats are not all they seem, neither are humans. In fact the blame for cats' deviance lies with humans, and nature would be harmless if it were not for the intervention of the human race. This view seems to derive partly from Romanticism, partly from the Old Testament. It appeals to Emily Brontë because of her sympathy for the animal kingdom, shown by the long trail of pets at Haworth, and the Law Hill remark about the house-dog.

The third devoir still surviving consists of a letter of invitation to a '*soirée musicale*', together with a reply. An '*élève respective*' writes to her music teacher and receives a letter full of ironic advice, part of which amounts to the suggestion: play a piece of music when people are too busy to notice how it is played. The implication is that the teacher has a very low view of the pupil's standard.[12] The tone of the letter is almost rude, and we must wonder how M. Heger felt about it. He could surely not overlook the unfriendly rebuke given by the music teacher, and nor should we. For pupil, substitute the naive guest, Lockwood; for scornful teacher, substitute Heathcliff, who rebuffs his tenant's would-be friendly approach. In this devoir, Emily seems to be taking no pains to commend herself personally to her master. This is in line with a great deal we have heard and shall hear about Emily's 'reserve': as in the cat devoir, she seems to think politeness is hypocritical and rudeness equal to honesty.

In an essay of 26 July Emily writes a letter to a mother. She apologizes for her long silence, and explains she is unable to come home because of illness. She has to keep to her room, deprived of the company of her friends. She begs her mother to come and see her. At the bottom, M. Heger has written that she should have sent some kind of remembrance to her father. How far this imagined letter corresponds with real life we cannot say. Emily seems to have been reluctant to write letters, later stating in a short note that she had never succeeded in penning a proper one, though Charlotte mentions one or two, for example the letter received from Law Hill in 1838, and one received from Haworth in April 1841.[13] We can't even be sure how much Emily wrote to Anne.

On 5 August Emily completed another essay, on '*L'Amour Filial*'. Its thesis is that men must be monsters in order to require a commandment to honour their parents. Still, one wonders if M. Heger had selected the title because he found a lack of interest on Emily's part in her family at home. Emily imagines in the essay the suffering of parents who have been disobeyed and disregarded. As for the son, he has brought on himself eternal torment. The tone is much like that in the relentless poem, 'Shed no tears o'er that tomb'. At times, it seems as though Emily considers herself an outcast, incapable of compromise with society.

The same day she wrote a dramatic fragment under the heading '*Lettre d'un Frère à un Frère*'. The writer says he has not written for ten years when both brothers left their father's house vowing eternal separation. (Yet another exercise on this favourite topic.) At last the exile returns to the gates of the park where he played as a child. He can just see a gleam of light indicating the place where his old home lies surrounded by trees. It is the discovery of Thrushcross, with the remembrance of Ponden and Shibden. The brother enters and finds his way to the library, where the fire is lit, and paintings and books surround him. The house seems to be deserted.

All at once a '*grand chien*' comes out of a corner of the room and recognizes the brother. It is, of course, the old dog they played with in childhood. But the archetypal moment haunts Emily as she records how the exile rebuffs his old dog's friendly advances. This Emily puts down to the '*dernier acte du tyran qui avait usurpé si longtemps la place de la nature dans mon sein*'. This seems to correspond with a pervasive inner sense Emily had about being usurped in her own selfhood by an interloper. The theme recurs in Heathcliff's usurpation of the Earnshaws, just as Welsh usurped the Pruntys. The word 'tyrant' occurs in many poems, e.g. the long poem 'The Prisoner' in which Emily may be seen as writing an allegory of a chained soul sustained only by a mystic hope. In this essay, Emily ends by demanding that the second brother should not merely write, but come in person to establish their reconciliation.

We might by now be feeling that Emily Brontë is on the side of 'Nature'. The cat is more natural than humans; King Harold becomes his natural self when set free from the pressures at court; Nature, not God's command, should ensure filial affection. Brothers should be reconciled and return to their natural relationship. But in '*Le Papillon*' Emily broods on the predatory aspect of Nature. She notes the chain of predation, one creature on another, and the way in which man completes the chain. In fact, Nature is inexplicable: '*elle existe sur un principe de destruction*'. But this essay closes on a hopeful note; a caterpillar seen on a flower will one day turn into a beautiful butterfly: so glory and happiness will arise from the destruction of the temporal world as the ugly caterpillar will be destroyed and reborn as a glorious insect.

In '*Le Palais de la Morte*', which Emily wrote on 18 October (two days after Charlotte's devoir of the same title), she returns to her suspicion of Civilization. The most powerful helpers in Death's kingdom are Age, Anger, Vengeance, Envy, Treason, Famine, Plague, '*La Paresse*', and Avarice, until Fanaticism and Ambition win the palm. But these themselves are overtaken by '*L'Intempérance*', aided by Civilization. Intemperance is handed down from father to son. By the time men have combined to ban her, she has control over them and '*changé toute leur nature*'. There could possibly be a suggestion that Branwell, adopting a family trait, is becoming deformed by indulgence. Unfortunately we simply do not know how original Emily was being here; John Hewish cites one of the *Fables* of Florian (1792), which also associates Intemperance and Civilization with Death.[14]

It is very unfortunate that we do not know how far Emily

progressed with her German during the Brussels period. We know she worked at it, then and later. It has frequently been suggested that it was during this period that a strain of German Romanticism entered her thought, and that this is evidenced by the apparent links of *Das Majorat* with *Wuthering Heights*. There is an undeniable flavour of Novalis about some later poems, but all these influences might possibly have been gained at second hand from *Fraser's* and *Blackwood's*. On the whole, it seems quite likely that Emily's interest in German literature deepened during her stay on the continent, but real evidence is hard to come by.[15]

The pensionnat, of course, was a much more splendid building than any of the other schools Emily attended. Charlotte's description in *The Professor* was endorsed by Frances Wheelwright, a contemporary in Brussels to whom Emily taught music. When the door into the street was opened, there appeared

> a passage paved alternately with black and white marble; the walls were painted in imitation marble also; and at the far end opened a glass door, through which I saw shrubs and a grass plot, looking pleasant in the sunshine.

To the left was

> a salon with a very well painted, highly varnished floor; chairs and sofas covered with white draperies, a green porcelain stove, walls hung with pictures in gilt frames, a gilt pendule and other ornaments on the mantelpiece, a large lustre pendant from the centre of the ceiling, mirrors, consoles, muslin curtains, and a handsome centre table completed the inventory of furniture.[16]

Beyond a second pair of folding doors was a carpeted room with a piano, couch and a huge window with a crimson curtain, through which the garden could be seen. Possibly this splendour contributed to Thrushcross Grange, and the alien feelings of Heathcliff reflect Emily's strangeness in its midst.

Charlotte's mind became full of all this detail and much more. The imperious yet genuinely benevolent character of M. Heger attracted her to him and we have her versions of him in her novels. But he is certainly not Heathcliff, though

Emily will have observed her sister's strong feelings for him, and her subsequent struggle to detach herself. Emily worked hard for him, as we have seen. She worked less hard for the Wheelwright family, to the youngest three of whom she taught music. The Wheelwrights 'admitted her cleverness' says Clement Shorter, 'but they considered her hard, unsympathetic and abrupt in manner'.[17] Shorter seems to imply in the same passage that Emily's deep reserve caused Charlotte to avoid going out socially. When she returned to Brussels without Emily, 'she was heartily welcomed into two or three English families'. The Wheelwrights 'never cherished any love for Emily', states Mrs Chadwick.[18] Letitia said she disliked her from the first: 'her tallish, ungainly ill-dressed figure contrasting so strongly with Charlotte's small, neat, trim person, although their dresses were alike'. It was Letitia who recorded that Emily could not take a joke against herself: 'I wish to be as God made me', she said.[19] Once again we see Emily's devotion to 'Nature' unvarnished, and her brittle pride.

The three youngest Wheelwrights, Frances (aged eleven), Sarah (aged eight) and Julia (aged seven) were taught music by Emily. They disliked this process, apparently because she taught them in play hours 'so as not to curtail her own school hours'.[20] We may suppose that the little Wheelwrights would be less than geniuses at the piano, and that Emily would tolerate their foolishness very little. Charlotte herself found stupid children hard to teach (though there is no evidence that the Wheelwrights were stupid), and Anne despaired of the children at Blake Hall. The Brontës seem to have had little patience with girls or boys who were not attuned to their own intensity of effort or enthusiasm. How they would have got on if the school project had ever been realized is very dubious.

However, Belgium does provide us with one clear example of a warm friendship between Emily and someone outside the Brontë family. Louise Bassompierre was then sixteen, a rather more rational age. Unlike the Wheelwrights, she didn't like Charlotte.[21] She found Emily '*plus sympathique*' though '*moins brillante*'. We might be tempted to think Louise had forgotten their names, but Emily had given her '*un joli paysage signé de son nom*', which is now at Haworth. Her picture shows an old pine tree, gnarled and rough. It seems that at one time there were twin trunks, but the rotten wood of the right-hand trunk has split, and the broken branch lies on the ground behind the tree.[22] This '*paysage*' hardly seems '*joli*', in fact there is a sinister air of decay about the sketch. A great deal of work has gone into the picture, and Emily must indeed have felt attracted to young Louise to have given her such a present, costly in time and emotional effort.

In '*The Life and Eager Death of Emily Brontë* Virginia Moore, in many ways an understanding biographer, despite her famous gaffe over 'Louis Parensell', claims that this pine was in the garden of the pensionnat.[23] There are no buildings in the background, and the suggestion seems unlikely. Even if that were the case, we should ask what it was that so attracted Emily Brontë about this broken pine tree. We notice a string of references to broken trees running through the Brontës' work in general, but Emily's more than the others. Of course, there is the riven chestnut in *Jane Eyre*; there is the song 'The Woodman', two versions of which are among the Brontë music collections. In this song, the woodman is about to chop down a tree, when the singer pleads with him to spare it. In writing about Emily and herself, Anne uses the metaphor of two trees, one on each side of an encroaching river: two trees that 'at the root were one'. The broken pine in Emily's picture has two trunks, though presumably only one root. (Anne, of course, did not see Louise's picture, which did not come to England until after the death of all the Brontë sisters.)

Then there is the poem, 'There let thy bleeding branch atone', a powerful and mysterious work of about 1840. It seems full of allusions which cannot be traced. A broken branch, apparently, will atone for tears shed in the past, and the poet cries out that guilty tears should not be everlasting. The pine tree in the picture is not exactly *bleeding*, but the personality of the tree stands out as almost animal, so that there seems to be pain in the fractured stump. It is almost as though Landseer hovers nearby. We recall that Emily once broke a branch off a fruit tree in the parsonage garden and (according to one odd rumour) confessed to her father only on her deathbed. This may be a legend, but it seems sure that a sobbing guilt was symbolized for Emily Brontë by the idea of a broken branch. The pine tree which scratches Lockwood's window in *Wuthering Heights* may also be connected.

In her editor's Preface to *Wuthering Heights* Charlotte underlines this tree symbolism with her own comment:

> Had she but lived, her mind would of itself have grown like a strong tree, loftier, straighter, wider-spreading, and its matured fruits would have attained a mellower ripeness and sunnier bloom; but on that mind time and experience alone could work: to the influence of other intellects, it was not amenable.

(Charlotte means *her* intellect, of course; Emily seems to have been perfectly amenable to the intellects of Shelley and Coleridge.) The two-trunk pine is a fascinating symbol and its parallel to Anne's poem suggests a meaning. From 1830, Emily and Anne grew together like twin trunks of a tree, but one trunk is now decaying, and surely that is the one representing Emily, in whom the 'bleeding branch' of the poem, the damaged pine of the present picture, and the broken fruit tree of her childhood all combine.[24]

It would be very valuable to know more about the friendship between Louise Bassompierre and Emily, in which Emily for a moment stanched her perpetual wound of separation, but the picture and the comments of Louise related above exhaust our evidence. Evidently Emily did *not* tell Louise she preferred the house-dog to her; she was '*sympathetique*'. Perhaps for once she let slip some of her 'reserve' and met another human face-to-face.

In the meantime she was (as Charlotte wrote in a letter to Ellen) 'making rapid progress in French, German, Music and Drawing', so that 'Monsieur and Madame Heger begin to recognise the valuable points of her character under her singularities'.[25] We note again Charlotte's motherly concern, always excusing, always looking for Emily's better side. M. Heger, as we have seen, called it 'anxiety' to make Emily contented. It amounted to an unconscious tyranny on Emily's part.

The strange interlude of Brussels was to end with three deaths. First, Martha Taylor, sister of Charlotte's correspondent Mary, caught cholera at school in Koekelberg, a little way from Brussels. She died almost immediately, before the danger had been fully recognized. Charlotte went out as soon as she heard of her illness, but arrived too late. Whether or not Emily went with her sister, the death was a great shock and underlined the transience of human life. In *Wuthering Heights* minor characters are removed with speedy surgery. Once they have played their part, such people as Frances Earnshaw are killed painlessly. This strikes the modern reader as heartless, but it accords with the reality in such cases as Martha Taylor's.

Much more vitally, by the end of October, Aunt Elizabeth had fallen ill in Haworth and died on 29 October.[26] Charlotte and Emily set sail from Antwerp on 6 November, the earliest they could reasonably manage but, despite a quick journey, arrived too late for the funeral. Aunt Branwell had been buried. Branwell apparently watched by her deathbed, and wrote to his friend Francis Grundy about the grievous loss he had sustained. The three Brontë sisters (Anne returned from Thorp Green, but also a little too late for the funeral) must have felt the loss very sharply. We have seen Elizabeth Branwell as a kindly influence, who may have missed her native Cornwall, and possibly failed to understand completely the literary absorption of her nieces. But she had provided an atmosphere of security in the house, and helped them financially. She was no Aunt Reed, and no dreadful Calvinist.

The third sudden death was one of which the girls may not have been informed, but which they would certainly mourn when they found out. William Weightman, the curate who had been an erratic ray of sunshine in the Brontës' ambit, died some weeks before Aunt Elizabeth.[27] Of the three girls, Anne thought most of him, and is linked with him in Charlotte's letter of 20 January 1842. Charlotte was alternately intrigued and maddened by the capricious affections of the man. Emily made him 'her only exception for any conventional courtesy' among the curates. It is not likely that she was totally unaffected by his death.

At the turn of the year – the will was proved on 28 December 1842 – Emily was told that she had inherited £350 from her aunt. This seemed to make it unnecessary to go back to Belgium, all the more so because Anne was returning to Thorp Green and Branwell with her. He was to undertake the education of the Robinson boy, Edmund. Charlotte meant to go back to Brussels. Her education was no more complete than Emily's and she had another motive which became apparent after her death – an emotional attachment to M. Heger, which Emily may have known about by now, and certainly recognized a while later. Emily had little option but to stay at home, to mull over and digest her new-found knowledge. This could be done in the midst of her practical tasks, as we shall see. The emotional grind of being exposed to the world was over. Emily must have acquiesced in her new role with great happiness.

M. Heger wrote to Mr Brontë, regretting that the girls had had to leave, and giving a kind of unofficial report. He ascribed their very remarkable progress to their '*amour de travail*' and '*persévérance*'.[28] This was due to Mr Brontë's influence, he suggested. Emily was about to embark on piano lessons '*du meilleur professeur que nous ayons en Belgique*'. She had been taking younger children as pupils for the piano (we have seen how they reacted). She had lost her ignorance and '*un reste de timidité*'. Optimistic as this statement was, it shows that M. Heger understood the origin of Emily's brusqueness and anti-social ways. The letter was, however, perhaps aimed more at getting Charlotte back to Brussels, in which it succeeded. The non-return of Emily, we can feel sure, was more of an academic than a personal loss.

12

Domestic Chores Lightened by Fancy

Yes, Fancy, come, my Fairy love!
These throbbing temples, softly kiss;
And bend my lonely couch above
And bring me rest and bring me bliss.

Apart from one or two excursions in Yorkshire, and a trip in 1846 to Manchester, to try to find a cure for Mr Brontë's blindness, Emily would not leave Haworth again. During the next two and a half years she was able to devote herself to domestic life. Thus she had the solitude to meditate on poetry and the themes which appear in *Wuthering Heights*. Before this period was over in mid-1845, when Anne returned for good, Branwell finally collapsed in disgrace, and Charlotte turned publishing agent, Emily had written some of her most enduring poems and perhaps started an actual manuscript of the novel. The first year of this period was spent in charge of the kitchen, with Tabby re-engaged, but Mr Brontë beginning to decline, feeling the effects of failing sight and perhaps a little lonely, now that it was harder to walk to the far ends of his parish.[1]

In religion, Emily was loath to support him. She had sedulously guarded her right to silence on everything to do with it, venturing the words 'That's right' (spoken tersely) when Mary Taylor had said that religious opinions were between the individual and God.[2] She apparently condemned Shelley's atheism, but was far from happy with what she saw of Christianity. This dissatisfaction is clearly shown in a poem finished in May 1843 and one dating from February 1844. The former, 'At such a time in such a spot', disavows the search for God 'in cell and cloister drear'. Of such people, perhaps met in Belgium, she says 'By dismal rites they win their bliss – By penance, fasts and fears'. The 1844 poem is even more forceful. It is entitled 'My Comforter' and will require attention soon. Three stanzas have not been given the prominence they deserve.

Was I not vexed, in these gloomy ways
To walk unlit so long?
Around me, wretches uttering praise,
Or howling o'er their hopeless days,
And each with frenzy's tongue –

A brotherhood of misery,
With smiles as sad as sighs;
Their madness daily maddening me,
And turning into agony
The Bliss before my eyes.

So stood I, in Heaven's glorious sun
And in the glare of Hell
My spirit drank a mingled tone
Of seraph's song and demon's moan –
What my soul bore my soul alone
Within itself may tell.

This is Shelleyan. It also reminds one of Blake, though there seems no way in which Emily could have read him. Clearly the 'wretches' must be Christians, 'howling' or 'uttering praise'. Anne was one; the divisions between the two girls, who hardly saw each other these days, were mounting. Her father was also one. His tolerance has many times been remarked. Surely he must have recalled his Irish youth, when he saw both sides of the denominational divide, and when communion with Nature on the Mourne mountains had been a valuable experience for his Presbyterian pupils.

However, Emily still attended church, even if she opted out of it spiritually.[3] She sat bolt upright in a corner of the family pew as motionless as a statue. 'Her compressed mouth and drooping eyelids, and indeed her whole demeanour, appeared to indicate strong innate power.' The observer adds that a large protruding tooth added to her peculiar aspect. In the Branwell picture of about 1835, her lips are shown pouting.

Perhaps even then she had rather large upper incisors, but it looks as though by the time this note was made one had fallen out. Miss Evans might have been hard pressed to recognize her pretty nursling.

Mrs Gaskell tried to discover more about Emily at home. She was somewhat alarmed to hear about Emily's relationship with dogs.[4] Charlotte told her that among many traits of Shirley, her adventure with the mad dog was taken from Emily's life. She had called out to a wretched creature which was running past with lolling tongue and hanging head, and the animal had bitten her when offered water. She had rushed into the kitchen, picked up a red-hot iron and cauterized the wound, telling nobody until the bite was healed. This was for the benefit of the family, who might be afraid for her; but we may also note Emily's general secrecy and unwillingness to share her troubles or her joys.

Keeper was always a great favourite with Emily. She sat with her arm around his neck as she read. But Mrs Gaskell unearthed a spine-chilling story of how she punished him. It will be best to quote in full.

> He loved to steal up-stairs, and stretch his square, tawny limbs, on the comfortable beds, covered over with delicate white counterpanes. But the cleanliness of the parsonage arrangements was perfect; and this habit of Keeper's was so objectionable, that Emily, in reply to Tabby's remonstrances, declared that, if he was found again transgressing, she herself, in defiance of warning and his well-known ferocity of nature, would beat him so severely that he would never offend again. In the gathering dusk of an autumn evening, Tabby came, half triumphant, half trembling, . . . to tell Emily that Keeper was lying on the best bed, in drowsy voluptuousness. Charlotte saw Emily's whitening face, and set mouth, but dared not speak to interfere; no one dared when Emily's eyes glowed in that manner out of the paleness of her face, and when her lips were so compressed into stone. She went up-stairs, and Tabby and Charlotte stood in the gloomy passage below, full of the dark shadows of the coming night. Down-stairs came Emily, dragging after her the unwilling Keeper, his hind legs set in a heavy attitude of resistance, held by the 'scuft of his

> neck', but growling low and savagely all the time. The watchers would fain have spoken, but durst not, for fear of taking off Emily's attention, and causing her to avert her head for a moment from the enraged brute. She let him go, planted in a dark corner at the bottom of the stairs; no time was there to fetch stick or rod, for fear of the strangling clutch at her throat – her bare clenched fist struck against his red fierce eyes, before he had time to make his spring, and, in the language of the turf, she 'punished him' till his eyes were swelled up, and the half-blind, stupefied beast was led to his accustomed lair, to have his swelled head fomented and cared for by the very Emily herself.[5]

The whiteness of Emily's anger or misery has been noted before. Here she reacts with steel nerves and enormous emotion to a minor crisis, but the event leaves an unhappy feeling in the mind. She had to punish Keeper, of course, but the particular manner and fury of the attack seem unwarranted by the crime. Emily's close identification with the dog has been evident; she put her arm round him when she was reading in the evenings. Her furious beating of the poor animal in the face and eyes seems aimed at herself, and her ruthlessness shows how she comes to write poems about iron-hearted young men. All the Brontës were closely concerned with animals. In 1844 (the Keeper incident may date from the same year, since Charlotte is present, but Anne is not) Charlotte records the death of a pet cat and says, 'Emily is sorry'.[6]

Emily was alternately an agitated companion or a restful one. Shirley's trait of wandering about on aimless quests is usually thought to be Emily's. When she starts sewing,

> her needle scarce threaded . . . a sudden thought calls her upstairs: perhaps she goes to seek some just-then-remembered old ivory-backed needle-book, or older china-topped workbox, quite unneeded, but which seems at the moment indispensable; perhaps to arrange her hair, or a drawer which she recollects to have seen that morning in a state of curious confusion; perhaps only to take a peep from a particular window at a particular view.[7]

More evidence of Emily's propensity to look out of windows! The objects mentioned were Emily's, and the restlessness sounds an accurately reported trait. The tidying and fetching seem very unlike reasons for the restlessness, which makes Emily seem rather like a caged tiger, or a person separated from a lover.

Of course, when this was happening, not much sewing would get done. We have seen Emily's lack of concentration with reading, which she conquered in Belgium. The manuscript evidence of broken poems is strengthened by her unwillingness to write long letters, as she says in one dated May 1843 (though the date does not appear to be Emily's own). Here she says to Ellen Nussey that she will get Anne to write 'you a proper letter – a feat I have never performed'.[8] She may not be quite serious about this; two previous letters have been mentioned, though neither survives. But it does seem that her 'taciturnity' extended as much to the written word as the spoken. It may appear all the more remarkable that she eventually wrote a full-scale novel, and less amazing that she never wrote a second one.

One reason for Emily's low poetic output during parts of 1843–4 must have been her involvement in domestic chores. John Greenwood, who was particularly interested in Emily, records that she baked bread and did the ironing. Even in these occupations she was often interrupted.[9] Mr Brontë was keen to teach her to shoot with a pistol, knowing her 'unparalleled intrepidity and firmness'. When her father was ready, she would come out of the kitchen and set up a mark at the bottom of the garden. Then she took the pistol from him and shot. She would then go down to the end of the garden and fetch the target, where her bullet was usually not far from the mark. Greenwood notes that his 'How cleverly you have done my dear girl' was all Emily cared for.

> She knew she had gratified him, and she would return to him the pistol, saying 'load again papa,' and away she would go to the kitchen, roll another shelful of teacakes, then wiping her hands, she would return again to the garden, and call out, 'I'm ready again, papa.' And so they would go on until he thought she had had enough practice for that day. 'Oh!' he would exclaim, 'She is a brave and noble girl. She is my right-hand, nay the very apple of my eye.'[10]

For the misunderstood Emily, this must have been balm. It is an interesting vignette, almost certainly from 1843, and illustrates another successful relationship of Emily's. Like her father, she was tall and like him she was more than courageous. John Lock is perhaps right when he suggests that Emily was for Patrick the son Branwell had failed to be.[11]

In view of her nickname 'the Major', and the frequency with which masculine attributes have been accorded her, we might also notice John Greenwood's description of her as 'this fragile creature' on an occasion when she had to separate Keeper from another dog which he was fighting 'down the lane'.[12] Emily picked up the pepper box and, after grabbing Keeper's neck, she covered the dogs' noses with pepper. She then drove Keeper in front of her, back to the parsonage, disregarding a group of men who had been watching all this with interest. As so often, Emily seems not even to notice human beings, especially males. In the earlier passage concerning her shooting practice, Greenwood mentions her 'most winning and musical voice' and her 'fairy-like' running to set up the target. We should see Emily in 1843 as lithe and willowy out of doors even if she became taut and miserable in the church pew.

Once she had settled to her home routine, Emily began to tidy up poetry that had been left unfinished before she had gone to Belgium. This process was to continue for a year, and Anne almost certainly became privy to it. It looks as if Belgium may have had the effect of giving Emily some self-confidence, perhaps because she had perforce mixed with other girls and knew that she had a gift they had not, and possibly because she had read the German Romantics and knew she had allies in thought. It seems sure that she went on reading now, deepening her knowledge of Shelley and probably taking in Coleridge and Wordsworth in more depth than previously. We shall find reflections of all these in the next batch of poems. Gondal was certainly not forgotten, despite Anne's growing doubts about it, evidenced by the fact that she hardly wrote Gondal poems when away from Emily. In February, two Brussels poems were rounded off and a Gondal poem about the fall of Zalona written. In April, a new stage was reached with a poem about the moon, entitled 'How clear she shines!'

This new poem is far from Gondal. It is full of philosophical

1 The old font at Thornton, in which Emily Brontë was baptized.

2 An early photograph of High Sunderland Hall, showing its exposed situation. In the field appears to be a heap of lime, reminiscent of one of Joseph's tasks in *Wuthering Heights*.

3 Haworth parsonage. The projecting rear wing, in which was the 'back kitchen', can just be seen.

4 The Clergy Daughters' School, Cowan Bridge, looking West. On the right hand are the 'pillars' which became transformed in Emily's poem, 'It is not pride, it is not shame.'

5 Ponden Hall, near Haworth.

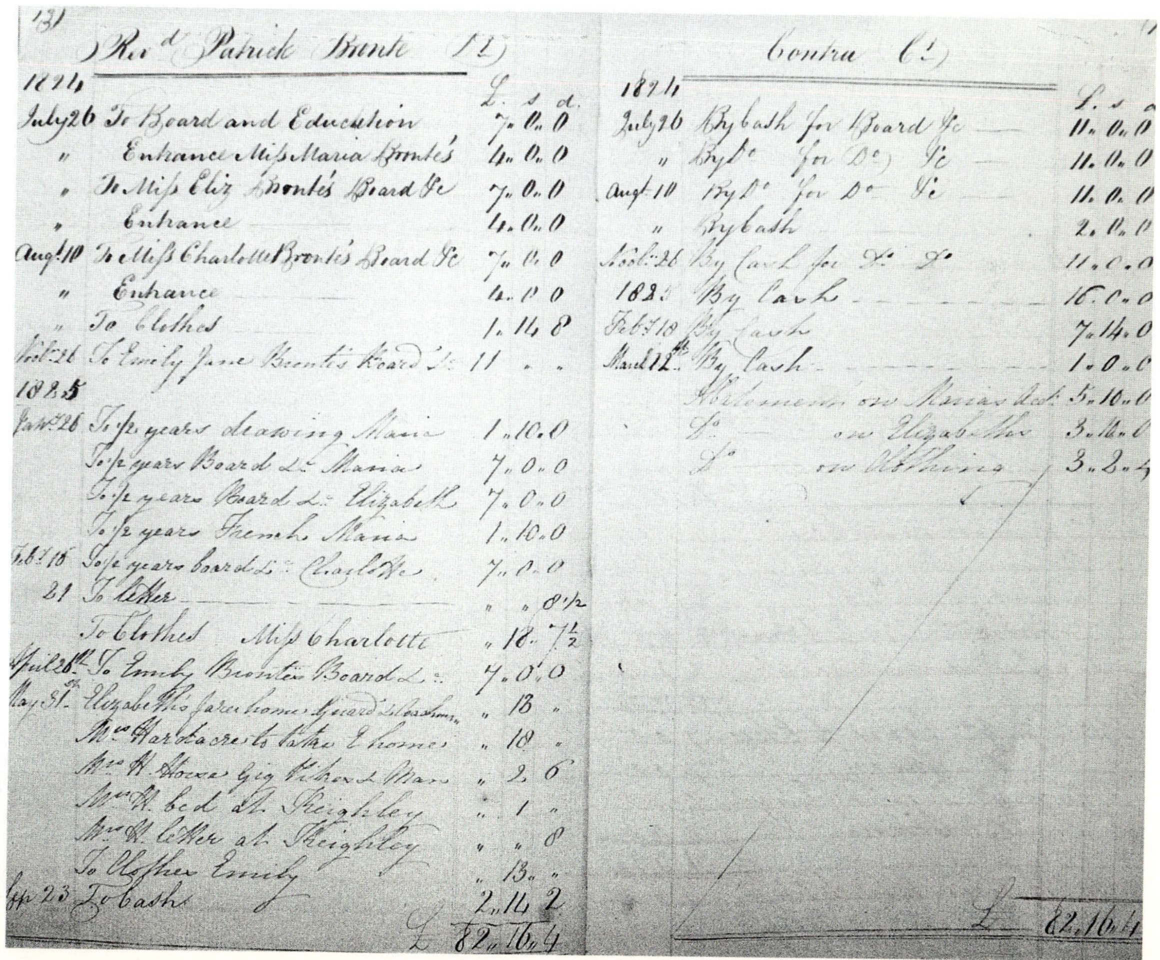

Revd Patrick Bronte (Dr)

		£ s d
1824		
July 26	To Board and Education	7.0.0
"	Entrance Miss Maria Bronte's	4.0.0
"	To Miss Eliz Bronte's Board &c	7.0.0
"	Entrance	4.0.0
Aug 10	To Miss Charlotte Bronte's Board &c	7.0.0
"	Entrance	4.0.0
"	To Clothes	1.14.8
Nov 26	To Emily Jane Bronte's Board &c	11 " "
1825		
Jan 26	To ½ years Drawing Maria	1.10.0
	To ½ years Board &c Maria	7.0.0
	To ½ years Board &c Elizabeth	7.0.0
	To ½ years French Maria	1.10.0
Feb 16	To ½ years Board &c Charlotte	7.0.0
21	To Letter	" " 8½
	To Clothes Miss Charlotte	" 18 7½
April 26th	To Emily Bronte's Board &c	7.0.0
May 31	Elizabeth's fare home Guard & Coachman	" 13 "
	Mrs Hardacre's to take E home	" 18 "
	Mrs H Horse Gig [illegible] & Man	" 2 6
	Mrs H bed at Keighley	" 1 "
	Mrs H Letter at Keighley	" " 8
	To Usher Emily	" 13 "
Sep 23	To Cash	2.14.2
	£	82.16.4

Contra (Cr)

		£ s d
1824		
July 26	By Cash for Board &c	11.0.0
"	By Do for Do &c	11.0.0
Aug 10	By Do for Do &c	11.0.0
"	By Cash	2.0.0
Nov 26	By Cash for Do Do	11.0.0
1825	By Cash	16.0.0
Feb 18	By Cash	7.14.0
March 12th	By Cash	1.0.0
	Abatement on Maria's Acct	5.10.0
	Do on Elizabeth's	3.16.0
	Do on Washing	3.2.4
	£	82.16.4

6 An extract from the ledger of the Clergy Daughters' School, Cowan Bridge, showing Mr Brontë's account, and the two different writing styles which may suggest two different authorities.

7 End wall of the schoolhouse at Law Hill, previously a warehouse. The bricked-up door may have been the entrance for children and teachers, and there was also an outside staircase.

8 Brussels, the Pensionnat.

9 The three Brontë sisters, painted about 1834, by Branwell. They are (left to right) Anne, Emily, and Charlotte. Branwell too was once pictured, between Emily and Charlotte, but was later painted out.

10 Title pages of the three-volume first edition of *Wuthering Heights* and *Agnes Grey*. Was *Wuthering Heights* rewritten to fill two volumes?

11 Drawing by Emily Brontë of a window similar to those at Wuthering Heights. Peering into and out of windows seems to have been a habit with her. It is possible that there is a figure in the central window.

13 Untitled drawing of a heroine, by Emily Brontë. She fits the descriptions of 'A.G.A.' in Emily's Gondal poetry. It is said that portraits facing to the right are likely to be done by left-handers.

12 Untitled drawing of a broken pine tree by Emily Brontë. The symbolism is worth pondering, though the origin could be a printed copy-book.

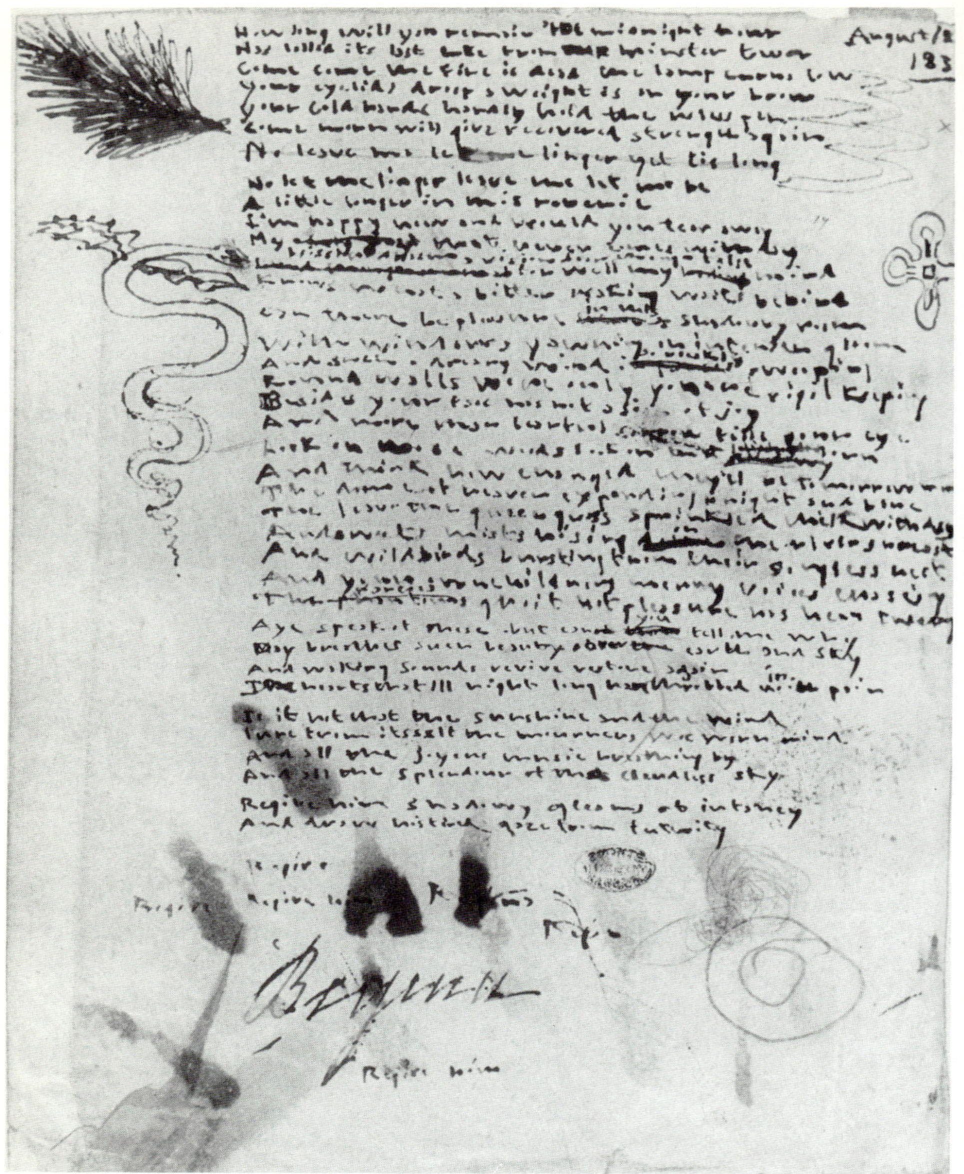

14 Manuscript of Emily's poem 'How long will you remain?', magnified. The marginal scribbles and blotting suggest the dreamy state of Emily's mind at the time.

speculation and begins the worship of 'Fancy' (later called 'Imagination') which may suggest a reading of Keats or Coleridge. 'Fancy' it is that will bring the poet 'rest' and 'bliss'. In stanza three we learn that the 'Grim world' is being replaced by Fancy, and in later stanzas details of the dream fed by Fancy are given. Of all the worlds in the universe, this is the only one in which Love is derided and Fate has her way. 'Pleasure' in this world will lead to wrong and Joy to Pain. Capitals, as often in Emily's work, are erratic. Joy and Pleasure may not be intentionally personified. The poem is pessimistic in its view that only in moonlight can the pain of the world be evaded. Emily seems in tune here with countless poets, before and after Shakespeare.

A little later, in May 1843, Emily wrote two Gondal poems, 'Where beams the sun the brightest?' and 'Thy guardians are asleep'. The first, which Mr Nicholls later entitled 'Grave in the Ocean', broods on a Gondal heroine lost at sea, while the second, written on 4 May, talks of a crescent moon at a time when the moon was in fact a crescent. It has alterations written by Charlotte in 1850, though she did not publish the poem. The last of this group, 'In the earth' (later 'Warning and Reply') was published by Charlotte after alterations had been made. It contrasts with the poem about burial at sea; in this poem the sunny hair of the heroine will 'with grass roots twined be'. We feel here that things are moving towards the burial aspects of *Wuthering Heights*.

Anne had returned for a short holiday in the summer. Some of her emotional energy was being absorbed by the Robinson girls these days, and some by an exploration of the meaning of Christian orthodoxy and its limits. She was unhappy about Calvinism this year, though perhaps the whole family, with their Wesleyan upbringing, had always been unfavourable to it. With Emily turning pagan, and Branwell irreligious, Anne thought more about the matter. She did not favour Gondal, and when she returned again in December the sisters seem to have had deep discussions about the future direction of their poetry. The previous month Anne had written in despair,

'Tis strange to think there was a time
. . . When speech expressed the inward thought
And heart to kindred heart was bare,
. . . And friendship like a river flowed,

Constant and strong its silent course,
For naught withstood its gentle force.[13]

Presumably she had in mind the 1830s, now passed into memory. It is likely that at Christmas she made an effort to renew this friendship. The evidence is circumstantial, and needs clear summary.

1 Like Emily, Anne began a new transcript book in the early months of 1844. (We shall return to Emily's transcript books in a while.) Anne began her poem 'Views of Life', a dialogue. It is not clear whether the poet's interlocutor is Emily or one of the Robinsons; the latter may be more likely.[14]
2 In this poem, there seem to be echoes of two poems by Emily. One is an old one, written as long ago as 17 May 1839, 'I am the only being whose doom'. The other is 'Hope', written on 18 December 1843, when both sisters were at Haworth, we may presume. Both sisters toy with the idea of Hope, Emily treating the idea lightly. In her poem the personified Hope disappears. Anne is more serious and (in part of the poem written later) maintains that 'hope itself a brightness throws/ O'er all our labours and our woes.'

Because of the way in which 'I am the only being' seems to affect Anne's 'Views of Life', it appears likely that Emily showed her poems to her sister that Christmas. Since both began to recopy poems, and Emily thought carefully about dividing Gondal from non-Gondal work, it may be surmised that they reviewed their future as budding poets. This implies that they also discussed Gondal. In view of her apparent disenchantment with it, and her failure to write anything much related to Gondal for years, it seems possible that Anne urged on Emily the need to collect her non-Gondal work together and develop it. This would account for the simultaneous adoption of new books at a time when Emily had not made a systematic attempt to collect or transcribe her poems for four years.

Anne had returned to Thorp Green by 26 January 1844.[15] Charlotte was back at Haworth, and Emily may have shared some rejoicing with her for a few days. It was not until 2 February that she felt like writing poetry, a scrawled and much altered manuscript of twenty-four lines. The poem appears to be called 'Castle Wood', but the Gondal signature is too vague to be certain of. It looks as if Emily has been reading Keats: she writes, 'I was *brede* the mate of care' and 'The foster-child of slow distress'. The poem ends, 'The heart is dead since infancy,/ Unwept-for let the body go.'[16] In this poem and many others, Emily stresses the liveliness felt as a child (by herself, surely?) and the subsequent death of the emotions. Eight days later she wrote the non-Gondal 'My Comforter'. It has not been fully understood, the misunderstanding beginning with Charlotte, at any rate if her reference to the 'Comforter' of 'Eva' in *Shirley* is based on this poem. This 'Comforter' of Emily's is not a pagan or animistic force, but a dead poet or philosopher.

'Well hast thou spoken', the poem begins. So this 'Comforter' uses words, and as we shall see in the next few lines, these express what Emily (as poet) has felt deep within her soul. The Comforter's words are not given, but are contrasted by implication with the three stanzas already quoted, in which Emily discusses her gloom in church. She has walked too long in these ways, and what her soul has borne cannot be told in detail, but the Comforter seems to her

Like a soft air above a sea
Tossed by the tempest's stir –
A thaw-wind melting quietly
The snowdrift on some wintery lea;
No – what sweet thing can match with thee,
My thoughtful Comforter?

In case we feel inclined to share Charlotte's view and see the Comforter as an airy spirit, we need to remember the first few words: 'Well hast thou *spoken*'. The Comforter is *like* a soft air; he is not actually one. He must surely be a poet, who wrote criticizing traditional Christian modes of thought and worship. Once again, the evidence points to Shelley.

At this point Emily did what Anne was also doing. She began to transcribe her poems, apparently making a permanent selection. She took two notebooks and began a rigid division into Gondal and non-Gondal categories of all the poems she then wished to keep. These two little manuscript books were called by C. W. Hatfield manuscripts A and B.

The former, sometimes called the Honresfeld manuscript, has been unavailable to the public for fifty years, though a full photocopy appears in the *Shakespeare Head* edition. Not a single poem in this manuscript has a Gondal name, set of initials, or reference in it. It is a book of poems written in Emily's own persona, and contains no fictional characters. The feelings contained in the poems are Emily's own, and the settings often precisely what Emily can see with her own eyes at the time of composition. After this, Emily copied all her personal poems but one into this A manuscript, perhaps quite soon after they were composed.

Poems, however, are not factual accounts. The precise relation between external events and poetic process is so complex that it is unwise, without the greatest care, to take any poem as a biographical source for an event.[17] Poems will always give emotional insight, but they cannot be used naively to trace a poet's life history. On the other hand, in tracing the growth of a poet's mind and understanding, the poems are a primary source which cannot be abandoned. We shall continue to use the poems in this way, noting the even clearer division that Emily has now established between Gondal and non-Gondal work.

All her Gondal material now went into manuscript B, the British Library manuscript, so often on show in the exhibition room. Its heading (surrounded by the type of scribble Shirley wrote in the margins of her devoirs) is a firm classification: 'Gondal Poems'; and the date, 'Transcribed Febuary [*sic*] 1844'. As in previous transcripts, the writing begins neatly but deteriorates. Almost all the poems prove the truth of the title with authenticating Gondal signatures or references. Like the A manuscript, this was written in Brontë small script, though very neatly. Whatever had made Emily use conventional handwriting for the 1839 transcript, she had evidently rejected such considerations now. Nevertheless, the very act of dividing and copying the poems suggests a secret knowledge of the worth of the non-Gondal ones at least.[18]

By now Emily's adult character was determined and set. In looking back over her life during the writing of *Shirley*, Charlotte harked back to the year 1844–5, as we have already seen. She remembered her sister's anger: 'A good, hearty quarrel always left Shirley's temper better than it found it', says Henry Simpson.[19] Whether she could view these quarrels with as calm a detachment at the time is open to a great deal of doubt. Anne calls them 'bitter quarrels'. The extent to which *Shirley* incorporates the character and mannerisms of Emily was explored by Ivy Holgate.[20] We have already taken two of the best-known examples of incidents in which Shirley is supposed to be modelled on Emily. The authority for this goes back to Mrs Gaskell. She noted the connection and tells us that Shirley is 'Charlotte's representation of Emily'.

> I mention this (she goes on) because all that I, a stranger, have been able to learn about her has not tended to give either me, or my readers, a pleasant impression of her. But we must remember how little we are acquainted with her compared to that sister, who, out of her more intimate knowledge, says that 'she was genuinely good, truly great', and who tried to depict her character in Shirley Keeldar as what Emily Brontë would have been, had she been placed in health and prosperity.[21]

There has been very little reference to physical illness throughout Emily's story so far, and there will be little in future. What can Charlotte have meant by the conditional clause in her remark to Mrs Gaskell? Was Emily Brontë unhealthy?

We may recall the solicitude with which Charlotte looked after Emily in Belgium. So obvious was it, that M. Heger considered Emily exerted an unconscious tyranny over her sister. The same solicitude occcurs in the notices published after Emily's death. Charlotte was afraid for her sister, and the fear could surely not have been for physical illness. Emily was as strong as the rest of the family, or stronger. Then the illness that Charlotte half feared was mental. Emily's 'peculiarities' amounted to an eccentricity so marked that her sister (and perhaps Emily herself) feared some form of dementia. Translated into the present context this means that when Charlotte is writing Emily into Shirley's part, she will tone down the eccentricity, as well as portraying it as the adjunct to a rich young lady instead of a poor clergyman's daughter. Shirley will be a calmer, less unusual person than Emily. We may say, with some caution, that when Shirley is eccentric or outspoken, Emily may well have been so, but when Shirley is conventional, this does not show that the same holds of Emily.

Ivy Holgate argues convincingly that while Emily was alive Charlotte could not have used her as a model.[22] Emily was 'grafted' on to the character after her death. The second volume begins to refer to Emily in the guise of Shirley, for instance in Chapter VII, where Emily's language of 1846 is used in her description of Nature as an 'undying, mighty being'.[23] But not until after the death of Anne, when Volume III was being written, does Emily take over the character widely. With both her sisters dead, the novel began to take on the character of a memorial to them. Charlotte was able to portray characteristics of Emily which would have been resented if Emily had ever read the book.[24] The mad dog episode is one such. I intend to discuss some of the others shortly.

Charlotte returned from Belgium in January 1844, and from then on she lived in the same house as Emily for almost five years. It is from the first four of these, probably even the first half of those four, that these impressions stem. There is, for example, the French devoir supposed to have been written by Shirley while being taught by Robert Moore. The memory of French devoirs goes back to 1842–3, but the internal references to the actions and thoughts of '*La Première Femme Savante*' suggest the mature Emily. Shirley scornfully refers to the devoir as 'that rubbish', just as Emily referred to her poetry as those 'rhymes'.[25] The mythological aura of the devoir is in tune with those we know of, both from Emily and Charlotte. In it, we encounter a young girl who has lost her tribe (the scene is set before the Flood). She takes up a position as the sun sets to wait for Night.

> The girl sat, her body still, her soul astir; occupied, however, rather in feeling than in thinking, – in wishing, than in hoping, – in imagining, than projecting. She felt the world, the sky, the night, boundlessly mighty. Of all things, herself seemed to herself the centre, – a small, forgotten atom of life, a spark of soul, emitted inadvertent from the great creative source.[26]

The girl cries out for comfort ('She had her religion: all tribes held some creed'). A 'Comforter' appears. The evening flushes full of hope, the air 'pants' and the girl addresses the 'invisible, but felt'. She 'drinks' from the evening and her 'arid heart revives'. Though 'Her eye received no image . . . a sense visited her vision and her brain as of the serenity of stainless air, the power of sovereign seas, the majesty of marching stars, the energy of colliding elements.'

When the devoir is examined by Moore and Shirley, she is reminded of her propensity to draw pictures in the margins of her work. We have already seen marginal drawings on Emily Brontë's manuscripts, for example the fragment which contains, 'How long will you remain?' There seems no doubt that in this passage of her novel, Charlotte is close to what she believes is the spirit of Emily. Doodling in the margins of books and exercises is a minor facet of it, Nature worship a major one.

There are also some echoes here from the poetry of 1843–5. The 'Comforter' seems to be a misunderstood version of the one we have seen in Emily's poem. Charlotte is writing *Shirley* with a new edition of Emily's poetry in prospect. She is re-reading these poems, but not necessarily with care, and not necessarily with total understanding. If the girl 'Eva' in this passage is Emily, she is only the Emily of Charlotte's external observation, except insofar as Emily may have told her sister how she felt. We cannot set aside Charlotte's observations. If she suggests, as she seems to suggest here, that Emily sometimes went into a silent ecstasy as Night approached, and this is corroborated by some poems, such as 'How long will you remain?', we may believe her. But Charlotte could misunderstand and seems to be wrong about the nature of the 'Comforter'. Her attempts at finishing 'Silent is the house' after Emily's death suggest that she had a ready-made recipe for understanding Emily, but this does not guarantee that the recipe is accurate. Her observations of what Emily *did* and how she *appeared* are correct enough, no doubt. But we cannot accept uncritically her explanations of what was happening inside Emily's mind.

Among the other observations in *Shirley* which may contribute to our understanding of Emily Brontë are the following. Chapter II in the last volume, written soon after Anne's death, is entitled 'The West Wind blows'.[27] In it the east wind is described as 'arid'; it seemed to 'rob of all depth of tone the blue of heaven'. We know that Emily considered the east 'a very uninteresting wind'.[28] But soon 'A little cloud like a man's hand arose in the west'. This led to gusts and rain.

After that, the sun broke out genially and 'heaven regained its azure'. The west wind is important as an agent of release. Emily calls it 'That wind' in a poem, and is closely following Shelley in her enthusiasm for it.[29]

Shirley is full of ridicule. When asked in Volume III, Chapter 5, whether she is ill, she retorts 'I *am not*'. She laughs at the idea of her spirits being affected. 'She had no spirits, black or white, blue or gray, to affect.' Soon, 'She peremptorily requested to be left alone.' Nevertheless, we are allowed to hear her self-castigation. She calls herself 'Fool!' and 'Coward!', and tells herself, 'If you must tremble, – tremble in secret. . . . How dare you . . . show your weakness and imbecile anxieties? Shake them off: rise above them: if you cannot do this, hide them.' The search for personal strength does seem to be a part of Emily Brontë's story, as it is of Anne's. The phrases used ring true, and may possibly have been heard by Charlotte when she was with Emily at various testing times.

There is some illumination, too, in Moore's remark that Shirley may accept his invitation to her 'like a child or like a queen. . . . Both characters are in her nature.'[30] He arms himself with the thought that Shirley's 'scorn' startles him from his dreams, and 'A sarcasm from her eyes or lips puts strength into every nerve or sinew that I have.' Both the two-sided nature of Emily and her propensity for scorn and sarcasm are attested at many points. Emily, 'placed in health and prosperity' still seems a prickly personality at times, though full of depth and character.

We have seen Emily and her father at gunnery practice. The life of the parsonage in 1843–4 was inevitably rather different from that when several of the Brontës were at home at the same time, but there would be many unchanged features. They seem always to have risen about 7 a.m.[31] Emily may have been awake already, in her small room above the hall. In 'Stars', she describes a summer wakening, when the morning sun intruded upon her part-wakeful dreams about the stars. When she does get out of bed, her first action will be to open the window and let the buzzing flies out, not to kill them with a fly swat. The 1845 diary paper contains a sketch of the bedroom; we need to remember that it was not as small as it is now, since Charlotte's alterations.[32]

Emily's bed lay beneath the window, parallel with it. She

could gaze out directly at the moon. The picture seems to show curtains and Tiger the cat appears to be asleep on the bed. Beside the bed is a hastily drawn chest of drawers, not very well in perspective. It must have been placed at right angles to the bed, though it is not easy to see this from Emily's sketch. She does appear, however, to have made an attempt at altering her earlier proportion, and in any case, there surely wouldn't have been room for a piece of furniture like this if it hadn't been at right angles to the bed.

There seems to be a rug on the floor, indicated by a swirl of the pen. On the rug sleeps Keeper, his head on his paws just as in the 'from life' picture of 1838. Seven years older, he looks no different. Emily draws herself from behind, as she usually prefers to do. She has hair bunched up in a bun and rather loose clothing, extending to the floor, so that to modern eyes it looks as if she is writing in her dressing gown, though this may not be the case. On her lap she has the desk box, tidied many times, surely, since it was mentioned in 1841. She appears to be sitting on a stool, but not the 'buffet' she used on the moors or in the garden. It is backless, but the legs can clearly be seen. The turn of her head as she looks down at the paper reminds me of the suspicion I have sometimes had (there is no external evidence) that Emily Brontë might have been left-handed. Both her hands are on the paper, but she does seem to be turning aside from the natural position for a right-hander.

It was from this bedroom that Emily went downstairs, after combing her hair. There is not a sign of a bedroom jug, so she may have washed in the back kitchen. The 'toilet' was, of course, a privy at the end of the garden.

Breakfast was in the kitchen, it seems. There Mr Brontë had told the wild and varied stories of his past when the children were young.

All the parsonage mornings we hear of involve domestic work. In a letter from Belgium, Charlotte, depressed one Sunday in 1843, wrote

> I should like uncommonly to be in the dining-room at home, or in the kitchen, or in the back-kitchen. I should like even to be cutting up the hash, with the clerk and some register people at the other table, and you standing by, watching that I put enough flour, not too much

> pepper, and above all, that I save the best pieces of the leg of mutton for Tiger and Keeper, the first of which personages would be jumping about the dish and carving knife, and the latter standing like a devouring flame on the kitchen floor. To complete the picture, Tabby blowing the fire, in order to boil the potatoes to a sort of vegetable glue![33]

Later, as Mrs Gaskell reminds us, Tabby, as she grew older, disliked giving up her work.

> Among other things, she reserved for herself the right of peeling the potatoes for dinner; but as she was growing blind, she often left in those black specks, which we in the North call the 'eyes' of the potato. Miss Brontë [Charlotte] was too dainty a housekeeper to put up with this; yet she could not bear to hurt the faithful old servant, by bidding the younger maiden to go over the potatoes again, and so reminding Tabby that her work was less effectual than formerly. Accordingly she would steal into the kitchen . . . and breaking off in the full flow of her interest and inspiration in her writing carefully cut out the specks in the potatoes, and noiselessly carry them back to their place.[34]

This anecdote is told of Charlotte; but it does show the kind of regard in which Tabby was held.

In 1843, Emily took on herself the principal part of the cooking, as Mrs Gaskell tells us. When Tabby grew too old,

> it was Emily who made all the bread for the family; and any one passing by the kitchen-door, might have seen her studying German out of an open book, propped up before her, as she kneeded the dough; but no study, however interesting, interfered with the goodness of the bread, which was always light and excellent. Books were, indeed, a very common sight in that kitchen: . . . in their careful employment of time, they found many an odd five minutes for reading while watching the cakes, and managed the union of the two kinds of employment better than King Alfred.[35]

After dinner, a formal meal, there would be some time during the afternoon which Emily might use for a walk on the moors. Some of the poetry written during 1843–4 must have been written at this time of day. Older people recalled Emily taking a little 'buffet', or stool, out with her on her walks.[36] On this she presumably sat to save herself getting damp. In earlier times, the first part of the evening might be used in music around the piano. We have no proof of this, but it seems likely that Emily would play by herself during the time when Charlotte was still in Belgium. During holidays, Branwell might still play his flute, and Anne join in singing with Emily.

There were family prayers at nine o'clock. After that, Mr Brontë wound the clock and went to bed, leaving the girls to begin their literature exchange.[37] When Emily was by herself, she may have retired to bed early. We remember from 'How long will you remain?' that Charlotte and Emily might otherwise sit round the table, and this would be an excellent time for composition. It may well have been after midnight that Emily finally slept, and if the nightmares of her adolescence still recurred, she might not even sleep then.

In March 1844 Emily took a stanza she had written in 1842 and began a new poem with it. It became the Gondal work 'This summer wind' and was ascribed to A. G. A. It then became the fifth in a series of seven poems concerned with the Gondal princess, copied into the new Gondal manuscript in spring 1844. By May, Emily was writing of her death in a long poem, hard to interpret. It has already been mentioned because of the passage in which many 'kinds of love' are distinguished. We may ask (but unfortunately cannot clearly answer) why Emily wished to kill off A. G. A. at this stage. The killing of an authorial self-identification is psychologically significant in the case of any writer. I should suggest that at this point Emily may have felt drawn to the idea of closing Gondal and perhaps was increasingly turning her mind, in some moods, towards self-negation or even self-destruction. We have seen that the guilty dog Keeper, a creature as close to Emily as was A. G. A., was punished ruthlessly. The guilty and blood-thirsty A. G. A. is treated even less well, and departs from the stage. It is perhaps a funeral ode for her that Emily pens on 1 May 1844 in a splendid poem, much praised by the early critics, 'The linnet in the rocky dells'. In the poem the feeling of calm at the end is very like the end of *Wuthering Heights*. Significantly, Emily has changed the direction of the light wind that was blowing, in reality, when she wrote it:

Blow, west wind, by the lonely mound,
And murmur, summer streams,
There is no need of other sound
To soothe my lady's dreams.

The Keighley meteorologist, Shackleton, records that it was a south-east wind that blew that day.

Emily was exploring the theme of transience and eternity in a non-Gondal mode too. In a curious poem written on 5 March she tells how she lay 'alone' on a 'sunny brae'. Unlike the other 'wedding guests' at the marriage of May and June, she feels sullen. Even the rocks treat her as a leper. She cannot understand her gloom, but she communes with her own heart, considering the speedy decay of the bright new creations of spring. 'The leaf is hardly green/ Before a token of the fall/ Is on its surface seen.' She then describes a vision, reminiscent of 'The Ancient Mariner' in several ways:

A thousand thousand glancing fires
Seemed kindling in the air;
A thousand thousand silvery lyres
Resounded far and near.

The Irish writer Cathal O'Byrne has singled out this poem as the one most reminiscent of Irish Gaelic poetry, and indeed the faint mockery mixed with the clarity of the natural description does seem akin to it, though it is very hard to see how Emily could have been aware of this strand of Celtic bardic verse.[38] The Coleridgean influence is more certain.

The final stanza is again significant. After the airy spirits in her vision have given her a message that eternity is brighter than the world, their music ceases. The 'noonday Dream' withdraws. Emily ends, 'But Fancy still will sometimes deem/ Her fond creation true.' In the last line the word 'fond' may have both its nuances, of 'dear' and 'foolish'. Thus Emily hangs between belief and scepticism, feeling eternity to be real, and perhaps obtaining some support from the Romantics, but urged on by a 'rationalist' part of her mind to be more pessimistic.

Two quite undatable stories recorded by A. M. F. Robinson (who also evidently found she couldn't place them chronologically) may be added here. The first asserts that Emily brought her own chair through to the kitchen whenever Martha Brown's invalid cousin came to visit her. This strengthens our observation that Emily could show concern for young children. The second mentions a shopping expedition when Charlotte, Ellen and Emily went to Bradford for some dress material. Emily chose 'a white stuff patterned with lilac thunder and lightning', which horrified her sister and friend. But according to Ellen's memory, it suited Emily, making her seem 'half-queenly, half-untamed'. The exact colour may have been quite dark; later Miss Robinson calls her skirts 'purple-splashed'. At this time Emily's face was clear and pale, her hair 'very dark and plenteous brown . . . fastened up behind with a Spanish comb'. Her eyes seemed 'grey hazel' and large, 'now full of indolent, indulgent humour, now glimmering with hidden meanings, now quickened into flame by a flash of indignation'.[39] It is possible that the story of the purple dress may relate to an earlier period.

Now, in late 1844, it seems unlikely that *Wuthering Heights* had reached paper, even so much as a plan. But the death of A. G. A. left a void. Very soon she is being resurrected, as Catherine Earnshaw.

13

My Darling Pain – Heathcliff in the Open

O Stars and Dreams and Gentle Night;
O Night and Stars return!
And hide me from the hostile light
That does not warm but burn.

The climax of Emily Brontë's artistic life was now at hand. During the years 1845–7 the three sisters will make the attempt to appear on a public stage, and by the end of the period, they will have done so. Charlotte's determination and her capacity to soften the most idiosyncratic elements of her sisters' work are the factors most potently behind its 'marketing'. In this period as much or more than any, external evidence of the methods and intentions of Emily is mediated to us through Charlotte. As often, we have to try to evade Charlotte's glossing filter in order to see Emily clearly, and then the evidence shrinks to a matter of scattered clues and guesswork.

There are major questions which cannot be answered definitively. Exactly when and by what processes was *Wuthering Heights* written? How far was it written and offered to the public in consultation with Anne and Charlotte, and how far against their wishes? How willing was Emily to enter the field of publication at all? Did she accept the joint poetic enterprise, or did she wash her hands of it, and leave Charlotte to manage the whole matter? Can the time scale, especially in the years 1845–6, be as short as it may appear? Not one of these questions can be given a final answer, but as our research increases, we may be able to offer more and more likely hypotheses, making use of the few firm landmarks to produce a tentative chart.

We might begin at Christmas 1844, when we see a continuation of the poetic co-operation between Emily and Anne which had flourished the previous year. By this time Anne was becoming weary of Thorp Green, partly because of the unsatisfactory progress of her pupils, and perhaps partly because she was worried by whatever was occurring between Branwell and Mrs Robinson.[1] Immediately after returning to Thorp Green in January 1845, she wrote, 'Call me away', a poem in which she proposes to escape to 'our beloved land' of Gondal. As Anne had been unenthusiastic about Gondal during most of the time since 1840, we may suppose that Gondal had been revived strongly during the Christmas holiday, and that it had been a happy time.

There is more internal evidence than this. On 16 December, at the start of the holiday, Anne had written a poem fictionally dated 1826; this is the same date as Emily's poem of 2 December. On 3 March 1845 Emily wrote 'Cold in the Earth', a poem to which we shall return. A poem by Anne dated 'early 1845' contains the phrase 'Cold in the grave' and praises night, as Emily might have done. Emily's poem 'Stars' of 14 April 1845 is the best of her poems on night, and Anne's 'While on my lonely couch I lie' continues the theme. There is a clear family likeness between the poems written by the two sisters at this time.

In July 1845 both girls wrote further diary papers, which will need to be examined carefully. Anne says she has begun 'the third volume of "Passages in the Life of an Individual"'. We need to consider briefly what this work was, as it has a bearing on Emily's work. The non-Gondal title of Anne's book has led critics to consider it was the first draft of *Agnes Grey*. Some have assumed this without discussion.[2] While this seems a slightly rash proceeding, the title does appear to suggest an autobiographical work, and *Agnes Grey* is a first-person narrative which looks like autobiography and contains identifiable references to Anne's life. The 'Life of an Individual', then, does seem quite likely to have been at least a practice run for the novel, and a new departure for the Brontës. It appears to be a non-Gondal work; and it was advanced as far as the third volume by July 1845.

Agnes Grey begins by dealing with events based on Anne's experiences during early 1839, six years ago, when she took her first steps into the world of teaching. If the 'Life of an

Individual' is an early *Agnes Grey*, then Anne was casting her mind back six years in the early months of 1845. I shall soon suggest that *Wuthering Heights* was beginning at the same time, and may have been at the point where an easily deluded stranger spends a snowy evening at the old farmhouse by about March. For the scene of *Wuthering Heights* Emily too retraced her steps six years, to the period when she set out in 1838–9 to try teaching and fell under the spell of a dilapidated hall with its statues and crumbling battlements. It seems likely that there was collusion between the two sisters, during the warmth of their relationship at the start of 1845, and that both intended to write about their experiences of 1838–9. If so, Emily's intentions were soon diverted.

Emily's poems of early 1845 surpass her previous ones and have the same tone as *Wuthering Heights*. She would be hearing from Anne of the disgraceful link between Branwell and Mrs Robinson, and this is one of the ambient factors of the poems. She also seems to be dwelling on memories of twenty years ago to the month, when she saw her sisters suffer and did little (we have supposed) to comfort them. From then on, Maria and Elizabeth have led a phantom existence just outside Emily's consciousness. When Lockwood sees the ghost of Catherine in his dream, she says she has been a waif for twenty years, though this does not fit in with Sanger's calculation of the dates in the novel.[3] But it seems likely that it fits in with Emily's thoughts as, perhaps, she writes the snowy passages during the snowy days of March 1845, when Haworth was covered by a white blanket.[4]

'Cold in the Earth' mentions *fifteen* wild Decembers instead of twenty. This takes us back to another crisis point in Emily's life when she exchanged her reliance on Charlotte for her twinship with Anne. Exactly where the 'fifteen' comes from we do not know; possibly it was subconscious, but it may have been accurately calculated from the Gondal Chronicles, which had been in the process of systematization from 1841.[5] It will be seen that I am suggesting here an interweaving, in the mind of the numerically inclined Emily, between Gondal dates and real ones. 'Fifteen' may sound better and fit Gondal chronology; 'twenty' is an anomaly in the novel, but is allowed to stand because of its subconscious resonance.

Another vital poem of the first part of 1845 is 'The Philosopher's Conclusion', dated 3 February. The first part of it reports a summer conversation in which an interlocutor addresses a 'space-sweeping soul'. The soul must be Emily, who is constantly represented as musing and dreaming into Eternity. The interlocutor represents, perhaps, the voice of Charlotte, as in 'How long will you remain?' The summer background fades as the philosophic 'soul' replies

O for the time when I shall sleep
Without identity,
And never care how rain may steep
Or snow may cover me!

The philosopher goes on to report that 'wild Desires' and a 'quenchless will' are the cause of the difficulty. Heaven, she says, cannot satisfy them. Three 'Gods' are warring inside one human body, and she wishes for the day when they will be at rest and 'I shall . . . never suffer more!' It seems perverse to deny that this is autobiographical and that Emily, as philosopher, is wishing for the reconciliation of three 'Gods' inside her. In stanzas 7–9 the interlocutor tells the philosopher that she has seen three rivers circling the feet of a 'Spirit'. One is golden, one 'like blood' and one 'like Sapphire': yellow, red and blue. The Spirit gazes on the dirty mixture of the three colours (as on one of the Brontës' paintbox lids) and the colours become crystal.

The glad deep sparkled wide and bright –
White as the sun; far, far more fair
Than the divided sources were!

But the philosopher cannot attain the vision. She cannot see the 'Spirit' and thus in reaction must 'call oblivion blest' and stretch eager hands to death. Obscurely and metaphorically, Emily is foreshadowing Catherine's unhappiness with Heaven as home. If my chronological suggestions hold any weight, within the month she is seeking another route to reconciliation, through the novel.

The 'bleeding branch' theme returns in a poem of 10 April, later simply called 'Death'. It is hard to interpret, but is concerned with a second death which has supervened at a time of positive enthusiasm, just when the poet begins to have faith in 'Joy to be'. We note the growing optimism of this part of

1845, which may have to do with the positive state of relations with Anne, or the flourishing creative urge. This double death seems to reflect the double death of 1825, when in May one sweet Anne-like sister followed a sharp-minded but dreamy sister to the grave: events which Emily's subconscious had been reworking for twenty years. We have only slight evidence for Anne's letters at this time, but it seems most probable that Emily pondered deeply on their news that Branwell's relations with Mrs Robinson are a cause of grief to Anne.[6] Added to the blighted love of Charlotte for M. Heger and Anne's love for Weightman, cut short by his death, this seems to have confirmed Emily's optimism and self-congratulation. On 2 June she writes cheerfully of the consolations of Nature in 'How beautiful the Earth is still'. Summer can obliterate the sullenness of December, she says. Though 'youth is past' the treasure of youth's delight remains. It seems likely she is thinking of childhood more specifically than youth in general. The next two stanzas are of acute interest:

When those who were thy own compeers,
Equal in fortunes and in years,
Have seen their morning melt in tears,
To dull unlovely day;
Blest, had they died unproved and young
Before their hearts were wildly wrung,
Poor slaves, subdued by passions strong,
A weak and helpless prey!

Because, I hoped while they enjoyed,
And by fulfilment, hope destroyed –
As children hope, with trustful breast,
I waited Bliss and cherished rest.

This cannot be a Gondal poem, of course; if it had been, it would have appeared in the B notebook.

Though we must make allowance for the imaginative poetic process, Emily is clearly writing about her siblings. The tone of her poem shares something with Anne's 'Views of Life', being worked on a little later. Anne had been the first 'poor slave' to submit by attaching herself to William Weightman. Charlotte had been grieving for M. Heger. Now Branwell too was involved in a romantic relationship which had little chance of success.[7] All three 'compeers' were seeing their mornings melt in tears. Emily distances herself from them, putting her trust in 'hope' instead of 'enjoyment' (a word which hardly describes the traumatic love longings of the three siblings).

There will be more to say about Emily's relations with Branwell. They seem to have been closest (and then not very close) about 1837. But those who say he contributed to *Wuthering Heights* are not quite wrong. Branwell could rant at times, though his ranting meant little. He shared with Heathcliff the interest in shooting birds, so that when Catherine is recalling the way in which Heathcliff liked to shoot lapwings, this may be an echo of conversations between Emily and Branwell.[8] But there was a good-natured side to Branwell quite unlike any of the Earnshaw group at Wuthering Heights. For the moment, it seems likely that the dramatic events of summer 1845 interrupted Emily in the early stages of work on what may have been a realistic novel.

Anne returned from Thorp Green for the last time about 11 June. Branwell came back about the same time, but he was to return to look after young Edmund while the family was in Scarborough.[9] There would have been some secret conversations between Emily and Anne as he left. They were renewing their old intimacy, though not quite successfully. They would certainly talk about Branwell's obsession. But Mrs Robinson herself was not at Thorp Green, but at Scarborough. This makes it unclear how Branwell came to be dismissed. In the reported letter which Mr Robinson sent, 'exposure' was threatened: a word hardly likely to have been used if he had merely discovered a liaison between Branwell and his wife. Possibly Branwell was drunk, or perhaps in some way he was degrading the not-very-bright Edmund whose tutor he was.

Back he came, and spent his time in sick complaints. As soon as possible he was packed off to Liverpool, where sea air might do him good. Charlotte returned from a visit to Ellen Nussey to find the parsonage in a state of gloom.[10] But we are overrunning our tale. It seems that when Anne first returned, she and Emily talked over the possibility of going on some excursion together. This was probably intended to be a regular feature, though in fact they only went on one such trip. It may have been in their minds to go to Scarborough, which Anne loved. In the event, they got as far as York; we know a little about their journey from the two diary papers and a fragment of an account book which will be mentioned. Perhaps Scarborough had become an embarrassing place if the Robinsons had been alienated. Emily's diary paper records:

> Anne and I went on our first long journey by ourselves together, leaving home on the 30th of June, Monday, sleeping at York, returning to Keighley Tuesday evening, sleeping there and walking home on Wednesday morning. Though the weather was broken we enjoyed ourselves very much, except during a few hours at Bradford. And during our excursions we were, Ronald MacElgin, Henry Angora, Juliet Augusteena, Rosabella Esmalden, Ella and Julian Egremont, Catherine Navarre and Cordelia Fitzaphnold, escaping from the palaces of instruction to join the Royalists who are hard driven at present by the victorious Republicans. The Gondals still flourish as bright as ever. I am at present writing a work on the First War. Anne has been writing some articles on this, and a book by Henry Sophona. We intend sticking by the rascals as long as they delight us, which I am glad to say they do at present.[11]

Not the slightest mention here of her poetic achievements, let alone any sign of a great novel! Some of the account is confirmed, but some undermined, by Anne's paper.

> The Gondals are at present in a sad state. The Republicans are uppermost, but the Royalists are not quite overcome. The young sovereigns, with their brothers and sisters, are still at the Palace of Instruction. The Unique Society, above half a year ago, were wrecked on a desert island. They are still there, but we have not played at them much yet. The Gondals in general are not in first-rate playing condition. Will they improve?[12]

The difference in tone between the two papers has been remarked on by other writers. Emily's buoyancy in the first half of 1845 was not shared by Anne. She goes on:

> Emily is engaged in writing the Emperor Julius's life. She has read some of it, and I want very much to hear the rest. She is writing some poetry, too. I wonder what it is

about? I have begun the third volume of 'Passages in the Life of an Individual'. I wish I had finished it.[13]

The poetry seems never to have been finished, unless it tottered to birth as the weak 'I know that tonight the wind is sighing'. But this bears an August date and mentions an August wind, so it seems unlikely. The Emperor Julius seems more promising. His identity with Heathcliff was urged by Mary Visick.[14] Julius Brenzaida (whose name is in part subconsciously developed from *Jane Brontë*, perhaps) appears in the Gondal poems from nowhere. Mary Visick says he is 'apparently of obscure birth'.[15] In the poems which seem to be first in Gondal chronology, he is a moorland wanderer courting 'Geraldine' across wild terrain, with the wind whispering and the moon shining.[16]

Wild the road, and rough and dreary;
Barren all the moorland round;
Rude the couch that rests us weary;
Mossy stone and heathy ground.

The meaning of the last line is roughly equivalent to *Heath + Cliff*. Like the setting for *Wuthering Heights*, these two Julius poems go back to late 1838. Brenzaida and Geraldine ('A. G. A.' if our identification was correct) appear to be soul-mates, who do not hear the tempest beating 'round our spirits' home'. Emily's mind, it seems, is still working at the roots of the novel.

In the second poem of the pair written in those far-off days at Law Hill, Julius has been 'slighted' by Geraldine, and he prepares to forget her. She has been faithless both to her soul-mate and to the moorland scenery where they have passed their time. Now, according to Anne, Emily is rewriting their story in prose. She is dwelling, then, on the detail of the moorland, and perhaps making more specific the Gondal scenery which stems from Ponden. The emperor of humble birth, Julius, moves towards being Heathcliff and his lover becomes Catherine. There is a hint of a reason in the poem for her desertion. 'Hard commands' are said to 'tame' her love. So Geraldine abandons Julius because of external pressures, just as one element in Catherine's rejection of Heathcliff seems to be social.

Like Heathcliff, Julius went on to become a harsh aggressor and betrayer. In 'The wide cathedral isles are lone' he takes an oath of kingship, but falsely, since it is made clear that he is about to usurp the rights of his kinsman, Gerald. Heathcliff does not take an oath of kingship, but he plots to undermine his adoptive kinsman, Hindley Earnshaw, who bears a name as similar to Catherine as Gerald does to Geraldine. (Catherine and Hindley Earnshaw are siblings and so may Gerald and Geraldine be.) The orphan archetype, which has been in Emily's mind since her father told her of the outcast Welsh, now begins to crystallize and take its place in the moorland background of Gondal/Wuthering Heights. Julius becomes a conqueror, but dies 'in the zenith of his fame' almost by stealth, as a treacherous dagger 'close by his side' does its deadly work.[17] He is mourned in 'Cold in the Earth' by Rosina, who may possibly be the same as Geraldine. This, presumably, was the outline of the story read by Emily to Anne during July 1845. Mary Visick comments that 'the love between Catherine and Heathcliff is Emily Brontë's way of giving expression to some all-devouring spiritual experience'. If Anne read her 'Passages in the Life of an Individual' to Emily, this may have proved the trigger which caused Julius to be redefined in terms of the landscape round High Sunderland. This, of course, is speculation; but some such process must have taken place this summer, when no poetry is produced for almost four months after a productive spring.

We have seen earlier how Emily listed Gondal characters and gave them height, physical appearance and habitations. This was a necessary stage before she could 'play' with them, it seems. The *Wuthering Heights* story now taking shape must have gone through the same process. Anne and Emily were used to looking back for the Gondal Chronicles; now Emily seems to have seen that if she was to make use of the Ponden date of 1801, she would need to go back to the 1770s for her crucial events; but as one strand in the novel is family history, and she had apparently heard the family history of Ulster in the 1770s *ad nauseam* from her father, this was not difficult. A skeleton chronology of *Wuthering Heights* must have been before Emily as she wrote; it would take some time to establish; this summer seems to be the most probable time for this to be done.

However, there was to be a diversion, both for the

'individual' developing into Agnes Grey, and for Julius as he turned into Heathcliff. For a short time Julius became Julian and Geraldine a sweeter captive, Rochelle (to be precise, 'A. G. Rochelle', whose second name is as likely to be Geraldine as anything else). This happened in October 1845 as Emily organized them into a long poem that has seemed to many not to be homegeneous. Though Jonathan Wordsworth, in an article for *Brontë Society Transactions*, redresses the balance somewhat, he may not quite prove his case.[18] Dated 9 October, the poem tells how Rochelle, a beautiful young girl prisoner, is kept in chains by a 'jailer grim' whom Jonathan Wordsworth likens to 'the older Heathcliff'. Rochelle is saved from despair only by the 'messenger of hope' which comes to her nightly. The passage in which she describes the messenger is among the best known of Emily's poems and goes back, significantly, to Shelley. 'He comes with western winds . . . And visions rise and change which kill me with desire', writes Emily.

Rochelle seems in some ways to be a symbolic figure which represents Emily's 'sweet' more 'feminine' self, aspects of which had been recognized at Cowan Bridge by Miss Evans, but which had gradually darkened to become 'gipsy' Blanche. She appears to be exploring the way in which her joyous persona is always chained by the ruthless, harsh, scornful mask she must exhibit to the outside world. The bright soul is imprisoned by the inflexible jailer. Just so in *Wuthering Heights* the young soul-mates are imprisoned in an outhouse by Catherine's father, 'pure' Catherine herself feels entombed by her body, Linton Heathcliff is locked in, and the younger Catherine forced by Heathcliff into a travesty of marriage.

Now we turn to Charlotte to remind ourselves of the famous words in which she explains how the 'Bells' came to publish their poems.

> One day, in the autumn of 1845, I accidentally lighted on a MS volume of verse in my sister Emily's handwriting. Of course, I was not surprised, knowing that she could and did write verse: I looked it over, and something more than surprise seized me, – a deep conviction that these were not common effusions, nor at all like the poetry women generally write. I thought them condensed and terse, vigorous and genuine. To my ear, they had also a peculiar music – wild, melancholy, and elevating.[19]

So reads her first paragraph, and we must examine it first before going on to the next one.

It has been thought, it seems rightly, that the manuscript Charlotte 'accidentally' lighted on was the B manuscript, with its Gondal poems. This would need to be out of its desk or tin repository in October or thereabouts, for the prison poem to be copied in. It is unlikely that Charlotte would actually pry into Emily's private containers, so we may assume that she found the book lying on a table, in the kitchen or somewhere else round the house. She says the find was 'accidental', but Charlotte had always hoped that one day the girls would appear in print like their father; she says as much in the same passage below. Now that they were all at home together she may have thought this was a good time to begin in earnest. The manuscript may have been accidentally left out, but Charlotte was looking for it. (One might also add, that if Emily required total secrecy, she would have known places to hide the poems.)

It was not strictly in Emily's handwriting. It was in Brontë small script, the style they had all used as children, but only Emily seriously maintained. Charlotte 'looked it over'. Was she afraid that Emily might walk through the door and find her? She then discerned the terse, vigorous and genuine note of Gondal verse, as chosen by her sister to appear in the B manuscript. Let us take up her tale again:

> My sister Emily was not a person of demonstrative character, nor one on the recesses of whose mind and feelings, even those nearest and dearest to her could, with impunity, intrude unlicensed; it took hours to reconcile her to the discovery I had made, and days to persuade her that such poems merited publication. I knew, however, that a mind like hers could not be without some latent spark of honourable ambition, and refused to be discouraged in my attempts to fan that spark to a flame.[20]

We may imagine, as so many people have, the approach Charlotte made, and the ruthless rejection on the part of the 'Heathcliff' guarding Emily's soul. Charlotte certainly had intruded; she had read material no one, unless it was Anne, might read. This saga expressed Emily's depths, laying bare the shivering captive on the dungeon floor, even going so far as to explain how the captive sustained herself. Perhaps the captive's beauty might not be recognized: a Heathcliff-like public would take over from the inborn Heathcliff and savage the 'peculiar music'. Ambition, in any case, was dangerous; Gondal heroes had died because of it. Emily wished to be 'as God made me', though in truth the three warring Gods might tear her to pieces.

The next day, we may suppose, Charlotte renewed the attack, and recalled that Anne also wrote verse. She tells us 'my younger sister quietly produced some of her own compositions', though she does not say whether this 'production' was spontaneous or not. The existence of three sisters in a family leads to subtle shifts in alignment. Until 1830 Charlotte and Emily had been close; from 1830 onwards Anne had become Emily's confidante, at times very close indeed. Fifteen years later we see a further move. Now Charlotte enlisted Anne's help, and Anne added to the pressure on her sister. How far Emily saw this as a betrayal, confirming her suspicions of human nature, is unknown.

It would be wrong to think of Emily as quite unwilling to publish her poems. She arranged them several times, beginning in the winter of 1838–9, under the influence of Law Hill and possibly Shelley. She admired her father, and was the apple of his eye. He had published poems, and as Charlotte says, Emily was not without a latent spark of ambition: hence her sparring with M. Heger, a worthy opponent. But the poems *were* intense beyond measure: they could be read as a way into Emily's soul. As a child she had exhibited her soul to Miss Evans, and been approved. But like Blanche in the poems, or like Wordsworth's growing boy (about whom she had surely read) she had found shades of the prison house closing on her, and so retreated to a scornful persona. In any case, she knew full well that she had 'corruption' within her: a mad destructive fury, treacherous impulses, gaunt and foul aspects, overlaid the beams of joy. This could never be shown to the public, whose forgiveness could never be relied on. (Emily may have judged the public by herself: she was implacable and unforgiving, so would her public be.)

In the 1980s our psychological knowledge has taught us that we are all many-sided. We can forgive more easily. But in the 1840s Emily could not trust her own sister, let alone the public at large. She and Anne may also have thought of their prose works, languishing for want of time. For all these reasons, Emily fought her sister hard. In 1848, when things were very different, Charlotte wrote to W. S. Williams: 'I was sternly rated at first for having taken an unwarrantable liberty . . . But by dint of entreaty and reason I at last wrung out a reluctant consent to have the 'rhymes', as they were contemptuously called, published.'[21]

Exactly how long and how ferociously Emily went on refusing no one knows. It used to be thought that she was so reluctant to publish that she did not even co-operate in Charlotte's project, but allowed Charlotte to edit and copy out the poems without taking any more personal action. It may well be that we should still be right to suppose Emily sulking some days, and possibly Charlotte herself making alterations in the text. There is no manuscript warrant for a number of changes made in the 1846 edition. But in 1984 Derek Roper made the discovery that some at least of the alterations to the 'rhymes' were directly attributable to Emily, however reluctant.[22] It became clear that whereas Charlotte had altered the poems published in 1850 entirely on her own initiative, Emily had written some suggestions later adopted in the Bells' edition in her own hand. For example, two of the verbal changes made in 'How clear she shines!' seem to be in Emily's handwriting and are not contemporary with the original writing of the manuscript. These are 'gardian' for 'silver' in line 2 and 'surest' for 'shortest' in line 36. Perhaps these revisions do not always improve the poems. In those taken from the B manuscript, they may have a purely de-Gondalizing function. But evidently Emily accepted in the end the need to modify her poems for public presentation.

Gondal then began to fade. Here was Emily, reluctantly agreeing to the verbal revision of her work for publication. The effect of this must have been to turn her mind to the question of how her poems could appear without any Gondal clues. This exercise reinforced the de-Gondalizing process in her fiction. Julius would be no less rewarding or relevant to her personal quest if he ceased to be called Brenzaida, and if Anne's 'realistic' approach of near-factual accuracy was attended to. In the intervals of selecting the twenty-one poems and making minor alterations to them, Emily must have turned more and more to the planning and writing of the fictional work. Charlotte's words, read literally, do not support this suggestion: she ascribes the beginning of the three novels to a period after the poor reception of the poems. 'Ill-success failed to crush us: the mere effort to succeed had given a wonderful zest to existence; it must be pursued. We each set to work on a prose tale.'[23]

According to this chronology, the novels could not have been started until after July 1846, when critical comment on the poems began to appear. The manuscript of the poems was delivered in February 1846, the proofs were being corrected in March, and copies were printed by 20 April.[24] In a letter to Aylott and Jones of 6 April, Charlotte says that the Bells 'are now preparing for the press a work of fiction, consisting of three distinct and unconnected tales . . .'. The fair copy of *The Professor*, Charlotte's contribution, was completed on 27 June 1846 and the three novels were sent to Henry Colburn on 4 July. Clearly, Charlotte is wrong. *All* the novels must have been well advanced by the time the poems were in print, and they must surely have been in the writing at the same time as the poems were being selected. Beyond altering some words and copying out her poems (twenty-one of them) in her own writing, it is not clear what part Emily would play in the preparation for the 1846 poem edition. Yet she produces little fresh poetry. The time is being spent in writing the novel.

But what was this version like? It is necessary to raise this question because, as Tom Winnifrith has pointed out, there is an anomaly. In July 1846 *three* novels were sent to Henry Colburn to make a three-volume set.[25] In 1847, *two* novels, *Wuthering Heights* and *Agnes Grey*, were published in a three-volume novel set, having lost *The Professor*, who had been supplanted in his author's affections by *Jane Eyre*. It hardly seems possible that the same version of *Wuthering Heights* should be worth one volume in 1846 and two in 1847. The clue, perhaps, is in the Emperor Julius's life. An early *Wuthering Heights* may have been largely the story of Heathcliff, influenced strongly by Emily's life-long absorption with the story of the outcast orphan, whom she had met first in the guise of the changeling Welsh.

We should do well at this point to recall several aspects of Emily Brontë's background and character. She saw herself, we remember, as an actor. As far back as 1829, the girls involved themselves personally in *plays*. Actors may act the same part many times, each time modifying slightly. The key to their success is a capacity for self-involvement in the part which they are currently playing. While on stage (in the case of the Brontës, on the moor, or in the parsonage garden) they must act the play to the best of their capacity. They play the same scene today as yesterday, only better if they can. They feel the same feelings, only deeper, and their facial expression deepens to convey their deeper understanding. The feelings are part of themselves, and in acting they give vent to those feelings.

Emily's grandfather was a ballad-singer and a story-teller. There is evidence that he lived his stories as he told them to his audience by the light of the fire in the logie-hole at Imdel. He could conjure up devils and ghosts, outcasts and soldiers. People were so scared they didn't wish to go home to bed. His children acted too. Whether it was Patrick preaching from his pulpit with 'nothing in his hand' or the young brothers going round the neighbourhood to scare people with their tales of the gorse on fire, or fairies in the glen, they played their parts with conviction.

A ballad-maker does not often make up his stories. He re-casts them. Sometimes he merely performs them, pausing and hurrying where necessary. He may compose new versions of old tales, but in essence he is a re-worker, a performer, whose belief in the stories he tells is intense. In Ireland, part of his repertoire is family history. As Patrick told the tales of Ireland, of ghosts and fairies and revolution, and as these stories became the basis of the children's play, and were added to by the tales of Tabby in the kitchen, the Brontë children knew by practice the interiorizing skills of ballad-makers. They wrote and re-wrote the legends of Angria, bringing characters alive after they had died, changing the course of history if it did not suit them. Characters were undoubtedly duplicated: hence the different names for the Gondal princesses: Geraldine, Rosina, Augusta, Rochelle, 'A. G. A.'. They are all facets of one haughty princess. Emily, we recall, was one of the pair of Brontës who chafed at allowing the plays to happen in an unrealistic African setting. She and Anne brought their stories home to the area between Haworth and Ponden, though they still called this by a fictitious name, and admitted fictitious detail.

The final stage in this evolution is now occurring. The Gondal characters are changing their masks and acquiring a

Yorkshire accent. Mary Visick has explored for us the way in which this is done.[26]

Geraldine (or A. G. A.), romantic, peevish, haughty, wayward, intense, becomes, by the change of a few letters in her name, Catherine. She will still lack constancy, and will try to hold both Julius (Heathcliff) and Alfred (who loses the start of his name and finds a new end to become Edgar). Like Geraldine, she will wreak peevish havoc on her friends and die in torment, which is partly due to the fear of being separated from Heathcliff, her soul-mate. All this takes place in a moorland setting like the 'common' of Gondal, which had long been identical with part of Yorkshire. The setting *is* the story, in the sense that the characters act as they do with the inevitable indifference of Nature: they wish to be 'as God made them'. There is a deep dialectic in the novel: Emily and Anne are twins, just as Maria and Elizabeth were similar sisters. But like these two pairs, Heathcliff and Edgar share one facet intensely (the love of Catherine), yet in other ways are opposite. Pairs of opposites are contrasted in *Wuthering Heights* as they have been in Gondal. We may imagine Emily, in the last months of 1845 and the first part of 1846, seething with these ideas. How far she had sorted them out by the time the 1846 version of the novel went off to Henry Colburn, we cannot know.

Emily Brontë's fascination with the figure of the pitiless man is fundamental. Heathcliff, the rocky, whinstone, wolfish man has other antecedents besides Julius. He surely descends from the reckless and harsh Welsh of the ancestral story, who marries into the true Brontë (Prunty) family by trickery and then usurps the family home like a cuckoo. But he has appeared in Gondal in various guises. He is almost superhuman in 'And now the housedog' of July 1839. As a visitor to the household, he freezes the hospitality of the shepherd family. Their blood is chilled, and they are glad when he turns away his basilisk eyes. Suggestions are made throughout the poem that the visitor is hardly human: a changeling, and a cuckoo. The modern equivalent of this visitant is the science fiction 'Man from Mars'. In *Wuthering Heights* Nelly and others express their doubts about whether Heathcliff is human. Emily may have seemed rather inhuman herself when beating Keeper's eyes with her fists; we thought it probable that she stayed obdurately silent when she could have saved her sister from unfair punishment. It seems likely that she knew what it was like to have abandoned human standards.

In the poem 'Shed no tears', which we have thought likely to be about Shelley, the final stanzas exhibit the same total inhumanity, this time predicated of the wrecked mariner's 'Maker'.

That wrath will never spare,
Will never pity know,
Will mock its victim's maddened prayer,
Will triumph in his woe.

In April 1839 Emily was writing of the way in which such cold sadism can be brought about. An unknown Gondal hero or heroine watches a companion in sleep. The poem is called 'The soft unclouded blue of air' and deals with the regress of an 'iron man' who was once a soft child. 'He was once an ardent boy' writes the poet. 'Perhaps this is the destined hour/When hell shall lose its fatal power.' But the iron man feels nothing for the beauty round him, despite the fine blue sky. The explanation is straightforward:

Oh, crime can make the heart grow old
Sooner than years of wearing woe;
Can turn the warmest bosom cold
As winter wind or polar snow.[27]

Crime committed *by* or *against* the iron man? This we are not directly told. In Emily's childhood, she saw crime committed against Maria, but it did not turn Maria's heart cold. Emily herself, if our interpretation is correct, betrayed her sister, at least in her own eyes. She then became the unloved child of the regressive poems, sometimes called Blanche. Modern readers often explain Heathcliff's ruthlessness by the way in which he was treated as a child, but possibly Emily Brontë means us to understand that his intense malice grew by what it fed on.

The iron man of the poem may possibly be Douglas, who occurs in 'Douglas's Ride' and kills A. G. A. As Mary Visick points out, he is the 'wandering Jew' of Romantic literature. He is exile and outcast, 'For men and laws have tortured me/Till I can bear no more'. He is a 'spirit lost in crime'. He is, up to a point, Heathcliff. But though we see Isabella responding to Heathcliff as a romantically wayward soul, Emily Brontë is quick to correct her impression. Heathcliff is filled with avarice on an almost squalid level. We may sympathize with him, but this lust for revenge is harder to excuse in the Yorkshire world than it would have been in a fairyland of romance.

Neither Charlotte nor Anne was happy with Heathcliff or the novel he features in. In her preface, Charlotte appears to describe her remonstration with her sister as she read parts of the novel aloud in composition. Unfortunately, we do not know when this happened. It is interesting that the Brontës' old habit of comparing their work continued at this stage, but the date could be either 1845–6, or later, if the novel was rewritten.

> If the auditor of her work, when read in manuscript, shuddered under the grinding influence of natures so relentless and implacable, of spirits so lost and fallen [almost a direct quotation from the words used about Douglas in 'The Death of A. G. A.']; if it was complained that the mere hearing of certain vivid and fearful scenes banished sleep by night, and disturbed mental peace by day, Ellis Bell would wonder what was meant, and suspect the complainant of affectation.[28]

Charlotte does not identify the unpleasing scenes, or say whether Emily changed them under pressure, as she may have changed some of the poems for the 1846 edition. It seems that Charlotte did not read *Wuthering Heights* when it was first printed, but when she did, in preparation for the second edition, she found she must make significant alterations. Anne found other ways to correct Emily, as we shall see.

There is a well-known passage from the 'Preface' in which Charlotte likens the novel to a granite block hewn by a sculptor. 'With time, and with labour, the crag took human shape' is a quotation from it which is not always attended to. But the metaphor as a whole suggests that Charlotte knew her sister had worked very laboriously and for a considerable time on the book. Sculptors do not use knitting needles. The feeling is that Emily toiled and sweated. On the whole this tends to support, though it certainly doesn't prove, the idea that *Wuthering Heights* had to be recast. A novel begun and sporadically fostered in early 1845, then written in the intervals of poem revision between October 1845 and June 1846, would surely be too quickly written.

Meanwhile, the temperature at Haworth may not always have been warm enough to allow the reading aloud of the sisters' productions. Anne, at any rate, seems to dissent from such a view. On 11 May 1846, she wrote a poem later called 'Domestic Peace', which deals with dissension in the Brontë family. It will be well to quote portions of it.

Why should such gloomy silence reign
And why is all the house so drear,
when neither danger, sickness, pain,
Nor death, nor want, have entered here?

We are as many as we were
That other night, when all were gay,
And full of hope, and free from care;
Yet, is there something gone away.

. . . Something whose absence leaves a void,
A cheerless want in every heart.
Each feels the bliss of all destroyed
And mourns the change – but each apart.

The fire is burning in the grate
As redly as it used to burn,
But still the hearth is desolate
Till Mirth and Love with Peace *return*

. . . Sweet child of Heaven, and joy of earth!
O, when will Man thy value learn?
We rudely drove thee from our hearth,
And vainly sigh for thy return.[29]

This poem is an interesting and unusually revealing one. The timing needs careful note. The poems have been in print for several months, but not yet reviewed. The novels are nearing completion: *The Professor* will be dated at its close six weeks from now. Charlotte has stopped writing her letters entreating M. Heger for a reply. Branwell has been writing literature; it is a fortnight yet before he will hear that his old employer has died, leaving Mrs Robinson free to marry him, but that she will not do so. As Anne says, except for Branwell's alcoholism, which may have been mild at this precise moment, there is no disease. Yet 'each feels the bliss of all destroyed'. What did she mean, and what had destroyed their bliss (for '*We* rudely drove', Peace 'from our hearth')?

It may be that *Wuthering Heights* was one cause of the friction, and that a subsidiary one was Emily's continuing doubt about the printing of her poems. *Agnes Grey* is not likely to have been attacked by the others in reading, though it included some frank scenes of child delinquency. But Charlotte never attacks these later. Emily knew why Charlotte was so enthusiastic in writing *The Professor*; she might have taunted or objected. Branwell was certainly on edge, and had been left out of their plans. Charlotte, it is alleged, would not speak to him. But the poem makes it clear that the problem was not with Branwell alone, but the whole family.

As we have seen, when *Wuthering Heights* was read aloud, Charlotte objected, and Anne, it will be shown, was unhappy. Emily's period of reluctance over the poems may have been followed by an even greater period of reluctance to change her story. We saw the differing views on Gondal expressed by Anne and Emily in July 1845. It may now have seemed to Anne that she was right to suspect that Gondal was a drug. Heathcliff (so 'lost and fallen') presented too powerful a portrayal of evil for Anne to be happy. She may have felt that Emily was slipping from her as Branwell had slipped. The shift in relationships, whereby Anne moved closer to Charlotte and further from Emily, is further associated with this period of turmoil. And as Charlotte abandoned Branwell, Emily may have warmed to him. In the next few months, with the novels finished and going out to publishers, Anne returned to Gondal, presumably to try to renew her intimacy with Emily. Ultimately this ploy did not work.

It was now, with the family at sixes and sevens, that a visitor arrived unexpectedly. Uncle James, fresh from a tour of harvest work, appeared on the doorstep. He was large and homely, an Ulster farmworker, who talked as freely as the Brontë girls wrote.

Connections between the Irish Brontës and the family at Haworth had been loose.[30] Since Hugh had visited, about 1837, there had probably been no personal contact, unless – as the rather inaccurate William Wright suggests – Patrick had been briefly to Ireland one summer in the early 1840s. Throughout his life Patrtick was ambivalent about his early home and background. Though he certainly transmitted to his children when they were young many attitudes that were typical of Irish culture, Charlotte was always reluctant to stress this. It seems possible, though, that Jamie had a share in *Jane Eyre*; Mr Rochester's dressing up as a fortune-teller seems to have been derived from an episode in the doings of the Brontë brothers at Ballynaskeagh.

It seems that James arrived on a Sunday, and was turned away from the door by Tabby. To her, he looked like an Irish tramp, though Charlotte later called him a 'respectable' yeoman from Belfast. Unfortunately, we have no record as to how Emily saw the visitor, and his impressions of her are not given. He seems to have stayed some time, helping to bring Branwell back from the Black Bull, possibly on several occasions. Whether he found his way at all into the revised *Wuthering Heights* is unsure. There may be traces of the Irish situation in the scene and feelings expressed in 'Why ask to know the date, the clime?', as there had also probably been Irish facets to Gondal's civil war. Jamie's 'bolt-from-the-blue' visitation seems not to have been mentioned to Ellen Nussey, and we should never have known of it from reports on the English side of the water. Uncle James was a strange visitor, but it would have been hard to make anything sinister out of him, with his light-hearted joking good-humour.

There is one really tantalizing piece of evidence about the life of Emily Brontë during 1845–7 which must be mentioned here. She had an account book, about 3½ inches wide and proportionately long, kept carefully in her small script writing. Only blank pages, and the stubs of the rest, remain. The accounts have been snipped out with scissors in what seems to have been a deliberate attempt to destroy them.[31] The top one-third of an inch gives some idea what must have been in the rest, as well as overall statements for 1845 and 1846 which happened to have been written on the tiny fragment which survives.

If the whole booklet were extant, it would have answered some of the questions about the writing of the novel which we have been considering, for evidently Emily wrote an account of all expenses in this tiny document. A full transcript of everything remaining is given in Appendix I.

We cannot be sure whether the book was begun in 1844 or

earlier, but certainly the entries for 1845 are not the first. The first detail of 1845 apparently refers to an existing balance of £1 12s. At the end of the second side and beginning of the third, Emily gives some expenses connected with the trip to York. Returning they went to 'Leeds by rail', for which Emily paid 4s, and took two omnibuses to Bradford, where it seems that their dubious experience (mentioned in the diary paper) caused them to pay 1s for wine. The cost of the bed at Keighley seems to have been 3s 6d, and they had tea before setting out, for which Emily paid 1s 6d.

At the end of 1845 comes proof of what Charlotte told Ellen Nussey, namely that Emily handled the railway shares in which the three sisters had invested the money they inherited from Aunt Elizabeth.[32] Even with the profit from some railway scrip (£3), Emily finds her expenditure £12 above her income. The final two items in the expenditure column show that she was buying shares in what she calls 'specs' (speculations). By the end of the next year, this may have paid off, since the income for 1846 was more than twice that for 1845: £305 10s, instead of £116 18s 4d. 'Speculations' seem to have been Emily's forte; perhaps she looked upon her novel in the same light. In the middle of the year (the date has not survived) she was buying a 'Collar for F', presumably Flossie, who has generally been thought of as Anne's dog. She also bought needles, and we find evidence of the wonderful cakes mentioned by Greenwood in the 'Walnuts Dates etc' and 'Seeds' purchased. At the start of 1847 she brought a new tin, perhaps the kind which we saw holding the Gondal saga. Was it for *Wuthering Heights*?

The rest of the page is destroyed until the first three entries for July 1847 in which £100 is paid out rather vaguely, and then some tiny amounts in sundries and to 'B' (perhaps Branwell). At the end of August, Emily totalled up her small expenses under headings which are just legible. She had spent 3s 2d on dress, 1s on gifts, 3s on sundries and nothing at all on journeys and books. The inclusion of the former, however, confirms the feeling of the 1845 diary paper, that the York trip was to have been the first of a series. In September 1847 Emily bought some lace and something which might have to do with beds. The rest of the book is gone, leaving us maddened at losing even this small scrap of personal data left by such a secretive young woman.

14

The Themes of Wuthering Heights

> *Only two winds blow through* Wuthering Heights*; the soft south wind that came from the region beloved of Branwell and Charlotte, that bore dreams, wealth and happiness; and the Gondal wind, breath of the icy region, the lonely region in which the tempests of Emily's secret history roared and strove.*
>
> – Romer Wilson, *All Alone*

About the third week in August 1846, *Agnes Grey* and *Wuthering Heights* (as a one-volume novel) were presumably returned to Haworth with *The Professor*. Charlotte told Mrs Gaskell that her rejected novel reached her in Manchester 'on the very day that her father was to submit to his operation' for cataract.[1] We may suppose that Emily or Anne unwrapped the parcel of manuscripts and re-directed *The Professor*. The eye operation was a success, and when Charlotte returned, decisions would have to be made about the three novels. Mrs Gaskell is our earliest source for this:

> The three tales had each tried their fate in vain together, at length they were sent forth separately, and for many months with still-continued ill success. . . . Not only did *The Professor* return again to try his chance among the London publishers, but she began, in this time of care and depressing inquietude . . . *Jane Eyre*.[2]

There follows an interesting account of Charlotte's methods of composition, which we cannot pursue. Then Mrs Gaskell enlarges on Charlotte's account in the 'Preface' of the sisters' 'workshop' sessions in the evenings.

> The sisters retained their old habit, which was begun in their aunt's lifetime, of putting away their work at nine o'clock, and beginning their study, pacing up and down the sitting room. At this time, they talked over the stories they were engaged upon, and described their plots. Once or twice a week, each read to the others what she had written, and heard what they had to say about it. Charlotte told me, that the remarks made had seldom any effect in inducing her to alter her work, so possessed was she with the feeling that she had described reality; but the readings were of great and stirring interest to all, taking them out of the gnawing pressure of daily-recurring cares, and setting them in a free place. It was on one of these occasions that Charlotte determined to make her heroine plain, small and unattractive, in defiance of the accepted canon.[3]

If Mrs Gaskell's story is true, we may reasonably ask what the other sisters were reading aloud in reply to Charlotte's first passages from *Jane Eyre* (that the occasion described followed September 1846 is implied by the final sentence: the early stages of *Jane Eyre* are being discussed). Anne was contributing the first outline of chapters of *Wildfell Hall*, probably. What else could Emily have been reading but a new version of *Wuthering Heights*?

There are problems in accepting this thesis. If Mrs Gaskell's earlier statement is right, the three first novels were still going the rounds of the publishers, in separate packets. Charlotte had moved on from *The Professor*, Anne from *Agnes Grey*; Emily might have nothing to read unless she left *The Life of the Emperor Julius* (in a Yorkshire setting), or whatever *Wuthering Heights* was called, and began again from memory or notes. Could she have done this? Possibly the two novels of the younger sisters were not being sent out until Emily had revised her contribution to fill the gap the third novel had left. Possibly some publisher had been attracted to *Agnes Grey* and suggested an expansion of *Wuthering Heights*, so that the two novels were both at Haworth, and Anne had no need to recast hers. Of course, these are only plausible suggestions: certainty is unattainable.

In any case, it looks as if the decision to persevere with the novels was not immediate. Almost as soon as the novels returned from London, both girls went back to working on Gondal. Anne's poem of 14 September 1846 may be considered to refer obliquely to Branwell. It is an interesting fiction, the full title of which has not been deciphered, but which deals with a man whose heart has grown bitter as he thinks back to his childhood. An incident in it is drawn from an incident in Branwell's youth. Emily's poem, begun the same day, is a thoughtful and complex ballad in which the name Gondal is not mentioned: 'Why ask to know the date: the clime?' She seems to have written about 150 lines of it before putting it on one side. When Charlotte returned from Manchester, the three girls must have made a decision about their novels, as we have suggested. As for the poem, we shall come back to it.

I have suggested that *Wuthering Heights* now began to be recast and expanded. It seems quite impossible to say what this revision added. We may speculate that the 1845–6 version of the novel, which was sent off to the publishers with *Agnes Grey* and *The Professor*, told the story of Heathcliff (who had been Julius in mid-1845), possibly through Lockwood's eyes. Catherine had been developed from Geraldine, Edgar from Alfred. Isabella, romantic and spoilt, takes a name that had been used in Gondal. It may be pure coincidence that an Isabella Linton is found in Glascar (Co. Down) meeting house registers, but perhaps Emily's long memory had recalled a name mentioned by her father when talking about his youthful exploits. The geography of Thrushcross and the Heights, drawn from North Halifax, must have been early in the novel. But it could possibly have been written without Nelly. The 'Chinese box' style of narrative is common to *Wuthering Heights* and *Wildfell Hall*. The two books have a complex relationship, but it may be that this structure was discussed by Emily and Anne during late 1846 in one of the workshop sessions mentioned. Nelly is not closely paralleled by any Gondal figure. She could be the inspired addition of 1846–7 who enabled the novel to seem acceptable to Newby. Verbally, she is an adaptation, descending from Eilís ('Alice'), Emily's grandmother. Nelly is Ellen and is obviously related to Ellis (Emily's pseudonym), and her Christian name. Like many of the parts conned by this actress, Nelly is a part of Emily, the well-read housekeeper at Haworth parsonage.

We may now be in a better position to see how *Wuthering*

Heights emerges from the life experience of its author and the poetry she has written. That the burning intensity of the book mirrors an almost self-consuming intensity in Emily we have clearly seen. The many themes of the novel, crystallizing about the demonic Heathcliff, all cast their shadows before, in earlier work or anecdotes about Emily. As Mary Visick shows, the book was in unconscious process as far back as the 1830s, though it could not have been guessed how it would look when complete. The themes, like Heathcliff, were 'always, always' in Emily's mind. Though planning of the actual book on paper may have begun in 1845, and been renewed in an 1846 revision, events and characters had been circling round Emily's imagination almost all her life. It is hard to see how she might write a second book without duplication, for *Wuthering Heights* is a chart of the inner country of her dreams. In this section, I propose to disentangle some of the threads of the tapestry to show the origin of each, as near as may be in chronological order.

Firstly, the fabric of the novel is *oral*. Though narrative techniques owe something, clearly, to Scott, Lord Lytton and other novelists, the story is heard, aloud, whether the speaker is Lockwood, Nelly, Joseph, or Catherine. From her earliest days, Emily heard stories told, as well as read. At the lowest, deepest level of her unconscious mind lies the layer formed when a fascinated little girl heard the magical and arresting tales told by her Irish father, who (despite eccentricity) loved to be with children, yarning to them. These tales formed patterns in her mind: she heard them over and over again and learnt them. Miss Robinson reports that even at fifteen Emily 'wore a strange expression, gratified, pleased, as though she had gained something which seemed to complete a picture in her mind' when her father told 'fearful stories of superstitious Ireland' in the parsonage at breakfast.[4] 'This was the same Emily who at five years of age used to startle the nursery with her fantastic fairy stories', comments Miss Robinson. Two topics dealt with by Mr Brontë were the stirring days of the 1798 rebellion and the ancestral legend of the foundling, Welsh. This was family history. Emily was half a little Irish girl, with a voracious appetite for such history, and living an intense and troubling inner life. She looked for clues to her own personality; in her ancestry, she found them.

Mr Brontë seems to have transferred to the family some of

his own inheritance of ballads. He is credited with composing some in far-distant Ballynaskeagh.[5] J. F. Goodridge suggests that 'Fair Annie' is the ballad mentioned in *Wuthering Heights*, Chapter 32, and we are throughout reminded of such ballads as 'Cold blows the wind', in which a mourning lover is apparently the cause of his sweetheart's inability to rest in the grave.[6] Ballad forms and ballad speech seem to underlie *Wuthering Heights*. The rapid movement of many ballads seems to influence the arbitrary way in which Emily Brontë treats time. As John Hewish points out, the childhood of the younger Catherine lasts only a paragraph or two. She reaches the age of thirteen without leaving Thrushcross Park (as Hewish wryly remarks, 'She has not had time!').[7]

At this level the live and dead meet and intermingle. We have seen examples of Emily Brontë's closeness to the dead, greater sometimes than her closeness to the living. Ballads such as 'Cold blows the wind' and 'The Grey Cock' combine the sense of the dead as decomposing body and as disembodied spirit in exactly the same manner as *Wuthering Heights*. For example, in 'The Grey Cock', the dead lover comes to his love's window at the dead of night. After they have kissed, shaken hands and embraced, 'Mary' asks,

> *'O Willie dear, O dearest Willie,*
> *Where is that colour you'd some time ago?'*
> *'O Mary dear, the clay has changed me;*
> *I am but the ghost of your Willie O.'*[8]

In such a stanza, the ballad-maker has it both ways. The dead man is a corpse and can be changed by the 'clay' in his grave; but he is also a ghost, who can fly to the loved one's window at night. The ambiguity is not resolved either here or in *Wuthering Heights*.

A number of writers have examined Emily's use of dialect in the character of Joseph, though there is evidence that this was changed by the printers even in the 1847 edition, and the whole was considerably modified by Charlotte in 1850. K. M. Petyt of Reading University concludes that 'she is surprisingly good – better than either of her sisters'.[9] He shows that she has consistent principles of transcription and generally holds to them. Branwell and Charlotte made attempts at Haworth dialect in the juvenilia, and of course there are dialect speakers in *Jane Eyre* and *Wildfell Hall*, but it looks as if Emily's superior ear and memory are responsible for her greater accuracy. The evidence underlines the oral nature of the novel, which is clearly meant to be spoken and heard rather than read silently.

Secondly, written literary exemplars played some part in the creation of Emily's novel, but the solid evidence, despite enormous labours, is hard to come by. So much is this so that there is still an occasional disposition to take Charlotte's view as the correct one. She presents her sister as a 'naive' artist.

> [*Wuthering Heights*] is rustic all through. . . . Had she but lived, her mind would of itself have grown like a strong tree, loftier, straighter, wider-spreading, and its matured fruits would have attained a mellow ripeness and sunnier bloom; but on that mind time and experience alone could work; to the influence of other intellects, it was not amenable.[10]

Charlotte is doubtless thinking of her own attempts to wrestle with Emily's intellect, and we understand why she considers her sister impossible to influence. However, the traces in her work of Wordsworth, Coleridge and Shelley, as well as of Byron and Shakespeare show that Charlotte misunderstood her sister's thought processes.

At one time Byron was considered the major influence on the work of all the Brontës and there can be no doubt that he is there quite strongly. Mention has already been made of Moore's *Life of Byron*, and John Hewish showed that the diary papers were inspired by Byron's example. From his life the name Augusta may have been picked up, and 'The Prisoner of Chillon' seems to have been an influence on such poems as 'The Prisoner'. Byron's personality seems also to have struck a deep chord in Emily. Winifred Gérin points to a similarity between Heathcliff's shock at his rejection by Catherine – so it seems to him at the time – and the occasion when Mary Chaworth, loved by Byron as a young man, said to a maid, 'Do you think I could care for that lame boy?' and was overheard by him.[11] Byron ran out of the house and vanished into the night. The parallel between this incident and Heathcliff's departure is not likely to be coincidence. But the incident had certainly been fully integrated into Emily's subconscious; there is no feel in the story of this being inconsistent or inappropriate.

Scott had been well known to the Brontës since childhood. Similarities between *The Black Dwarf* and *Wuthering Heights* have many times been remarked, and John Hewish notes the influence of *Old Mortality*.[12] Scott's wide moorland scenes and emphasis on adventure fed into Gondal; he was one of the sources of the Brontës' absorption with things Scottish. The Gothic horror novel also leaves traces on *Wuthering Heights*, and their avid reading of *Blackwood's* did not cease when the Brontës grew up. Hewish notes parallels between Emily's novel and *The Bridegroom of Barna*, by Bartholomew Simmonds, published in *Blackwood's* in November 1840.[13] If such stories were used deliberately in the construction of *Wuthering Heights*, we have to think of Emily either re-reading back numbers of the magazine in 1845, or casting back in her long memory. But there is no suggestion that they were used deliberately; only that Emily had a much more receptive attitude to other intellects than Charlotte realized.

The evidence that Emily was interested in German literature is circumstantial. It was German she learnt in the parsonage kitchen during 1843–4, but it is not clear what she hoped to do with her knowledge. We cannot possibly know how far she had been able to progress with the subject during her stay on the continent or whether she had ever read a novel in that language. This was perhaps unnecessary. There were frequent articles on German literature in the magazines such as *Blackwood's* and *Fraser's*. Her account of Heathcliff's revenge, through the acquisition of the Earnshaw property, suggested to early commentators that she had read E. T. A. Hoffmann's *Das Majorat*, reviewed in *Blackwood's* in December 1826. Another Hoffmann story, *The Devil's Elixir*, had been reviewed two years earlier. An excellent account of the influence on *Wuthering Heights* of these and other literary sources can be found in Hewish's book.[14]

Thirdly, there is *the theme of duality*. In his book, *The Mind of Emily Brontë*, Herbert Dingle notes what he calls her 'positive' character.[15] He points out that there are few similes, few comparisons, either in the poems or the novel. Emily *states*, she does not compare. What is more, she states contradictory thoughts or feelings in adjacent poems, as we have observed. We have noted a similar duality, or ambiguity, in her attitude to life after death. But sometimes her dualities constitute poles of mythic intensity. Such duality sometimes seems to be a constituent of the human mind: so at any rate a host of philosophers have thought. Plainly, Emily sees these dualities as cosmic.

For many people the primal duality is that of father and mother. In some ways there is not a strong opposition in the Brontës' works between male and female. One could parallel Charlotte's observation in other contexts:

> . . . for an example of constancy and tenderness, remark that of Edgar Linton. (Some people will think these qualities do not shine so well incarnate in a man as they would do in a woman, but Ellis Bell could never be brought to comprehend this notion: nothing moved her more than any insinuation that the faithfulness and clemency, the long-suffering and loving-kindness which are esteemed virtues in the daughters of Eve, become foibles in the sons of Adam.)[16]

What echo of past arguments lurks in this comment? The only men who are on record as being 'kind' to Emily, except for her father and brother, are Robert Heaton and William Weightman. The comment does, however, square with a general tendency in the Brontës to play down sex-differences, as in their choice of neutral pseudonyms, or Anne's insistence in *Wildfell Hall* that boys and girls should have the same education.

Emily's father was strong, kindly, short-tempered, scholarly, fond of children, romantic and dutiful. Her mother was kindly and intelligent, but died too soon for Emily to know her well. If she recalled her, it may have been as a fretful invalid. The 'good' characters in *Wuthering Heights* have a peevish, feeble side to their constancy.

The next duality was that of Maria and Elizabeth. As I have tried to show, the two sisters differed quite markedly. Maria was apparently thought of as an intellectual. She was very much her father's daughter, striving hard to fulfil his loving ideal for her. She had great determination, but was rather unworldly, and she may have courted disaster stubbornly. She knew her role, and she played it to death. Elizabeth was patient too, but not an intellectual. Where Maria could not be bothered with the feminine arts such as sewing, Elizabeth (who, however, also sewed badly) may have provided a less self-confidently intellectual leadership. These two alternative mothers may have provided differing models, and even when they died alternative allies were presented to Emily by her two remaining sisters, Charlotte and Anne. We have seen how in fact she fluctuated between the two, collaborating with Anne in Gondal, but going to Belgium with Charlotte.

It is sure that Emily began to see things in terms of pairs, which might contrast. This is so in Gondal. In May 1845, when perhaps *Wuthering Heights* was already beginning, she wrote two contrasting poems called later 'The two children'. The two are 'A. E.' and 'R. C.', who might be anyone. It is symbolic that the two poems have sometimes been thought to be one only, with contrasting parts. In a sense the two children are one child: the boy and his 'guardian angel'. Early in the poem, we hear that

Never has a blue streak
Cleft the clouds since morn –
Never has his grim Fate
Smiled since he was born

But as the metre changes and we reach the second half (or second poem) we meet a seraph, a 'Child of Delight! with sunbright hair . . .'. This spirit denies that she comes from heaven, but

I, the image of light and gladness
Saw and pitied that mournful boy,
And I swore to take his gloomy sadness,
And give to him my beamy joy . . . .

Guardian angel, he lacks no longer;
Evil fortune he need not fear:
Fate is strong, but Love is stronger;
And more unsleeping than angel's care.[17]

The two children are two sides of the same being, just as Catherine and Heathcliff are two parts of a whole. Even more, this reminds us of the two second-generation protagonists, Hareton and the second Catherine. We must be right in concluding that Emily saw herself thus divided: these two children are two sides of Emily's own nature.

Elsewhere in the poetry, Emily does not compromise. She embraces *both* alternatives. 'Yet my heart loves December's smile/As much as July's beam.' To some extent, the opposition and reconciliation of extremes appears to be a commonplace of philosophy and sub-philosophic thought. It is certainly a strong feature of Emily Brontë's work, strongest of all in the novel.

Fourthly, and linked to this, is the emphasis on separation and reunion. Separation from the beloved was a recurrent experience in Emily's childhood. The loss of her mother must have remained as a subconscious trauma. Such a loss is sometimes perceived as incurring guilt, and any such guilt feeling would have been accentuated by the loss of the two sisters in circumstances where Emily could perhaps have palliated matters. We have seen that bad temper caused discord between Emily and her surviving sisters. As Anne says in 'Self-communion': 'there was cruel bitterness/When jarring discords rose between'.[18] But Anne was as patient as Elizabeth, and reconciliation was possible. The lines which follow in 'Self-Communion' tell us that the relationship between Emily and Anne was not all peace. It is possible that Emily was compelled to play tricks on her 'twin' sometimes, just as she played tricks on Charlotte.

Still, for significant periods Emily and Anne did achieve a close and joyous affection. We have seen Ellen's picture of them physically intertwined, and we have Anne's strong 'Oh, I have known a wondrous joy/In early friendship's pure delight'. We have seen the two sharing the moors and the dining room table, and the glorious secret of a 'Tin Box' with Gondal magic in it. We have Anne's bright poem about Alexander and Zenobia, who cannot be for ever parted. These two are in a sense 'lovers', but they are very young, sharing a romantic and sentimental attachment. The attachment between Emily and Anne may well have been sentimental, and when they played at Gondal lovers, it was probably romantic. Heathcliff and Catherine, similarly, are soul-mates; it is Edgar who marries Catherine for the normal satisfactions of family life, as Mary Visick notes.

The fifth point to be considered is that many Gondal themes, worked and reworked, found their ultimate place in

Wuthering Heights. The most obvious is infidelity. 'A. G. A.' seems to work her way through three lovers in the Gondal poems: there is Alexander, Lord of Elbë, who appears in such poems as 'Lord of Elbë, on Elbë hill'; Lord Alfred, who becomes Edgar; and Julius Brenzaida. Infidelity was of great interest to the little Brontës as they played in their nursery. To Charlotte and Branwell the theme appears to have been eternally attractive, and Branwell may have dabbled with the practice in real life. Anne encountered infidelity at Thorp Green, surely in more cases than just that of her brother: the topic became a major element in *Wildfell Hall*. There was a great deal of infidelity among the four children, not of course in love, but in taking sides and playing one off against the other. Translating this into the sphere of marital love, Anne seems to imply that in heaven such problems will be ironed out by the introduction and encouragement of plural affections. Emily allows Catherine to see no problem at all in retaining and monopolizing the love of both Edgar and Heathcliff. The arguments propounded by Shelley seem to have been an influence.

There are a number of mysterious children in Gondal. Some are 'unblessed, unfriended', like Alexandria, who is abandoned in 'I've seen this dell in July's shine', possibly by A. G. A. There is the venom-spitting girl of the final Gondal poem, involved in civil war; pretty Blanche, who turned into a gipsy; 'A. A.', the subject of 'This shall be thy lullaby', and many more. They are all isolated, appearing from nowhere, and unloved: the relevance to Heathcliff is obvious. That they are all *children* is also important: we shall soon turn to examine Emily's view of childhood.

Wuthering Heights is set in a haunted landscape. If Heathcliff walks, as they say he does, he is the successor to the ghost of Aspin Castle:

Yet of the native shepherds none
In open day and cheerful sun,
Will tread its labyrinths alone;
Far less when evening's pensive hour
Hushes the bird and shuts the flower,
And gives to Fancy magic power
O'er each familiar tone.

For round their hearths they'll tell the tale,
And every listener swears it true,
How wanders there a phantom pale
With spirit-eyes of dreamy blue.[19]

A Gothic ghost, whom Emily is half dismissing here with her use of the word 'Fancy'. But he is the lighter part of a much deeper theme, which arises from Emily's deep feeling that the dead do not leave the earth.

We recall her two contradictory views on death. The dead body itself remains important:

Beneath the turf my footsteps tread
Lie low and lone the silent dead;
Beneath the turf, beneath the mould –
Forever dark, forever cold.

This is acceptable, because 'Heaven itself, so pure and blest,/Could never give my spirit rest'.[20] We have Catherine's account of her dream ringing in our ears. On the other hand, in 'Aye, there it is', we have the Platonic and Shelleyan

Thus truly when that breast is cold
Thy prisoned soul shall rise,
The dungeon mingle with the mould –
The captive with the skies.[21]

Emily does not reconcile these two views of death, and however many times we read and re-read the closing pages of the novel, we cannot be sure what her final conclusion was as none is reached. She could not reconcile opposing views, as 'Enough of thought, philosopher' tells us. That the dead live perpetually in the sense that they are always pervading our thoughts is a view that Emily constantly portrays, in the poems as much as in *Wuthering Heights*.

The sixth, and final point, is that Nature is a Gondal theme too, in a way. Emily's absorption in it is the chief cause of her moving her fictional world to a Yorkshire climate. In fact, her close geographical knowledge of the 'lone green lane' suggests that she transfers Yorkshire features lock, stock and barrel to Gondal, though this should not be taken to mean that the lane is necessarily the path from Haworth to the moors, as is often suggested.

Charlotte made Emily's love of the moors a main plank in her apologia for her sister. Emily did indeed adore (in a real sense) the world of nature, but in an interesting way. It is not correct to think of her as a nature poet in the manner of John Clare, for instance. She does not produce the minute descriptions of the plant and animal kingdoms which we have from the Shropshire writer, Mary Webb. On the other hand, weather, times of day, seasons, clouds, winds, sunlight, grey stones, masses of heather, the wheeling lapwing, imbue a great deal of her work. They are not described in set pieces. Emily's technique is almost 'dead-pan'. For example, when in Chapter 21 the young Cathy drags Nelly across the moor on 20 March for an hour's 'ramble', the following words help us to visualize the wild, open scenery:

> I found plenty of entertainment in listening to the larks singing *far and near*, and enjoying the *sweet, warm sunshine* . . . *moor-game*, so many hillocks to *climb* and pass . . . *cloudless* pleasure . . . a *great way off* . . . I began to be weary.[22]

In this passage, and many others, Emily conveys the feel of a bright spring day in the Pennines, but she does not particularize. Ellen Nussey testified to the way in which Emily lost her inhibitions in these wide open spaces, far from human habitation. But her love of nature goes further than simply 'escaping from the palaces of instruction' to be with the lapwings and moor-game. In the last analysis Emily is truly a Stoic in valuing nature in every form. *Secundum naturam vivere*, the Stoic motto, might well be hers. You must not interfere with me, she seems to say; 'I wish to be as God made me'. This needs to be taken into account when we watch her dying, as she might consider, '*secundum naturam*'.

This view of nature is often called nature mysticism, or pantheism. The Romantics taught something like it to a whole generation, and Mr Brontë was not untouched by it. The question is often posed, 'Was Emily Brontë a mystic?' It is not always clear what kind of answer can be given to such a question, but it cannot be evaded. In the passage from *Shirley*, originally in French, where 'Eva' has an ecstatic experience before the world is properly formed, we have Charlotte's view of what Emily might possibly have felt, and a second clue is generally thought to be found in the central passage of 'The Prisoner', in which the captive speaks of her nocturnal visitant, that takes away her normal human senses.

As an aside, however, it must be said that we have to be very careful in commenting on the latter passage. At least one well-known Brontë commentator quotes Charlotte's 1850 additions to explain the nature of the visitant:

What I love shall come like visitant of air,
Safe in secret power from lurking human snare;
Who loves me, no word of mine shall e'er betray,
Though for faith unstained my life must forfeit pay.

Burn then, little lamp; glimmer straight and clear –
Hush, a rustling wing stirs, methinks, the air;
He for whom I wait, thus ever comes to me;
Strange Power! I trust thy might; trust thou my constancy.

These well-known lines are *not* by Emily Brontë. They show, once again, what Charlotte thought Emily might be feeling; and once again they are apologetic: we shall return to them.

It seems likely that when people ask 'Was Emily Brontë a mystic', they are seeking to understand her personal attitude to religion and love. They are also trying to probe the nature of the ecstatic moments she seems to have experienced, and which seem to be evidenced both in her poetry and in Charlotte's accounts of her sister. The subjective evidence for these experiences is strong in the poetry, and objective evidence is not lacking. We do have to be most careful, however, in extracting evidence from poems, some of which are intended to be fictional. All the same, no one would doubt that the experiences Wordsworth dwells on in 'Tintern Abbey' and 'The Prelude' are not fictive, and Emily Brontë is entitled to a careful reading of her poetic accounts of similar experiences, especially since the principal actors in *Wuthering Heights* feel similar emotions.

I have already suggested that the first trace of these feelings occurred when Emily was six, perhaps at Cowan Bridge. Romer Wilson, indeed, links the onset of the 'visions' with a fit Emily is supposed to have suffered. I should not exclude this possibility, though it seems more likely that Emily's account of a lonely child withdrawing from cheerful, lively society betokens an emotional rather than a physical crisis. We must always bear in mind the volatility of Emily's emotions, shown in her childhood tempers. The deprivation of her mother could not be glossed over in her mind, and perhaps a joyous moment would soon turn to sorrow even while the nursling is being petted. She writes of a 'voice', and the characters in *Wuthering Heights* often seem to act as though interior but separate forces are motivating them. The impression is ambivalent: in 'I saw thee, child, one summer's day', dated July 1837, the child of the poem is struck by the passionate desire to know the future, but is overcome instead by an almost physical presence. The description foreshadows Heathcliff's intuition in the presence of Catherine:

> *A fearful anguish in his eyes*
> *Fixed strainedly on the vacant air;*
> *Heavily bursts in long-drawn sighs*
> *His panting breath, enchained by fear.*[23]

Such a description would be hard to write for anyone who had not experienced something like it. It seems that Emily's mind visualized an unknown, unspecified entity which could terrorize her. How near this feeling was to epilepsy or hysteria we cannot know. Terror was not the only emotion it might convey; when the visitant appears in other poems, it is benign, and of course Heathcliff welcomes it.

The intellectual force in *Wuthering Heights* is gigantic. As we see Emily Brontë now in 1846 struggling with the form of the novel we may recall M. Heger's opinion of her as a supreme intelligence. We may be inclined to place more emphasis on her emotional power, but in the novel she succeeds in channelling this through rational construction to a masterpiece. Once she had endured these moments of intense and surprising emotion, she needed to wrestle with them and try to formulate some theories which would satisfy her own questioning. One possible explanation she toys with is ghosts; we have seen how Aspin Castle has its ghost, and the final pages of *Wuthering Heights* repeat this solution rather wistfully. The literary convention of the ghost was a little overworked; Emily could not always take it quite seriously. She is equally unconvinced by Charlotte's orthodoxy and Anne's universalism.

'How clear she shines!' of 13 April 1843 showed us how Emily worked herself into this kind of vision, just as Heathcliff tries to induce a vision of Catherine. Emily invokes 'Fancy', who is bending 'my lonely couch above'. The metaphor is from the goodnight kiss of a mother (or elder sister) for her child. 'Fancy' is seen as a sort of latter-night Maria or Elizabeth, who can comfort and placate the wounded spirit of the wakeful Emily. She gazes fixedly out of the window, at the stars that glow 'Above me in that stormless sea', and allows herself a waking 'dream', under the patronage of Fancy. A year later, Emily is more inclined to call her faculty 'Imagination' and to set it against 'Reason', which will 'tell the suffering heart how vain/Its cherished dreams must always be . . .'. Imagination is

ever there to bring
The hovering visions back and breathe
New glories o'er the blighted spring
And call a lovelier life from death,
And whisper with a voice divine
Of real worlds as bright as thine.[24]

At this point Emily seems to consider 'heaven' or some such further dimension a 'real' world. She does not, however, 'trust' to Imagination's 'phantom bliss', but at evening, she finds it a solace.

All these poems lead to *Wuthering Heights*, because they speak of a deliberate attempt by Emily Brontë to cultivate methods of approaching the once-spontaneous experience. As a Wordsworthian, she realizes that 'the glory and the dream' is fitful, but a semblance of it can be restored. 'O thy bright eyes' of 14 October 1844 is more intense. She calls the faculty 'God of Visions' and says she had chosen it beyond Wealth, Power, Glory and Pleasure. It is 'ever present, phantom thing' and has become a 'King' to her. The account of imagination here is much more intense and emotional. The vision is 'My slave, my comrade, and my King' and even more emotionally

My Darling Pain that wounds and sears
And wrings a blessing out from tears
By deadening me to real cares.

Emily is writing of a mentally induced vision, willed as an intense pleasure, but surprisingly also an intense pain. Heathcliff shares this pain and pleasure; for Emily in 1846 it may be that he came to represent them.

Sometimes the description of these visions is most distanced and sceptical, as though Emily would withdraw from the title of 'mystic' or cannot in honesty attain it. In 'A day dream' of 5 March 1844, a Shelleyan cosmic dream is recorded, but in slightly mocking terms. Sometimes, the vision is apparently in human shape. In 'My comforter' of 10 February 1844, a writer is being described whose printed words 'heard' by the person whose audial memory and visualization had once enabled her to read 'very prettily' seem to become a vision of that person. Gradually, it may be, the envisioned poet became the envisioned hero of *Wuthering Heights*.

Whether such an intense imaginative life, sometimes willed and sometimes spontaneous, can be called mystic is for the reader to decide. Certainly the novel could not be the same without this bodily withdrawal and emotional dynamism, which became focused on Heathcliff and Catherine. Judging by the dates of poems which express the same compressed feeling, Heathcliff was already potent in the version of *Wuthering Heights* sent to Colburn in 1846. Emily was at her 'mystical' height in 'The Prisoner', already mentioned as the poem she may have been copying into her B manuscript on the day Charlotte discovered it. 'Rochelle' (earlier 'Geraldine', later Catherine) is specific about a wild visionary experience:

He comes with western winds, with evening's wandering airs,
With that clear dusk of heaven that brings the thickest stars;
Winds take a pensive tone, and stars a tender fire,
And visions rise and change which kill me with desire –

But will Emily be precise about these 'visions'? What does she mean by saying that they 'rise and change'?

There may be some clue in the next stanza, which continues

Desire for nothing known in my maturer years
When joy grew mad with awe at counting future tears;
When, if my spirit's sky was full of flashes warm,
I knew not whence they came, from sun or thunderstorm.

David Cecil considers that the family at the Heights are 'children of storm', and Heathcliff the most so.[25] Here Rochelle–Emily says that emotional heat constitutes the greatest value, whether the heat is sunny or stormy. One effect of *Wuthering Heights* is to leave the reader believing in the moral value of emotion as such, whether it issues in conventionally good or bad acts. 'Rochelle' recalls the most powerful instances of this heightened feeling as taking place in childhood, as Catherine and Heathcliff yearn to return to their free days of rambling on the moor. 'Mysticism' involves a stormy communion with the self of the past, and the natural world where it lived. In adulthood, 'Rochelle' works herself up to a point where she is beyond humanity. The frantic passion of Heathcliff also takes him beyond humanity, to a point where he is sure that his lost love is situated 'within two yards' distance'; he gazes at her while the vision 'communicated, apparently, both pleasure and pain, in exquisite extremes'.[26]

Mysticism perhaps also implies intense love; we commonly use the word of a religious communicant who expresses his or her love of God. As we have seen earlier, Emily expressly says she has not been involved with any earthly love. As a violently emotional child, she was nursed by Maria and Elizabeth, petted by Miss Evans, cuddled in bed by Charlotte while they made up their very special plays, then transferred her affection to Anne, with whom she is found intertwined as a young teenager. A voracious reader and dweller in the land of poetry, she takes to Byron and develops a passion for Shelleyan ideas so intense as to bring the writer before her eyes. I have suggested elsewhere that *Epipsychidion* may have been a special favourite, as it seems to address Emily directly. She loves her animals, but is so extremely shy that she hardly stops to nod to any curate she sees. The persona she adopts is so dense that only children can penetrate it. In writing *Wuthering Heights* she can elude all communication difficulties, and become legitimately absorbed in frenzied, heart-warming creativity.

We should not leave *Wuthering Heights* without re-emphasizing the recurrent images of childhood in it. Deep in the poetry we have found many references to lonely, imprisoned, emotional children. One vital element in the novel is the terrible yearning for lost childhood, Wordsworth's idea of the extension of heaven. 'The child is father of the man' could be

Emily's theme song. Stevie Davies points out the centrality of the image of the lapwings, abandoned in their nest to become winter skeletons, remembered and contemplated by Catherine as she nears her own end, in a state of dementia and mystic vision.[27]

This nest destroyed is a metaphor for the Brontë family itself, with one parent dead and leaving two of her children to become tiny skeletons. Stevie Davies goes further, and points to the emphasis on motherhood in the centre of *Wuthering Heights*; at the central axis of the novel Catherine, erstwhile child, who, with Heathcliff, 'pictured Heaven so beautifully . . . in their innocent talk', suffers, dies and gives birth to a regenerated new Catherine. So, too, Emily Brontë, at one time busy pairing off fictional characters in a Gondal plan, does not attain motherhood except through building her novel on the skeletons of past pain, and brings to birth her resurrected A. G. A.

The biographer cannot explain *Wuthering Heights*. The process of using the novel to understand the life, and the life to understand the novel, can easily become circular. I have tried to remain aware of the trap. What is clear, surely, is that *Wuthering Heights* is in all ways consistent with Emily's life as we know it and in particular with her inner life, as that emerges before us in her rare oracular statements, and especially in her poetry.

15

Heathcliff on a Public Stage

He does repay and soon and well
The deeds that turn his earth to hell,
The wrongs that aim a venomed dart
Through nature at the Eternal Heart.

Wuthering Heights was now completed. We shall soon see how it was published and received by critics. During its final stages it seems as though the divisions between Emily and Anne were further accentuated. Emily herself never comments on these divisions; in fact from now until her death there is an almost total lack of direct evidence on her feelings and opinions, though in the very last months of her life Charlotte will record some impressions of the stubborn, inward-looking girl. On the face of it, she wrote almost nothing, a circumstance so odd that we shall need to consider it most carefully. One of our best indicators may be Anne's attitude to her sister, as reflected in poetry and prose, beginning at a time when *Wuthering Heights* was finished but not yet printed.

We have heard ominous rumblings of dissension at Haworth during 1846: 'Why should such gloomy silence reign?' The Anne Brontë of 1846 is not the 'twin' of 1835, nor yet the shy retiring 'Maiden' of her own poem written in early 1840. Anne has been out into the world, and witnessed 'unpleasant and undreamt of' aspects of human nature, in particular at Thorp Green.[1] One of her pupils has eloped with an actor; the other two are writing to her, asking her advice on how to run their lives.[2] She has acquired enough knowledge of the world to feel able to comment on Emily's work.

Meanwhile, she has also fought her way to a commitment to traditional Christianity, though she is adding some unorthodoxy in her current novel. Anne now believes she understands the purpose of art: to serve the turn of the moralist (though certainly in no narrow partisan way).

From this position, Anne begins to offer a critique of Emily's attitude to life. This she does in three works: *The Tenant of Wildfell Hall*, which we have seen progressing alongside *Wuthering Heights*; 'The Three Guides', a poem written in August 1847; and 'Self-Communion', begun in November 1847. The three works have other aims besides commenting on Emily's philosophy; *Wildfell Hall* incorporates a great deal of material from Thorp Green. But one of Anne's aims is surely to look dispassionately at Emily's attitudes. She was the closest of all humans to Emily, and what she says must have great interest for us.

It may be worth recalling that as far back as 1835 Anne had been called upon to stand in for Emily. Anne was an asthmatic, whose health Charlotte worried over. Emily, physically, seemed to be strong. Yet Anne was called upon to replace her at Roe Head. One thinks of the 'unconscious tyranny' that M. Heger says Emily exercised over Charlotte in Belgium. We might see her refusal to endure life at Roe Head, and the subsequent arrival of Anne, as another example of unconscious tyranny. Quite probably Anne would not object; the chance of proving herself hardier than Emily, and even more learned, might be eagerly seized. But if there was self-sacrifice involving one sister or the other, it was Anne who sacrificed her home comforts for Emily's mental peace.

In 1836–7 the two collaborated on Gondal, giving us in the 1837 diary paper a charmingly unselfconscious picture of life at Haworth during a holiday. But Anne is being led. So far she is content with that role. In 1840, she realizes that William Weightman exercises a pull over her heart; nevertheless (or possibly because of this) she goes for a second exile to governess-ship.[3] Emily stays at home again. During her unhappiness at Thorp Green, Anne writes personal poetry, abandoning Gondal. The twins are drifting apart. In 1845–6, it is Charlotte who decides they will all try to publish their poems. Then Charlotte makes the decision to send out their fiction works. When she removes *The Professor* from the publication race, Anne apparently supports Emily; but we are not to suppose that she accepts Emily's presuppositions. As for 'playing' bad Gondal characters on the way to York, it is likely that the evangelical Anne shared the scruples of Fanny Price in *Mansfield Park*: to play the part of a bad character might lead to becoming one. Emily seemed set on that road, and Branwell was living proof of it.

We may suppose that these attitudes are uppermost in Anne's mind as *Wuthering Heights* is read aloud. 'The mere hearing' of the worst episodes 'banished sleep by night, and disturbed mental peace by day', as we have heard. Charlotte remonstrates; is Anne to remain unmoved by this wild play-acting, bordering on the wilful description of evil, which allows her mind no peace? Meanwhile Ellis Bell 'would wonder what was meant'. The tone of Charlotte's comments in her letter to W. S. Williams over the next two years suggests that she feared Emily and puzzled over her sanity. Anne did not fear Emily, and she disliked her philosophy. She was determined to say so, in print. Hence while Charlotte and Emily remained satisfied with their poetic output in the 1846 collection, Anne sought the public ear again, in 'The Three Guides'.

It was Muriel Spark who first noticed that the character of 'Spirit of Pride' in the poem is very similar to that of Heathcliff (and thus also Julius, Emily's Gondal companion). His eyes 'like lightning shine' (they might be called basilisk eyes). But their blaze is 'false' and 'destructive'. Such spirits have climbed mountains and stood silhouetted at the top. They have bounded, 'fearless, wild and free' over the hills. But at evening, they are forced to ruin: they cannot find the track again, since the Spirit of Pride has led them astray and abandoned them. As well as *Wuthering Heights* Anne may be thinking of 'The Prisoner', and of Emily's wild behaviour on the moors when she led Charlotte into physical dangers.

What emerges is what Anne *thought* her sister was trying to say in her work. These criticisms began before the novel was published, in the summer and autumn when Anne had time to spare while she waited to see her own *Agnes Grey* in print: it would share three volumes with Emily's extraordinary and explosive book. Meanwhile in the parsonage, Branwell showed in his life the results of trusting to Pride. Anne knew too that Emily was not being made happy by her beliefs. She had surely read 'The Philosopher's Conclusion' in which

Emily suggested the torment of being divided into three incompatible parts: her 'Three Guides' is an answer to this poem.

As we saw, in late 1846 there was an attempt to renew Gondal. At this time there was a considerable number of Gondal papers in existence. They included the poems we have considered, most of which were gradually copied into the B manuscript, and Anne's poems, which were copied into her corresponding copy books. In addition, there were presumably the voluminous prose works of which we have heard in the diary papers. Not one of these prose works has ever been found. We need to consider their state in the critical days of 1847, when Anne and Emily were absorbed in writing for the external public. What happened to these Gondal prose works?

It is possible that Charlotte destroyed them after the deaths of her sisters, and that in 1847 they languished in their tin box. But Charlotte did not destroy her own or Branwell's bulky sagas. Nor did she destroy Emily's poems, neither the copy books nor the tiny fragments Emily had kept. She kept all Anne's poems, even a small fragment about a prisoner, which had a list of Gondal names on it. That Gondal poems could be turned into poetry fit for adults had been proved by the 1846 edition, but perhaps the same was true of some Gondal prose, if we have been right in suggesting how Heathcliff emerged from the Emperor Julius.

One clue may be deduced from the fate of the birthday notes. These were all kept by Charlotte. The 1845 notes both suggest 1848 as the opening date; it seems the sisters had agreed to change their previous four-year span to three. A new note, or pair of notes, was due in July 1848. No such note seems to have been written, or it would presumably have been kept with the others. This suggests that the decision to destroy Gondal may have been taken during 1847 or the early part of 1848. The 'tin box' may have been emptied into a bonfire, or possibly thrown down the parsonage well.[4] A great change had evidently come over the relations between the sisters, perhaps partly feared in 1845 when Anne wrote, '. . . shall we be much changed ourselves? [by 1848] I hope not, for the worst at least. I for my part cannot well be *flatter* or older in mind than I am now.'[5]

It was not only Gondal poetry and prose which ceased. Emily's last known non-Gondal poem was written in January

1846, and here the A manuscript breaks off. It is possible that the undated 'Often rebuked', the only poem of Emily's which does not exist in manuscript, was written later. It is a difficult piece to draw conclusions from, since Charlotte almost certainly made changes to it before publication in 1850. It does, in a way, renounce Gondal.

> *To-day, I will seek not the shadowy region;*
> *Its unsustaining vastness waxes drear;*
> *And visions rising, legion after legion,*
> *Bring the unreal world too strangely near.*[6]

This, of course, was half of Anne's objection. The shadowy world *was* too near for comfort: it acted like a drug.

Emily continues: 'I'll walk where my own nature would be leading:/ It vexes me to choose another guide.' The three spirits in Anne's poem of August 1847 are called 'guides'. Here Emily appears to be rejecting all of them. We might guess (but it is pure guesswork) that Emily wrote this in answer to Anne's poem, in late summer 1847. In the end, with Gondal abandoned, she falls back on Nature as the only safe inspiration: 'The earth that wakes *one* human heart to feeling/ Can centre both the world of Heaven and Hell.' We note that there is no hint here of any spiritual comforter, human or supernatural. Imagination is, if anything, distrusted; the feeling is much different from the poems of 1845.

The chronology of the other late poem, the work begun as a Gondal poem in September 1846, is impossible to discover. The manuscript contains few alterations for the first 150 lines, not many more than in any poem copied up into the B manuscript. There are some, of course, even in the first four lines. It looks as if Emily wrote the first 149 lines in late 1846, copied them up into the B manuscript, and then abandoned the poem, presumably to carry out whatever processes on the novel were necessary (re-writing, we have supposed). Perhaps she took up the poem again late in 1847, with the novel sent to the printers, and Anne's 'The Three Guides' completed. This time she composed straight into the copy book, not on a separate sheet. Lines 150–265 are thus an unedited jumble, ending abruptly. A further attempt was to be made in May 1848.

The poem is therefore one of the few documents – the only

first-hand document – to tell us about Emily's mind in the period 1847–8. Jonathan Wordsworth and Mary Visick are among the commentators who have written about the poem.[7] The latter writes, 'if she were successfully reaching out towards a new novel, she would have left *Wuthering Heights* behind her: but this is just what she was not doing.' For the themes of the poem considerably overlap the newly finished or revised novel. For example, there is the 'pampered' versus 'hard-living' theme, in this case translated to a world in which the equivalent of Thrushcross Grange has become a military hospital. The dead royalist possesses a locket in which there are two strands of hair, one black, one brown: two women for one man, instead of two men for one woman.

The scene in Emily's mind during the writing of this poem mirrors the actual scene in 1846 to some extent. The weather is unduly hot, with a fierce sun beating down upon the revolutionaries. September 1846 was an unusually sunny month. We recall the visit of Uncle James, who may have been asked to retell what he knew of the 1798 rebellion. As on other occasions in Gondal, the revolutionaries are dealt with sympathetically. If Patrick Brontë was now a Tory, his daughter was not. She seems to have gained a new image of the enthusiasm of a rebel, almost political in its stamp. Though she may have gained some such ideas from Shelley and Byron, the conviction in the present poem suggests closer acquaintance with the sectarian rebel. The poem goes well beyond Emily's previously expressed personal rebelliousness, and makes the cause almost one of class warfare.

Jonathan Wordsworth emphasizes the poem's bitterness.[8] This begins soon after the start. In lines 1–3 we are tricked into believing this is a low-key poem, but at the end of the first stanza there is a shock. The 'clime' and 'date' of the poem are when 'Men knelt to God and worshipped crime/ And crushed the helpless, even as we.' This is not the writing of a proud, relentless person, such as Anne may have considered to be under the spell of the 'Spirit of Pride'; or if Emily is under that spell, she knows it. The adventurer who narrates the poem, apparently a mercenary in the Gondal army, is delighted when the west wind blows, but only because it gives him the strength to rob the dying captive. Emily thus uses '*that* wind', her inspirer, to motivate a diabolical crime.

After the point where Emily begins to compose straight on

to the page (we have supposed this to be in late 1847) her mercenary first broods on his haunting conscience. It tells him how many times he has spoken words of 'gall' to (as she originally wrote) 'helpless things'. Emily's conscience was tender, but that did not prevent her from uttering scornful words: she used them, and then repented too late. The mercenary turns to prayer, and wonders whether God will repay his wrong actions. The next stanza is crossed through. In it, Emily was exploring the cruelty of her mercenary, who has taken on some of the characteristics of the 'cruel boy' who appeared earlier in her poems. He says (writing later) that he was adamantine stone, and that God would repay the 'deeds that turn his earth to hell'.

So we have one more reworking of the 'guilt repented too late' theme, in which the sinner is a man too hard-hearted to be moved by any prayer. We have seen examples of this in Emily, among them the broken fruit tree and the beating of Keeper, in which she seems to have bitterly regretted her violent and destructive actions, but too late. One can only speculate on whether Emily saw her 'unconscious tyranny' appearing in many other incidents, and was more conscious than M. Heger thought. In the present poem, the mercenary allows his prisoner to die while he slips away to drink from a nearby fountain – but it is dyed with the red of human blood. A child is near the fountain. She is 'helpless' and begs to see her father's face before he dies. The mercenary spurns 'the piteous wretch away', and lies to her that he is already dead.

When he returns to his prisoner, he finds him in terrible pain and ask him 'why he would not die'. At this point a messenger, like one in Greek tragedy, arrives and tells that the enemy has captured the mercenary's own son, and will kill him. There is nothing for it but to beg the dying captive to intercede. The captive is grudging:

I lost last night my only child;
Twice in my arms, twice on my knee
You stabbed my child and laughed at me
And so, with choking voice, he said,
I pray to heaven – I trust she's dead.

We know that she is not; she has already washed her wounds in the blood-red fountain and asked to be allowed to see her dying father. However, as a supreme and final gift, the captive sends word that the mercenary's child shall not be hurt. Thereupon he dies and cannot be rewarded for his generosity. Death has robbed the speaker of all chance of balancing the books: he can never match the loving impulse. We may again be inclined to refer the source of this feeling to some treachery Emily considered she might have performed against Maria or Elizabeth.

The mercenary makes an effort, however. He finds the dead man's daughter and nurtures her. But she grieves perpetually and hates him. The manuscript ends in blots and scribbles, with 'One moonless night I let her go'. And indeed Emily seemed to be in a mood for letting go at that time: letting everything go, as far as we can judge by this muddled, messy piece of tragedy. It is as though she is weary of beating perpetually at her sensitive conscience, and of the blood lust that warred with the kindness in her. Possibly it was at this point that Gondal's sagas were destroyed.

Meanwhile the published poems had made little progress. On 16 June 1847 Charlotte, writing under her pseudonym, sent out copies as gifts to a number of critics and poets of the day, including Wordsworth and Tennyson. Ellen Nussey came to stay, perhaps in July, and the four women walked on the moors. There they witnessed a strange natural phenomenon, recorded by A. M. F. Robinson.

> A sudden change and light came into the sky. 'Look', said Charlotte; and the four girls looked up and saw three suns shining clearly overhead. They stood a little while silently gazing at the beautiful parhelion; Charlotte, her friend, and Anne clustered together, Emily a little higher, standing on a heathery knoll. "That is you!" said Ellen at last. "You are the three suns." "Hush!" cried Charlotte, indignant at the too shrewd nonsense of her friend; but as Ellen, her suspicions confirmed by Charlotte's violence, lowered her eyes to the earth again, she looked a moment at Emily. She was still standing on her knoll, quiet, satisfied; and round her lips there hovered a very soft and happy smile. She was not angry, the independent Emily. She had liked the little speech.[9]

The occurrence of the 'parhelions' at Haworth was well attested through history.[10] But what can Ellen have meant by likening the three sisters to three suns?

A. M. F. Robinson seems to imply that Ellen had guessed somehow that the Brontës were authors. At this time, they only had their poems in print, and (as we have seen) these were being disposed of as free gifts. Perhaps Ellen had seen a letter from Newby or Smith, Elder, addressed to members of the Bell family. On the other hand, perhaps she was not suggesting anything about authorship, but merely likening the three suns, with their similarities, to the three girls with theirs. Emily is standing at some distance from the rest: the 'independent' Emily, she is called. On the other hand, she has come for a walk with them all for old time's sake, and is blest by this visitation from Nature. 'She was not angry', says A. M. F. Robinson. Why should she be? Nevertheless, it looks as though anger was a response to be expected from Emily, which the others feared.

However it came about, the two younger Brontës were now committed to publish with Thomas Cautley Newby of Mortimer Street, Cavendish Square, London.[11] Such evidence as we have of the terms on which the works were to be published comes from Charlotte's correspondence with W. S. Williams and with George Smith, both of Smith, Elder.[12] She said that Newby required them to pay a £50 deposit to be refunded on the sale of a sufficient number of copies. If 250 copies were sold, this would leave £100 to be divided between them. The money appears not to have been paid. Some proof sheets had been sent back to Newby by August, but he seemed in no hurry to proceed.[13] Meanwhile Emily's 'taciturnity' was not improving. On 25 September 1847 Charlotte wrote to Ellen, from whose house she had just returned. Ellen had sent Emily some apples as a present.

> Emily is just now sitting on the floor of the bedroom where I am writing, looking at her apples. She smiled when I gave them and the collar to her as your presents, with an expression at once well pleased and slightly surprised.[14]

We can only interpret the expression subjectively. It may mean, 'How strange that I haven't alienated her yet!'

However, we note that Emily says nothing, as usual.

The precise publication date of *Agnes Grey* and *Wuthering Heights* is uncertain, but on 14 December Charlotte could write that Newby had sent the authors their six copies. He had doubtless been speeded to the post office by the runaway success of *Jane Eyre* after two months on sale. The *Critic* of 4 December 1847 listed *Wuthering Heights* under 'books received'; that paper's review of the poems had been encouraging.[15] We cannot know how Emily reacted to the reviews of her book, but they could not have discouraged her. Five reviews were found in Emily's writing desk. They were those in the *Examiner* (January 1848), *Britannia* (15 January 1848), *Douglas Jerrold's Weekly Newspaper* (15 January 1848), *Atlas* (22 January 1848), and an unidentified review first transcribed by Charles Simpson.[16] We shall summarize the main points of these. Unfortunately we can do no more than imagine Emily's thoughts as she read them.

The *Examiner* wrote that the book had 'considerable power'. Heathcliff was 'an incarnation of evil qualities; implacable hate, ingratitude, cruelty, falsehood, selfishness and revenge'. He has nursed up wrath until 'it becomes mature and terrible'. Some of the incidents 'look like real events', but (and here he puts his finger on a telling point) 'The hardness, selfishness, and cruelty of Heathcliff are in our opinion inconsistent with the romantic love that he is stated to have felt for Catherine Earnshaw.' The review praised Ellis Bell for going 'at once fearlessly into the moors and desolate places for his heroes', but begged that not all the coarseness found there should be incorporated in the novel.[17]

Britannia called the work 'strangely original'. The reviewer compared it to German stories in which supernatural influences are exerted on individuals. Mr Bell 'displays a considerable power in his creations. They all have the angularity of misshapen growth. . . . They are so new, so wildly grotesque, so entirely without art, that they strike us as proceeding from a mind of limited experience, but of original energy.' The main idea of the work is a 'passionate ferocity', and the narrative leaves an unpleasant effect on the mind. The story has the 'force of a dark and sullen torrent, flowing between high and rugged rocks'. There is much to blame in the story: the scenes of brutality are unnecessarily long and frequent, but the passion is well portrayed. 'The anguish of Heathcliff on the death of Catherine approaches to sublimity.' The reviewer interestingly notes a point that Anne seems to have noted in her 'critique' in *Wildfell Hall*: that character is often spoilt in childhood, and that Heathcliff is a supreme example.

Douglas Jerrold's reviewer compared *Wuthering Heights* with *Jane Eyre*. Emily's work was not 'equal in merit' to it, but it did have (in company with *Agnes Grey*) 'somewhat of the fresh, original and unconventional spirit'. The style was 'simple, energetic and apparently disdainful of prettiness and verbal display'. There can be no doubt of the powerful effect made by the new novel. The writer 'wants but the practised skill to make a great artist'; the reviewer strongly recommends the readers to get the story, 'for we promise they have never read anything like it before'.

> In *Wuthering Heights* the reader is shocked, disgusted, almost sickened by details of cruelty, inhumanity, and the most diabolical hate and vengeance, and anon come passages of powerful testimony to the supreme power of love – even over demons in the human form.

It is hardly surprising that Emily kept the cutting containing this review until she died.

The *Atlas* noted 'a sort of rugged power', which was not turned properly to account by the author. The book contained, in the reviewer's opinion, 'shocking pictures of the worst form of inhumanity'. Heathcliff 'sheds a grim shadow over the whole', but despite the inconceivable degradation of the characters, reality is 'admirably preserved'. 'The reality of unreality has never been so aptly illustrated as in the scenes of almost savage life which Ellis Bell has brought so vividly before us.' Nevertheless, there was little to be said for either male or female characters. The females are beautiful and 'loveable in their childhood' but turn out badly. To sum up, 'The work of . . . Ellis Bell is only a promise, but it is a colossal one.'

The unidentified review considers that *Wuthering Heights* is a work of great ability, the result of a talent 'of no common order'.

> It is not every day that so good a novel makes its appearance; and to give its contents in detail would be

depriving many a reader of half the delight he would experience from the perusal of the work itself. To its pages we must refer him, then; there he will have ample opportunity of sympathizing, – if he has one touch of nature that 'makes the whole world kin' – with the feelings of childhood, youth, manhood, and age, and all the emotions and passions which agitate the restless bosom of humanity. May he derive from it the delight we ourselves have experienced, and be equally grateful to its author for the genuine pleasure he has afforded him.

The reviewers all found faults in *Wuthering Heights*, with the exception of the last quoted. They reacted in a very similar way to Charlotte, if we are to go by her defence in the 1850 edition, and her attempts to tone it down. But all wrote encouragingly. Some saw freshness and truth in the novel, others noted the emphasis on love as redeemer. The last review quoted has understood Emily's identification with nature, and has been delighted by the work. A new author could not reasonably demand more. The impression has sometimes been given that just as the poems failed to find readers, the novel also failed. These reviews show that this was not the case, and that Emily could take heart from what was written about her book. These reviews, reaching her in January and February 1848, would surely encourage her to write more. Yet we have only the twenty-five revised lines of 'Why ask to know the date?' written in May.

The question therefore arises, whether she was beginning a second novel. To discover a possible answer, we must return to the writing desk. We shall be basing our examination on the description given by Simpson nearly sixty years ago, when the process of change and decay in the contents of the desk had had less time to operate. Two items found in the desk are crucial. They are a letter beginning 'Dear Sir' and signed by Thomas Newby, and an envelope with the name 'Ellis Bell, Esq.' on it, into which the letter fitted; however, it was not in the envelope when found, at least in Simpson's day. Newby, apparently writing on 15 February 1848, expresses himself pleased to be making arrangements for Ellis's next novel.

I would not hurry its completion for I think you are quite right not to let it go before the world until well satisfied with it, for much depends on your next work, it if be an improvement on your first you will have established yourself as a first-rate novelist, but if it fall short the critics will be too apt to say you have expended your talent in your first novel.

Provided the letter was really in the envelope addressed to Ellis Bell, and Newby could tell the two sisters apart, this seems conclusive evidence. But Newby had spent some time trying to confuse the Bells in the minds of his customers during the previous few weeks, and we may wonder whether he had confused himself.[18] Perhaps he really thought they were one person, and so was actually writing to Anne about *Wildfell Hall*. It may be argued that the time-scale would allow of this, since *Wildfell Hall* was first published in June 1848, some copies being held back and appearing with Anne's preface, dated 22 July, as a 'second edition' in August. If this were so, it would suggest that Anne had not yet finished her novel by February 1848. Against this we have the *prima facie* evidence of the closing date, 'Staningley, June 10th, 1847'. Perhaps it might be allowed too that if *Wildfell Hall* was not complete by February 1848, Anne would have had to work very fast, and Newby exceed his general speed, to have the book in print by June. We cannot rule out this unlikely possibility.

Several points tend towards the view that *Wildfell Hall* (which, after all, was probably started at the same time as *Jane Eyre*) is more likely to have been finished by late summer 1847. Among these are the tentative chronology at the start of this chapter, in which I suggest that *Wildfell Hall* is to some extent an answer to *Wuthering Heights*, and that the answer is continued in 'The Three Guides', possibly answered in turn by Emily's 'It vexes me to choose another guide'; Ellen Nussey's visit, probably in July; the earliest mention of proof sheets in August. If this is so, the letter is more likely to have been written to Ellis than Acton.

Further, there is a point which may be crucial. The letter almost certainly does belong in the envelope. Simpson says that it had been 'folded to a small size which exactly fits the envelope'.[19] However, there is no address on the envelope, only the name. It therefore follows that it was enclosed in another, larger envelope, which would have to have the direction to 'The Parsonage, Haworth' on it. There would be no point in putting in a second envelope if the outside envelope was addressed to Ellis Bell. It seems then that the main package must have been addressed to Acton. In it, as well as the envelope to be passed on to Ellis, there must have been some communication intended for Anne, possibly the acceptance of *Wildfell Hall*. It seems, then, that Newby did understand that there were two Bells and sent his letter to Ellis under cover addressed to Acton.[20]

If I have argued correctly here, it must seem probable that Emily was planning another novel and had told her publisher so, possibly through Anne. It looks as if she may have been heartened by the reviews and willing to begin again the major process of constructing a novel. February, March and April may well have passed during this process, but perhaps the return to poetry, a regression to Gondal, signals Emily's difficulty in exploring new themes. In the absence of first-hand accounts, we shall need to turn to Anne for evidence of the atmosphere during this period.

It has been impossible here to deal in detail with *Wildfell Hall* as a critique of *Wuthering Heights*. As we saw, the cumulative evidence of 'The Three Guides' taken with the novel and 'Self-communion', inclines us to consider that it has elements of parody which I have explored in some detail elsewhere.[21] But we do need to look at 'Self-communion', which was being completed at the time of the Newby letter and is rounded off by April. Some lines from the poem have already been quoted. Anne complains of the death of love in her heart. In part, she may be referring to the debacle over Weightman, but she is also surely mourning the loss of intimacy between herself and Emily. Even in childhood, she says, 'My fondness was but half returned.'

And as my love the warmer glowed
The deeper would that anguish sink,
That this dark stream between us flowed,
Though both stood bending o'er its brink.
Until, at last, I learned to bear
A colder heart within my breast;
To share such thoughts as I could share,
And calmly keep the rest.
I saw that they were sundered now,

The trees that at the root were one:
They yet might mingle leaf and bough,
But still the stems must stand alone.[22]

The close communion of the 'twins', observed by Ellen Nussey when the two girls were young teenagers, does *not* recur in the 'parhelions' picture which has been noted. Emily now stands alone, surprised when a family friend sends her some apples and a collar. Had Anne's poem been written during a period of rapprochement between Emily and herself, the passages dealing with their friendship would surely have been more optimistic.

The last communication we have from Emily's own hand comes in the rewritten beginning of 'Why ask to know the date?', composed on 13 May 1848. After eighteen months she returns to the beginning of the poem once more, though we saw that she probably wrote over a hundred lines towards the end of 1847. It was now to have a new first line: 'Oh, idle words, what date, what clime', or so we may guess from the manuscript as it stands.[23] The first four lines of the original are expanded to ten, in which the theme of the deceit and injustice of the fictional citizens is dwelt on. More detail is introduced: these are 'Foot-kissers' who deride righteous misery; they shed blood and tears; they are 'Self-cursers, greedy of distress', who mock heaven with 'avid' (later 'senseless') prayers. The mercenary tells us a little about himself: he is fighting 'neither for my home nor God', but at that point Emily's patience expires, the booklet is hastily shut and a blot spreads from side to side, making the last few lines almost impossible to read.

This last piece of work by Emily reveals her in gloomy, almost paranoid mood, and there can be no doubt that at the end she is overcome by wild impatience. Yet there is nothing the matter with the work itself: some lines seem to be an improvement on the earlier version, while none appear to be worse. However, they are not new, either in detail or in concept. Emily has returned once again to one of her eternal themes: the corruption of human nature in betraying and stifling the weak for material gain. If she was writing a second novel, we can see it may have cost her great effort and self-torment and is likely to have progressed slowly. Perhaps it simply would not progress: it may have refused to be written in a way that most authors have encountered. If so, Emily, trying hard to live up to the encouraging words of the critics and worried by Newby's warning, may simply have given up as she does with this poem, and flatly denied her spirit and emotions a way out on to paper.

The stage is now set for one of the oddest developments in the whole Brontë story: the persistent and wilful walk towards death of the once exuberant Emily Jane.

16

Living According to Nature: The Last Stage

Something corrosive had laid hold of Emily's being, and it seems most likely that is she had not died of consumption, she would have died mentally deranged.

– Muriel Spark, *Emily Brontë, her Life and Work*

Picking up a word used in one of her poems, Virginia Moore wrote in the 1930s of Emily's 'eager' death. We shall find that this is an exaggeration. But if Emily's death was not eager, it was at least wilful. This is, in fact, the adjective used by Martha Brown's sister, Tabitha (Mrs Ratcliffe), in an interview with *The Cornhill* for July 1910: she was 'that wilful like she would wait on herself'.[1] Martha said, 'Miss Emily died of a broken heart for love of her brother.' This seems to have been the only cause ever propounded for her rapid decline by those who knew her; all other authorities remain baffled. However, there are problems about accepting Martha's comment at its face value.

Branwell had been in poor physical health for years. Daphne du Maurier suggests that he may have suffered from epilepsy.[2] Certainly he was frequently in a state of collapse following his dismissal from Thorp Green in 1845, and turned as often as he could to alcohol. Undoubtedly he influenced *Wildfell Hall*, and many authorities consider the drunken behaviour of Hindley in *Wuthering Heights* to be partly based on him. It is a matter of dispute whether he knew much about the writing projects of his three sisters. It seems hard to believe that he knew nothing, though Charlotte, at any rate, had practically disowned him.

Unfortunately a mare's nest of rumour has grown up

concerning Emily's thoughts on Branwell, none of which appears to have any contemporary basis beyond the sentence quoted from Martha Brown above. The development of the legend appears to have been roughly as follows. It was doubted, in the early days, whether 'Ellis Bell' was a man or a woman. When it was discovered that the author was female, there was speculation on how she came to write such an 'unfeminine' book, apparently glorifying a repulsive and violent man, who dies after torment. Hints in Charlotte's preface were interpreted to mean that Emily's and Anne's heroes, Heathcliff and Arthur Huntington, were based on Branwell. Hence it was supposed that the wildness of *Wuthering Heights* could be accounted for by a passionate and protective love felt by its author for her depraved brother. Miss A. M. F. Robinson accentuated Branwell's wildness, calling forth a reply from Leyland, brother of his friend.[3]

Emily once put out a fire which threatened to kill her brother. This happened late at night, a time when Emily's mind was active.[4] In 'How long will you remain?' and 'Stars' we have seen two poems which clearly assert her habit of wakefulness at night. Branwell is known to have visited the Black Bull late in the evening. If only Emily was awake when he returned, clearly she was the one to let him into the house. When Uncle James was over from Ballynaskeagh, he helped Branwell back from the pub; when he was not there, it is reasonable to suppose that Emily would be called upon to help her brother. She was taller and stronger than he was. Charlotte later said that Emily was 'full of ruth for others' and contrasted this attitude with her severity towards herself.[5] One of the 'others' was surely Branwell; differing sisterly attitudes to him may well have been one of the factors in the dissension pointed out by Anne in 1846.

But this does not mean that communion between Emily and Branwell was close. It is not likely that when he was rescued from the Black Bull in a drunken stupor, deep philosophical conversations could be held between them. Her only recorded comment was that he was a 'hopeless being'.[6] Daphne du Maurier contrasts the behaviour of the sisters in 1846, when Charlotte took her father to Manchester for his eye operation, which turned out so successfully, with their attitude now, when Branwell was dying in front of their eyes of alcohol poisoning on top of consumption.[7] They did nothing. The local Haworth doctor, Dr Wheelhouse, was indeed consulted, but his recommendation, that Branwell should stop drinking, was insufficient direction. 'The rapid loss of weight, the continuing cough, the appalling insomnia, were left to take their course.' She guesses, I think shrewdly, that Charlotte's view prevailed. 'If Branwell was ill, he was ill through his own fault. There was no remedy.'

Throughout his life, Mr Brontë cared for his own health assiduously. He had great faith in the restorative powers of all kinds of medicine; his frequent annotations in his copy of Graham's *Modern Domestic Medicine* are well known.[8] He used this book to make notes on his children's illnesses, and possible remedies, as well as his own. It is fair to call him a valetudinarian, and the early deaths of Maria and Elizabeth, as well as that of his wife, gave him very good cause. But the children themselves seem to have reacted against this. Branwell, at any rate, took no care of himself, and we shall soon find Emily wilfully ignoring medical science.

If Emily cared for Branwell, then, this care amounted to retrieving him from the Black Bull, and seeing he got to bed. It did not extend to taking medical steps to help him, nor overruling Charlotte's indifference on his behalf. In his rambling letters to various friends, he never mentions the sustaining power of his second sister, and he does not seem capable by 1848 of carrying on any kind of reasoned conversation or exchange of views. He was an object of pity, the mental and physical causes of his illness unrecognized. Emily's poems seem to suggest she found it hard to exhibit pity in due time; we have suspected that guilt over the death of her two sisters in 1825 may have remained with her. She had not acted in time to help: now she was about to suffer the pangs for the third time. Emily did not die 'for love' of Branwell, but a factor in her death may have been guilt over his.

Branwell died on 24 September 1848. His funeral was held on Thursday 28 September, and was attended by all the family, Emily among them.[9] This was the last time, according to tradition, that she ever left the parsonage.

We have already seen evidence of Emily's attempts at literary activity during the first few months of 1848, and her mental turbulence. It is possible that the seeds of her physical decline could have been activated as early as January, when Anne wrote to Ellen Nussey,

> We are all cut up by this cruel east wind, most of us, i.e. Charlotte, Emily and I have had the influenza, or a bad cold instead, twice over within the space of a few weeks.[10]

As a number of authorities have pointed out, the onset of tuberculosis is not easy to spot, and Emily may have contracted it at this point.

In February, Emily may have written to Newby. In May she worked briefly at the frustrating revolutionary poem. On 7 July a letter reached Charlotte which caused her panic. Smith, Elder had heard that Newby had approached the American firm of Harper's with *Wildfell Hall*, offering it as a new work by the author of *Jane Eyre*. George Smith wrote to Haworth to say that they would be glad to be in a position to contradict Newby.[11] Charlotte and Anne decided to make a speedy dash to London in person to assure Smith, Elder that Newby was quite wrong. Notoriously, Emily did not go. She must surely have been asked, and dissociated herself politely or impolitely. Charlotte and Anne hurried south and met their publishers for the first time, though there are no details of Anne's confrontation with Newby.[12]

Emily was fulfilling a prophecy made by Charlotte in a letter to W. S. Williams of 15 February.[13] He had, in a previous letter, 'raised the veil from a corner of your great world – your London – and shown me a glimpse of what I might call loathsome, but which I prefer calling *strange*'. Charlotte, at that moment, wished to take a 'quiet view' of the world, though at some future time she might give herself the treat of visiting.

> Ellis, I imagine, would soon turn aside from the spectacle in disgust. I do not think he admits it as his creed that "the proper study of mankind is man" – at least not the artificial man of cities. In some points I consider Ellis somewhat of a theorist: now and then he broaches ideas which strike my sense as much more daring and original than practical; his reason may be in advance of mine, but certainly it often travels a different road. I should say Ellis will not be seen in his full strength till he is seen as an essayist.

This remarkable judgement shows how far Charlotte was from understanding the main merits of *Wuthering Heights*, and the passage also shows how far Emily had drifted from Charlotte as well as from Anne. It would be interesting to know what Ellis's 'daring and original ideas' were. In view of the 'Oh idle words' fragment, they seem likely to have been politically radical or even revolutionary. Emily's refusal to go to London with her sisters probably caused them no surprise.

Then came Branwell's death and Emily's alleged final walk from the parsonage door. The progress of her disease is well documented, but we should beware of how we interpret Charlotte's letters to W. S. Williams, Ellen Nussey and others that autumn. As we see from the preceding letter, Charlotte was already very puzzled about her sister's attitude to life. Though ultimately Emily did die, Charlotte could not have known that these letters would be studied closely by posterity in order to find a clue to Emily's mental attitude in the year of her death.

Charlotte generalizes a good deal in the letters, but she does not once suggest that the picture she is giving of Emily's character portrays a new Emily, suddenly overcome by the tragedy of Branwell's death. Emily's decline seems to have been part of a pattern, her submission to her own death not uncharacteristic. The detailed letters of Charlotte at this period throw light on Emily's adult character at all periods. (We may recall her white withdrawal from Roe Head, her 'unconscious tyranny' in Belgium.) It will be necessary to quote some of these letters in detail.

Emily was in a state of high dudgeon before Branwell's death. Charlotte had told Mr Williams, and Mr Smith, in London, that the Bells were 'three sisters'. On 31 July she was forced by Emily to write a disclaimer.

> I committed a grand error in betraying his [Ellis's] identity to you and Mr Smith. It was inadvertent – the words 'we are three sisters' escaped me before I was aware. I regretted the avowal the moment I had made it; I regret it bitterly now, for I find it is against every feeling and intention of Ellis Bell.[14]

Here, certainly, is uncompromising, unconscious tyranny. Charlotte must grovel before her publishers, and she does so.

On 29 October, Charlotte wrote to Ellen. By this time she was beginning to worry about Emily.

> I feel much more uneasy about my sisters than myself just now. Emily's cold and cough are very obstinate. I fear she has pain in the chest and I sometimes catch a shortness in her breathing, when she has moved at all quickly. She looks very, very thin and pale. Her reserved nature occasions me great uneasiness of mind. It is useless to question her – you get no answers. It is still more useless to recommend remedies – they are never adopted.[15]

Within a month, Emily has declined to the state of being 'very, very thin'. As for Emily's 'reserved' nature, this has many times been remarked on. The frequent monosyllabic or non-verbal response is something we are used to; we have seen her laconic on the subject of a person's religion, and non-verbal over apples and parhelions. This is the same Emily steering obstinately into troubled waters as clearly as did the romantic Shelley, or her own infatuated brother.

Charlotte addressed W. S. Williams on 2 November. Emily had, she said,

> something like a slow inflammation of the lungs. . . . I would fain hope that Emily is a little better this evening, but it is difficult to ascertain this. She is a real stoic in illness: she neither seeks nor will accept sympathy. To put any questions, to offer any aid, is to annoy: she will not yield a step before pain or sickness till forced; not one of her ordinary avocations will she voluntarily renounce. You must look on her and see her do what she is unfit to do, and dare not say a word – a painful necessity for those to whom her health and existence are as precious as the life in their veins. When she is ill there seems to be no sunshine in the world for me. The tie of sister is near and dear indeed, and I think a certain harshness in her powerful and peculiar character only makes me cling to her more. But this is all family egotism (so to speak) – excuse it, and, above all, never allude to it, or to the name Emily, when you write to me. I do not always show your letters but I do not withhold them when they are enquired after.[16]

Emily's behaviour is torturing Charlotte, just as Heathcliff tortures weaker 'helpless' creatures, and Emily knows this, of course. To Anne, this must have seemed one more example of the Spirit of Pride, and indeed we see her own answer to the problem of approaching death the next year, when she eagerly grasps at every positive straw. But as we have seen many times in Emily's verse, the iron, inflexible man is incapable of yielding until it is too late. Heathcliff tortures Isabella, Linton and the young Catherine; the grim jailer tortures the sweet captive; Eemala roars like a 'bellaring bull'; and, in all cases, not because they wish to but because it is their nature. Even in the final ballad the mercenary grasps at the dying man's jewels, and is incapable of relenting until it is too late. Emily knew her power, but felt herself incapable of restraining it.

Harshness, Charlotte calls it. This harshness had caused the rift between the two sisters at the end of their childhood and Emily had taken to Anne, who could sometimes guide her, not through a clash of wills, but by a softer influence shared through Gondal. Charlotte saw this as a failure on her part. She wished to be influential with Emily, to move her away from her 'impractical' and unconventional ideas, for Charlotte was in the ultimate a Christian, and could not accept the nihilistic side of Emily. It is too late for her to try charming compliance on her sister; nevertheless she shows Emily letters addressed to her by W. S. Williams, despite Emily's attempted choice of opting out of any contact with him.

In due course, this letter provoked a reply from Mr Williams too. He suggested Emily might like to try homoeopathic medicine. On 22 November Charlotte tells him what became of his kind suggestion.

> I put your most friendly letter into Emily's hands as soon as I had myself perused it, taking care, however, not to say a word in favour of homoeopathy – that would not have answered. It is best usually to leave her to form her own judgement, and *especially* not to advocate the side you wish her to favour; if you do, she is sure to lean in the opposite direction, and ten to one will argue herself into non-compliance. Hitherto she has refused medicine, rejected medical advice; no reasoning, no entreaty, has availed to induce her to see a physician. After reading your letter she said, 'Mr Williams's intention was kind

> and good, but he was under a delusion: Homoeopathy was only another form of quackery.' Yet she may reconsider this opinion and come to a different conclusion; her second thoughts are often the best.[17]

There are further references to Emily in this letter, but we need to comment on this part first.

We note Charlotte's tactics: do not try to persuade Emily of anything, or she will take the opposite line. Here the author of *Wuthering Heights* seems like a sulky fourteen-year-old, who is this time playing with fire. The implication is that Emily does not consider a question rationally, but takes delight in adopting views opposite to those of her friends, purely out of malice. I cannot see how such an implication can be escaped. In this particular instance, Emily does offer a justification for her rejection of the friend's proposal: medicine is quackery, and this is only another form of it. We have seen Mr Brontë's lifelong devotion to self-cures, which seemed to work. On the other hand, we recall Emily's first encounters with doctors, those who tried to cure her mother. Part of a doctor's skill perhaps lies in persuading his patient that things are improving; to which end he smiles and beams, falsely, as Emily might see it. And Mrs Brontë was not healed.

And, if she did have any care for Branwell, she might well contrast Charlotte's behaviour now with what had happened earlier that year. Branwell had only seen Dr Wheelhouse, who was ineffective. Why should she, guilty Emily, have any more expert treatment – especially as there was every likelihood that a false smile covered everthing? It is interesting, nonetheless, to have Emily's words reported in November 1848 and see that she is calm and polite.

In the letter sent by Mr Williams was a cutting from the *North American Review*. This Charlotte read aloud to Emily and Anne; it was ferocious and damning. Charlotte says she thought it might 'amuse' Emily.

> As I sat between them at our quiet but now somewhat melancholy fireside, I studied the two ferocious authors. Ellis, the "man of uncommon talents, but dogged, brutal and morose" sat leaning back in his easy chair drawing his impeded breath as best he could, and looking alas!

> piteously pale and wasted; it is not his wont to laugh, but he smiled, half-amused and half in scorn as he listened.[18]

'Riches I hold in light esteem, and love I laugh to scorn', Ellis had written. He also laughed to scorn, it seems, bad reviews and good medical help; or at least he smiled them to scorn.

Mr Williams continued his efforts to help Emily towards a cure. He sent a book by Dr Curie on homoeopathy, which Emily read.[19] However, she still refused to give the proposed cure a trial. Mr Brontë was at this point 'very despondent'; he had had a long acquaintance with such symptoms. Charlotte, however, refused to be daunted by the fate of Maria and Elizabeth, and continued to hope. She goes on (in her reply of 7 December):

> Much would I give to have the opinion of a skilful professional man. It is easy, my dear sir, to say there is nothing in medicine, and that physicians are useless, but we naturally wish to procure aid for those we love when we see them suffer; most painful is it to sit still, look on, and do nothing. Would that my sister added to her many great qualities the humble one of tractability! I have again and again incurred her displeasure by urging the necessity of seeking advice, and I fear I must yet incur it again and again.[20]

There follows a discussion of the iniquities of Thomas Newby, during which it is said that Anne will not have him for a publisher again; she has 'had quite enough of him'. Meanwhile, 'Ellis Bell is at present in no condition to trouble himself with thoughts of writing or publishing.' Even now, however, it is clear that Emily would not say directly that she would reject Newby: she 'reserves the right' to decide.

Mr Williams wrote back in haste to give Charlotte the address of a Dr Epps, who would give advice by post, provided the details of the character and symptoms of the patient were forwarded to him. By good fortune, we have Charlotte's account of her sister, written dispassionately to a medical man. Naturally, the letter gives details of the disease, but in addition, Charlotte tells him about Emily as a person.

> A peculiar reserve of character renders it difficult to draw

> from her all the symptoms of her malady . . . her pulse – the only time she allowed it to be felt – was found to be 115 per minute. . . . Her resolution to contend against illness being very fixed, she has never consented to lie in bed for a single day - she sits up from 7 in the morning till 10 at night. All medical aid she has rejected, insisting that Nature should be left to take her own course . . . .
>
> The patient has hitherto enjoyed pretty good health, though she has never looked strong, and the family constitution is not supposed to be robust. Her temperament is highly nervous. She has been accustomed to a sedentary and studious life.[21]

In the first letter, to Mr Williams, Charlotte admits that she has frequently been scolded by Emily for attempting to suggest that she try some cure. She goes as near as she ever does to agreeing that Emily's sin is pride: her intractability is the reverse of 'humble'. In the second, we have the familiar word 'reserved' being applied. Emily is praised for her 'resolution' to contend against illness, but that is exactly what she refuses to do, unless cure can be effected by 'Nature'. All this is entirely consistent with what we have read of Emily through the years, at any rate since she became an adult. Her attitude cannot be dismissed as a fear of doctors; it is more a brittle contempt. She is exerting a subtle emotional blackmail on her sister; if Charlotte suggests any form of help, she will turn it down, yet she must see that she is ruthlessly deriding her sister's affection. But that, of course, is exactly what she has told us, through many fictional characters, the internal Heathcliff would do, holding in subjection the kinder side of his creator. It is all a re-run of the basilisk-eyed visitor who derides his kingly hosts in 'And now the housedog'.

On 9 December Charlotte wrote to Ellen that her sister was 'as dear to me as life. . . . She is too intractable. I *do* wish I knew her state and feelings more clearly.'[22] She was never to know any more about her sister's feelings, and went to her own grave knowing no more, always puzzled and deprecatory about Emily's wilful end. There was to be no 'poisoning doctor' near Emily. She continued to feed the dogs every night. Miss Robinson records that on the evening of 14 December she rose to do this and

> got up, walking slowly, holding out in her thin hands an apronful of broken meat and bread. But when she reached the flagged passage the cold took her; she staggered on the uneven pavement and fell against the wall. Her sisters, who had been sadly following her, unseen, came forwards much alarmed and begged her to desist, but, smiling wanly, she went on and gave Floss and Keeper their last supper from her hands.[23]

Martha Brown told a number of people what happened on the final day of Emily's life. She persisted in getting up and dressing, then sat by the fire in her room to comb her hair. Miss Robinson says her plenteous dark hair was 'all that was not marked by the branding finger of death'.[24] As she sat combing her hair, the comb slipped into the fire. She could not pick it out, and had to sit there while the smell of burnt bone filled the room. Apparently this alerted Martha, who came in and took the comb out of the fire. Emily is alleged to have said to the servant 'I was too weak to stoop and pick it up'; though dying, she did not address these words to her sister, but to the servant.

In the end, she did come downstairs, but as the day wore on she seemed worse. At noon she said, gasping, 'If you will send for a doctor, I will see him now!' Charlotte and Anne begged her to let them put her to bed, but she refused and according to Miss Robinson, died about two o'clock, leaning with one hand on the parlour sofa. It was 19 December 1848.

Emily Brontë's funeral took place on 22 December. Charlotte wrote to Ellen, 'She died in a time of promise. We saw her taken from life in its prime.'[25] She then spent some proportion of her own remaining years thinking over her sister's life and death. Left with a sense of guilt which was hardly deserved, Charlotte saw herself as Emily's protector and interpreter in death, just as she had seen herself as a substitute mother after the deaths of the two eldest girls. She frequently recalled her sister, and began to see her through rose-coloured spectacles.

To Ellen, Charlotte wrote, 'I cannot forget Emily's death-day; it becomes a more fixed – a darker, a more frequently recurring idea in my mind than ever: it was very terrible, she was torn conscious, panting, reluctant though resolute out of a happy life.'[26] Already a legend is being woven round Emily Brontë. Certainly her death was terrible, but it is hardly true to say Emily was torn out of a happy life. There were indeed signs of happiness and even serenity in 1845, a time when the rest of the family were in various states of upset. The good press reviews may well have led to a temporary satisfaction with the artistic state of her soul during January and February 1848, but this was a precarious peace. We have seen that the hesitant efforts to revise a poem in early summer led on to a sulky refusal to join the others in their negotiations with Newby or Smith, Elder: there are hints in the letter of 7 December that this is still a bone of contention.

Charlotte was most sincere in her expressions of love for her sister, but she was also bound by the Victorian convention of *de mortuis nil nisi bonum*, so that these letters and descriptions of late 1848 are the only evidence of the 'unconscious tyranny' being recognized. And the longer Emily was dead, the better her reputation became.

Muriel Spark and Derek Stanford have traced the way in which Emily Brontë became an inscrutable legend, the 'sphinx of modern literature'. Once this view was established it became the received wisdom that we cannot know anything about her for certain, and indeed it is almost an act of impiety to try. *Wuthering Heights* becomes a book produced by a 'mystic' genius, far removed from ordinary humanity. Certainly its author was unusual, and in many moods wished to remain concealed behind her persona. She makes no attempt to explain herself to Newby, for example; and even worse, she will not explain herself to her own sister, as she dies, proud and inviolate, as much as to emphasize that she prefers the housedog to humans, as always. Despite this, the continued and deserved popularity of *Wuthering Heights* shows her as a superb communicator, who did, after all, consider that mankind, at least in some major aspects, is a 'proper study'.

17

Emily Brontë: A Child's Savage Woe

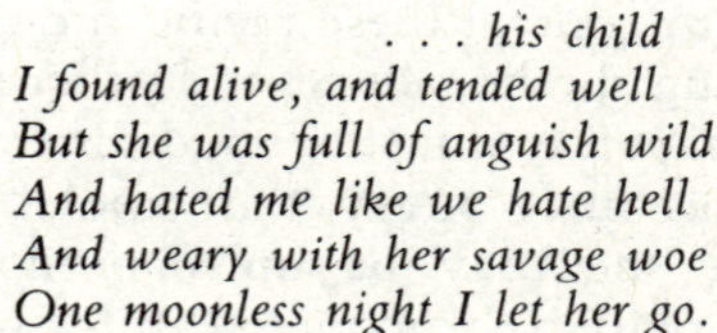

. . . his child
I found alive, and tended well
But she was full of anguish wild
And hated me like we hate hell
And weary with her savage woe
One moonless night I let her go.

Mr Brontë had 'considered Emily the genius of the family', said Mr Frank Peel of Heckmondwike, who talked to him in 1850.[1] Signs of this belief emerge in Emily's childhood. When the children try on the mysterious mask, Emily alone is asked for advice on what to do with another member of the family. Soon, if my reasoning is right, she is helping her father to read through proof copies of his book. At Cowan Bridge, she excels not only the other Brontës, but everyone, not only in intellect, but in vivacious appearance and character. Emily is precocious, like Maria. She is the 'pet nursling', 'a darling child'. A rosy glow settles over her childhood, despite the hardships suffered by her sisters. Such a child will be very acute in feelings as well as learning.

'But clouds will come; too soon they came', writes 'rosy Blanche' in Emily's poem of June 1838. Without tying ourselves rigidly to a precise Freudian or Jungian theory of psychic development, we can understand that childhood experiences and traumas must have had their effect. We seem to have discerned one at Cowan Bridge, which constituted rejection on the part of Miss Evans, and we have also noted the likelihood that Emily may have incurred great guilt by failing to use her charm to intercede for her sisters. This is not quite provable, yet it seems that if Emily had interceded, we should have heard of it through one of Mrs Gaskell's informants. So Emily leaves Cowan Bridge shaken and guilty, beginning to trust the inner voice of 'Gabriel' rather than other humans or herself.

Death then strikes once again, following the early death of her mother. A double death in early 1825 deprives her of her two models, Maria for clever saintliness, Elizabeth for domesticity and comfort. From this point on, it is inevitable that death will be a major theme in Emily's thought: she has been forced to acknowledge its primacy at the age of just under seven. She is a precocious, volatile, ardent seven, whose eyes reflect the emotional mobility of her selfhood. She is far from being able to control these racing moods, which include elation at surviving the bog burst and other perils, jealousy of Branwell, wild anger at injustice, and also at being thwarted herself. If she becomes angry the whole family begins to wonder whether she may be unbalanced, and she knows herself as a potentially destructive creature, who can annihilate with her scornful wit and physical strength. A few of her exploits as a young girl are on record: the day of the 'childer' going mad, the broken fruit tree (which Emily perhaps never forgot), the domestic chores that led to a knife being wielded, possibly an experiment with the beer in the cellar.

Emily liked to portray herself as a reckless daredevil, but she was not reckless. On the moors she could behave like an outlaw, taunting Charlotte with her fear of animals, poring over the whitening bones in the green dell. But remorse lay close at hand; she was not amoral, and she must have shocked herself as she discovered the 'same corruption' in her own soul as in those other people.[2] Hence, very early, a retreat to the love of animals. With Charlotte, she thought up 'bed plays', which were very strange ones, as Charlotte tells us. By this time, Emily was eleven, and had gone beyond the fairy tales which she had made up as a five-year-old. Charlotte, as we have seen, was a sharp and hasty girl, whose strong personality would not have easily been beaten down by a younger sister, even a tall one. It is a fair conjecture that in 1830 there were more quarrels than the one when Parry stamped on Charlotte's favourite.

We are in the realm of guesswork when we try to fathom how this lanky young slip of a girl will react when she begins to encounter the tensions and restraints of a Victorian adolescence. She is perhaps aided a little by the fact that there are elements of pre-Victorian Romanticism in the house, and the story-telling tradition of the Ulster ballad-singer is not forgotten. Drama has been a live art during their childhood, and the Brontës are not inhibited during their first teenage years. Emily forms a close liaison with Anne. We have Anne's word that this was a fine, but not untroubled, friendship. Possibly the two sisters shared a passion for Shelley, if I am right in thinking Emily discovered him during what she describes as her 'early years'.

We see little of the softer side of Emily Brontë as she reveals herself through her fiction and poetry. But it seems that once there had been such a sweet, gentle Emily; perhaps this girl surfaces again in the year when Mr Brontë taught shooting to the 'apple of my eye'. At the age of twelve, this quality called to a like quality in Anne, which survived so much better. Exactly how the relationship between Emily and Anne developed we cannot know. We have Anne's suggestion that fourteen is a suitable time for young love, and we could imagine Emily and Anne playing at romance during their early explorations of Gondal, which they discovered near its phonic echo, Ponden. We have a hint in 'The death of A. G. A.' that a strong, loyal childhood friendship was a kind of love known to Emily, and it seems likely that some of the adolescent Heathcliff/Catherine scenes may be based on this. On the other hand, there sometimes seems a hint that Emily is to Anne as Geraldine is to Christabel in Coleridge's poem. Emily is acutely aware of her own darker side. She may have chosen to write in the person of 'Geraldine' for several reasons: Geraldine is Christabel's temptress; she is also a romantic Irish heroine. Somewhere not too far below the surface it seems to me that Emily equated her Irish side with a daredevil person she wished to be; and Heathcliff, found wandering as a child in Liverpool, and only able to speak in a strange foreign lingo, may be an Irish changeling.

Emily developed into what the Haworth villagers called a 'slinky' girl.[3] The adjective seems to imply quiet and even graceful movement, but it also suggests someone a little underhand. Emily's protagonists are sometimes masculine: but, like Heathcliff, Emily is often *passive*, despite her fierce intensity.[4] We have no external hint of how Emily grappled with this inner flame as a young teenager. She formed some kind of friendly relationship with the Heatons at Ponden: this seems to be attested by her use of the library, which extended to Charlotte and Branwell, and the story of the pear tree planted by Robert Heaton. It would be very rash to infer a romantic incident there.

Roe Head made Emily physically sick. In part, this must have been a reaction to loss of freedom, as Charlotte says. Emily's whiteness perhaps stemmed partly from the need to relieve a situation fraught with guilt, partly from a white-hot anger. Ten years on from Cowan Bridge, Emily has become hopelessly divided and self-hating; she is likely to have resented discipline and rebuffed social advances. Possibly she pined for Anne; but when Anne replaces her she does not seem to complain. She could, of course, physically return to Gondal, if we have been right in seeing its actual location as between Haworth and Ponden.

There have been writers who saw Law Hill as the crucial period in Emily's life: they have discerned some experience there which burnt itself into her. Their evidence, however, is sometimes based on the poems of 1837 and early 1838, which do not fit in with the Law Hill timing. All the same, we have found that Law Hill sowed the seeds of *Wuthering Heights*. The constant brooding presence of High Sunderland, the archetypal castle, viewed from bedroom or classroom, seems to be one of the starting points of the novel. Emily must have arrived at Law Hill prepared to try again. She met Miss Elizabeth Patchett, who seems, if our deductions based on those of Hilda Marsden are right, to have told Emily a great deal about the topography and history of Southowram. Miss Patchett's character suggests that she befriended Emily warmly. In after years, she would not talk about her one-time teacher, allegedly because of Mrs Gaskell's publication of the letter from Charlotte reporting the physical hardships Emily had to suffer there. Was that Miss Patchett's only reason for not talking?

One may speculate whether Emily tried to recreate Cowan Bridge conditions at Law Hill. She couldn't quite be the 'pet nursling' again, but she may have wished to reincarnate Miss Evans in the guise of Miss Patchett. It is not impossible that Miss Patchett could have been the companion implied by the conversation in 'How still, how happy': 'Come, sit down on this sunny stone'. This is pure speculation, but it does seem a possibility that Elizabeth Patchett, the independent horse-rider, would seem attractive to Emily, and serve for a while as a focus for her idealistic affection. But eleven days later than the previous poem, she is mourning the fields of home. The effect of Law Hill was to encourage Emily to take her poetry seriously. During the following year, she twice began fair copies of her poetic output. Perhaps Miss Patchett acted as patron; just possibly she had somehow got to know that Emily wrote verse, and expressed her encouragement. It may be significant that it is in January 1839 that Emily writes her only poem in which the inspiring supernatural genius is clearly female.

In Belgium Emily worked 'like a horse'. In this way she gained self-respect. She now became a teacher for the second time, irritating the Wheelwrights by her devotion to hard work, but quite marvellously forming an attachment to Mlle Bassompierre. Was she trying to model herself on Miss Elizabeth Patchett, and trying to see her young pupil as a girl who was thirsting as much for learning and approval as she herself had been during the Law Hill period? Something in the sixteen-year-old caught at Emily's sympathy. If the fir-tree picture is an indication, it looks as if, consciously or unconsciously, Emily tried to tell her friend something about her inner life. The attempt seems in part to have succeeded, in that Mlle Bassompierre remembered Emily very warmly for the rest of her life. This appears to have been a real attempt at self-revelation on Emily's part, and perhaps it was the last.

Returning from Belgium, Emily seems numb. As she writes in 1844, 'The heart is dead since infancy,/Unwept-for let the body go.' Emily's heart had shown signs of revival on a number of occasions, though perhaps severely wounded in infancy. As often, Emily exaggerates an emotional point. But letting the body go, in several ways, may have been her neurotic reaction. On the moors she can let go in one way; she can act girlishly without inhibitions. But she lets her body go in another sense; she allows it to fall into disrepair: one of her front teeth drops out. She also leaves her body behind, and lives in imagination.

Of Mr Brontë's brothers, two married, and of the sisters only one. Hugh and James were bachelor brothers who lived in their imaginations, story-telling, playing the fiddle, constructing ghost stories and earning a pittance by labouring. The sisters danced and sang, picked the apple crop and worked around the farm. The family were isolated and lived a spirited existence. Their exploits strike one as retaining the irresponsibility of childhood and its naivety and zest. This background suggests a precedent for the non-mixing, non-marrying character of the young Brontës at Haworth. Much of Emily's varied and intense emotional life caused only ripples on her skin, expressions flitting across her face, and the kindling of her 'kind' eyes. She could be passionately sad, blissfully happy, torn with bitter anger and jealousy, without those feelings issuing in any overt action. Sometimes they did spill over, and then there was quarrelling, but more often they were translated into poetry, if only the poetry would come.

We have considered Emily's 'mystic' experiences, as exemplified in 'The Prisoner' and her previous colloquies with a shade who may be the poet Shelley. The mystic transport was not entirely biddable, and in the last few months there is no record of it. The heights experienced by Rochelle are rarely attained.

Working through Emily's poem manuscripts and those few relics of anything else she wrote, we note the small, concentrated, intellectual cast of the writing, so angular and so erratically spaced. Each word is dashed off at speed, but there are pauses for reflection. There is power in the darkness of the ink, economy in the tiny sheets of paper used. Letters and words are blotted and blurred, as if this communication is self-communication. There are wavering lines to divide each poem from its neighbour in the A and B copy manuscripts. The bare minimum is written by this restless, overtaxed pen.

The adult Emily writes:

And am I wrong to worship where
Faith cannot doubt nor hope despair
Since my own soul can grant my prayer?
Speak, God of Visions, plead for me
And tell why I have chose thee![5]

It was a deliberate choice, or so it seemed, to contain all her desire and hope within her own mind. Yet it did not work. Emily did not manage to have a single vision of the 'Spirit' that might integrate the warring factions inside her; or at least, no unequivocal and lasting one.

> *Had I but seen his glorious eye*
> Once *light the clouds that wilder me*
> *I ne'er had raised this coward cry*
> *To cease to think and cease to be.*[6]

So she writes in February 1845.

On 2 June 1845 Emily contrasts herself with her 'compeers'. She says they are 'subdued by passions strong' but she 'hoped while they enjoyed'. 'Enjoyed' is a strong word to use of Anne's loss of William Weightman, Charlotte's parting from M. Heger, and Branwell's muddled love for Mrs Robinson. But Emily seems to be saying that she has not suffered a parallel disappointment because she has not been involved in such an entanglement. It is fair to point out that poems are not autobiography, but the autobiographical interpretation here does not seem unduly strained. It looks as if we must conclude that she bases on emotional and spiritual experience the vast passion of Cathy for Heathcliff and vice versa, being worked out in her mind at that very time, when the Gondal characters were regrouping in a Halifax/Haworth landscape. The passion has no foundation in physical experience, except insofar as Emily calls on her early rovings with Anne, her passionate longing for the security of her dead sisters' presence, and the physical violence she may herself have exerted as a child.

It is undoubtedly disappointing that no lover can be found for Emily Brontë, orthodox or unorthodox; we can never rule out the possibility that at Law Hill and/or in Belgium someone might have appeared who incarnated Emily's ideal for a short while. But the roots of her passionate emotion go deeper than that, to the crucial year of 1824–5, when Emily Brontë was almost overwhelmed by the muddy waters of the Crow Hill bog, then was deprived of her home, after being for a short time the only girl who could read her father's proofs. She became the 'pet nursling' at Cowan Bridge, then saw her sisters misunderstood and ill-treated, and finally felt she had betrayed them as they died and she lost them for good. In these many ways the matrix of *Wuthering Heights* is a return to the intense and absorbing feelings of childhood and early adolescence.

rooted in abandonment & death. — Alice Miller

Notes

Abbreviations used in Notes

(Complete titles and publication dates of books are given in the bibliography.)

Chadwick: E. A. Chadwick, *In the Footsteps of the Brontës*
Chitham & Winnifrith: E. Chitham and T. Winnifrith, *Brontë Facts and Brontë Problems*
Gaskell: E. C. Gaskell, *The Life of Charlotte Brontë*: page references are to the Everyman edition
Leyland: F. Leyland, *The Brontë Family*
Lock & Dixon: J. Lock and W. T. Dixon, *A Man of Sorrow*
SHB: Shakespeare Head Brontë

AB = Anne Brontë; BB = Patrick Branwell Brontë; BL = British Library; BPM = Brontë Parsonage, previously known as Brontë Parsonage Museum; *BST* = Brontë Society Transactions; CB = Charlotte Brontë; EB = Emily Jane Brontë; EN = Ellen Nussey; PB = Patrick Brontë; WG = Winifred Gérin; WSW = W. S. Williams.

Notes to Introduction

1 Gaskell, p. 277.
2 Until there is a published edition of Charlotte's letters in which confidence can be placed, there must be chances of error, but I have tried to check MSS or xerox where possible.
3 J. Erskine Stuart, *The Brontë Country*, introduction, p. vii.
4 Letter from CB to EN, 21 February 1855. SHB, *Lives and Letters*, Vol IV, p. 175.
5 For Martha Brown, see Whiteley Turner, *A Spring-Time Saunter*, p. 224.

6 Emily's coffin is said to have been very narrow. It measured only 16" by 5' 7", according to WGEB, p. 259.
7 Extracts in J. Kellett, *Haworth Parsonage*, pp. 77–80.
8 The tracing is at BPM, but it may be made up from part-tracings of two different pictures. See discussion in E. Chitham, *The Poems of Anne Brontë*, pp. 24–5.
9 The confusion was finally cleared up by Tom Winnifrith in *BST* 85 (1975), p. 364. An 'A. H.' had written to the *Leeds Mercury* in 1855. The initials were taken to be those of 'Mrs' Harben, a later superintendent. They were in fact the married initials of Mrs Hill.
10 Chadwick, preface, p. V.
11 Ibid. See discussion in Chitham & Winnifrith, Ch. 3.
12 H. Dingle, *The Mind of Emily Brontë*, pp. 103 ff.
13 Chitham & Winnifrith, Ch. 4.

Notes to Chapter 1

1 I have examined the validity of reports of the family ancestry in *The Brontës' Irish Background*, and make assumptions here which are argued in detail there.
2 One source is Elizabeth Wilson, mentioned in Chitham, *Irish Background*, pp. 79, 83.
3 Robinson, *Emily Brontë*, pp. 26–7.
4 For a detailed, slightly imaginative, account of their courtship, see J. Lock and W. T. Dixon, *A Man of Sorrow*, pp. 122 ff.
5 This part of the Thornton evidence is from I. Holgate, 'The Brontës at Thornton' in *BST* 69, pp. 327 ff. She includes a plate of a decorated cast-iron fireplace by which the children probably played in cold or wet weather.
6 W. Scruton, *Thornton and the Brontës*, p. 58.
7 Lock & Dixon (quoting Mrs Gaskell's daughter, Meta) p. 520.
8 For evidence of the persistence of very early childhood memories in all human beings, see A. Janov, *The Feeling Child* (London, 1977). In Ch. 4, we shall deal with apparent examples of Emily's memories of school.
9 Lock & Dixon, (quoting Elizabeth Firth's diary) p. 166.
10 An imaginative account, which however includes many carefully researched details, is in Lock & Dixon, Ch. XI.
11 Scruton, *Thornton and the Brontës*, p. 79.

Notes to Chapter 2

1 J. Kellett, *Haworth Parsonage*, esp. pp. 19–36, 41–4, 47, 77–80.
2 Ibid., plan on p. 24.
3 Ibid., p. 32. For a suggestion that Mr Brontë himself had extensions built in the 1840s, see Lock & Dixon, p. 219.
4 J. Horsfall Turner, *Haworth Past and Present*, p. 95.
5 Ibid.
6 Kellett, *Haworth Parsonage*, plan on p. 24, showing both old and new parts of the house; cf. also p. 64, where 'two points' for well water to be pumped are mentioned.
7 Ibid., p. 64. Shown in a plan drawn for the General Board of Health in 1853.
8 *The Yorkshire Directory*, 1823, under 'Haworth'.
9 Lock & Dixon, pp. 226–9, reproducing entry in parish register.
10 See evidence of Cowan Bridge records, to be discussed in Ch. 4.
11 Letter from Patrick Brontë to John Buckworth, quoted (with supplementation) in Lock & Dixon, pp. 230–1, from Buckworth's *Cottage Magazine*, Vol XI, 1822; Gaskell, p. 33.
12 Gaskell, p. 30.
13 Ibid., p. 31.
14 Ibid.
15 Ibid., p. 32.
16 Ibid.
17 Leyland, p. 46 ff.
18 Ibid., p. 48.
19 See Chadwick, p. 226, for a description of Emily's clothes in Brussels.
20 Quoted in Lock & Dixon, p. 508.
21 Gaskell, pp. 29–30.
22 Ibid., p. 29.
23 Ibid., p. 30.
24 Lock & Dixon, p. 231.
25 Chadwick, p. 63.
26 Lock & Dixon, p. 232.
27 Ibid.

Notes to Chapter 3

1 Chadwick, p. 63.
2 Ibid., p. 48.
3 Ibid., p. 68.
4 Whiteley Turner, *A Spring-Time Saunter*, pp. 208–10.
5 Leyland, p. 54.

6 *BST* 74 (1964) p. 28 ff.
7 Gaskell, p. 124.
8 PB to Mrs Gaskell, 30 July 1855.
9 Gaskell, Ch. 3, gives original phrasing of the questions.
10 Daphne du Maurier, in *The Infernal World of Branwell Brontë*, treats the upbringing of Branwell imaginatively.
11 Mr Brontë's two accounts of the Crow Hill bog burst, originally printed by Inkersley, were reproduced in Horsfall Turner's *Brontëana* (Bingley, 1898), pp. 201–19.
12 Ibid., p. 211.
13 Supplementary material is from Whiteley Turner, *A Spring-Time Saunter*, p. 186.
14 Whiteley Turner, quoting The *Leeds Mercury*.
15 Quoted in E. Raymond, *In the Steps of the Brontës*, p. 205.
16 R. Skelton, *The Poet's Calling* (London, 1975), p. 19.
17 Lock & Dixon, p. 249.
18 J. Horsfall Turner, *Haworth Past and Present*, p. 154.
19 W. Scruton, *Thornton and the Brontës*, pp. 66–7.

Notes to Chapter 4

1 Gaskell, p. 39. On p. 44 she writes that 'Helen Burns is as exact a transcript of Maria Brontë as Charlotte's wonderful power of reproducing character could give' and notes that contemporaries of the Brontës at school knew who must have written the book before the world knew. However, there are some differences between Maria and Helen, for example, their ages. Nor did Maria die at Cowan Bridge, as Helen died at Lowood.
2 W. H. Chippendall, *A History of the Parish of Tunstall* (Manchester, 1940), especially pp. 73 ff.
3 M. Williams, *Notes on the Clergy Daughters' School*, pp. 7–8. Miss Williams based her notes partly on printed reports, copies of which are at Kendal Record Office, and partly on MS documents, some of which seem to have disappeared.
4 Ibid., pp. 8–18; some information derived from Mrs Chadwick, and some part-quoted from the school Ledger.
5 Ibid., p. 23.
6 Original at Clergy Daughters' School, Casterton; xerox copy at Kendal Record Office.
7 Much clarifying work was done by Brett Harrison in *BST* 85 (1975), who suggested that Miss Andrews was in charge for some months of 1824, and was followed by Miss Evans. On pp. 362–3 he explains how he traced more details of Miss Evans.

The married identity of Miss Andrews, as the wife of Hamilton J. S. Hill, Ohio, USA was clarified by Tom Winnifrith in *BST* 85 (1975), p. 364, quoting a letter of Mrs Gaskell.

8 CB to WSW, 5 November 1849, SHB, *Lives and Letters*, Vol III, p. 34.

9 Gaskell, p. 45.

10 Ibid., p. 48.

11 Reprinted in, for example, *The Brontës: Their Lives, Friendships and Correspondence*.

12 'Ledger', Clergy Daughters' School Records, Kendal Record Office.

13 Wilson, *All Alone*, pp. 27–31.

14 The poem is probably not earlier than 1839.

15 Wilson, *All Alone*, pp. 27–31.

16 Ibid., p. 50.

17 W. W. Carus Wilson to *Halifax Guardian*, 18 July 1857.

18 A. B. Nicholls to *Halifax Guardian*, of 6 June 1857. Authenticity is established by the correct number of girls being given ('about forty') in contrast with Charlotte's inflated number in *Jane Eyre*.

19 M. Williams, *Notes on the Clergy Daughters' School*, pp. 25–6. Leck chapel has since been rebuilt, but there was an earlier building on the site.

20 Gaskell, p. 48. Clergy Daughters' School Records, Kendal Record Office.

21 Clergy Daughters' School Records, Kendal Record Office.

22 Chadwick, p. 78.

23 Clergy Daughters' School Records, Kendal Record Office.

24 *Wuthering Heights*, Ch. 3.

25 P. 12.

26 Ibid., p. 69.

27 See Ch. 8, below.

Notes to Chapter 5

1 C. Alexander, *The Early Writings of Charlotte Brontë*, pp. 28–9.

2 Ibid., pp. 27–8.

3 CB, 'History of the Year', cancelled p. 1 (verso), BPM.

4 C. Alexander, *Early Writings of CB*, pp. 28–9.

5 CB, 'History of the Year', p. 3, BPM.

6 C. Alexander, *Early Writings of CB*, p. 29.

7 Ibid., pp. 42–3.

8 Ibid., p. 25.

9 I have been unable to trace this Bible, mentioned in Lock & Dixon, p. 264.
10 We must suppose that Mr Brontë had a letter from Cowan Bridge, which he would have received on 13 February 1825.
11 A photograph of this sampler is in B. Wilks, *The Brontës*, p. 41. The whole family were inclined to ignore the I before E rule until they were published authors. Charlotte's alphabets were accurate, Maria's, Elizabeth's and Anne's inconsistent.
12 J. Kellett, *Haworth Parsonage*, p. 57.
13 Emily's and Anne's piano music collection, BPM.
14 C. Alexander. *Early Writings of CB*, p. 32.
15 Diary paper, 26 June 1837.
16 Revised transcription by C. Alexander, *Early Writings of CB*, p. 20.
17 Photograph in *Woman and Home*, 1897, p. 909, in 'Relics of Emily Brontë' by Clement Shorter.
18 At BPM. Whinchat reproduced in WGEB, facing p. 44. On 25 April, a copy of a woman with geese was made, also from Bewick.
19 CB to PB 23 September 1829, SHB, *Lives and Letters*, Vol. 1, p. 82.
20 Leyland, pp. 63–4.
21 J. Erskine Stuart, *The Brontë Country*, pp. 18–19.
22 Chadwick, p. 87.
23 By Anne in 'Self-Communion' and by Charlotte after Emily's death, quoted in WGEB, p. 261.
24 C. Alexander, *Early Writings of CB*, p. 63.
25 *Young Men's Magazine*, October 1830, quoted in F. Ratchford, *Gondal's Queen*, p. 14.
26 The point is first made in WGEB, p. 16.
27 'The Foundling', in SHB *Miscellaneous & Unpublished Writings*, p. 228.
28 *History of the Young Men*, Ch. 6. SHB, ibid., p. 91.

Notes to Chapter 6

1 The event is usually dated from Ellen Nussey's 'Reminiscences' in *Scribner's*. WGCB quotes Chadwick (without page reference) to the effect that Ellen arrived on 25 January, a week after the rest. (WGCB, p. 61). This would suggest term began about 18 January 1831.
2 R. Wilson, *All Alone*, p. 130.
3 WGAB, p. 64.

4 'Fair sinks the summer evening now', 30 August 1839, stanza 3.
5 *Wuthering Heights*, Ch. 6.
6 See maps on pp. 286 and 287.
7 Lock & Dixon, pp. 337, 341.
8 WGBB, p. 31.
9 WGBB, p. 43.
10 WGBB, p. 44, Chitham & Winnifrith, p. 83, note 2.
11 Ibid., p. 79.
12 WGEB, p. 32. M. A. Butterfield, *The Heatons of Ponden Hall*, p. 17 gives Robert's birth date as 2 May 1822.
13 WGEB, p. 44.
14 Butterfield, *Heatons of Ponden Hall*, p. 19.
15 Ibid., pp. 15–16.
16 Whiteley Turner, *A Spring-Time Saunter*, pp. 192–4, including pen and ink drawing.
17 Reprinted, e.g., in SHB, *Lives and Letters*, Vol. I, p. 112.
18 Quoted C. K. Chorter, *CB and her Circle*, pp. 178–80.
19 Ibid., p. 179.
20 Ellen Nussey, 'Reminiscences', reprinted, e.g., in SHB, *Lives and Letters*, Vol. I, p. 112.
21 In 'Self-Communion,' lines 78 ff.
22 'The Death of A. G. A.', begun January 1841, finished May 1844.
23 Chitham & Winnifrith, pp. 59–60. The circulating library has been researched by Ian Dewhirst of Bradford Public Libraries Dept.
24 Ibid., pp. 60–1.
25 In 'Alexander and Zenobia', p. 52.
26 Lock & Dixon, p. 325.
27 SHB, *Lives and Letters*, Vol. I, p. 103.
28 Ellen Nussey to Wemyss Reid, discussed in Chitham & Winnifrith, pp. 128–9, where, however, the date is misprinted 1838 for 1833. On the same page is reported the rare *obiter dictum* of Emily that it was a vain attempt to try to teach the Sunday School pupils good manners. Also WGBB, p. 60.
29 CB to EN in SHB, *Lives and Letters*, Vol. I, p. 117.
30 W. Reid, *Charlotte Bronte, a Monograph*, p. 29.
31 Leyland, p. 115.
32 Gaskell, p. 81.
33 A. M. F. Robinson, *Emily Brontë*, p. 48.
34 C. K. Shorter, *CB and her Circle*, pp. 178.
35 Ellen Nussey, 'Reminiscences', reprinted in SHB, *Lives and Letters*, Vol. I, pp. 112–13.
36 See maps on pp. 286 and 287.
37 Shorter, *CB and her Circle*, pp. 179.

38 Discussed in E. Chitham, *The Brontës' Irish Background*, esp. Ch. 10.
39 'Well, some may hate, and some may scorn', 14 November 1839, stanza 4.
40 A. M. F. Robinson, *Emily Brontë*, p. 51.
41 Discussed in E. Chitham, *The Brontës' Irish Background*.
42 J. Kellett, *Haworth Parsonage*, p. 72.
43 Ellen Nussey, 'Reminiscences', reprinted, e.g. in SHB, *Lives and Letters*, Vol. I, p. 114.
44 CB to Dr Epps, 9 December 1848 in, e.g., Shorter, *CB and her Circle*, pp. 173.
45 CB to EN, 11 September 1833, in, e.g., SHB *Lives and Letters*, Vol. I, p. 117.
46 SHB, *Miscellany*, Vol 2, pp. 11,12. WGBB, pp. 69–72, implies that the writing is Branwell's. C. Alexander, *The Early Writings of CB*, pp. 16–17, may be right to consider it Charlotte's. The text in SHB is facsimile.
47 E.g. recto in B. Wilks, *The Brontës*, p. 73; verso in N. Brysson Morrison, *Haworth Harvest* (London, 1969), facing p. 136. Both are enlarged.

Notes to Chapter 7

1 Patrick Brontë to Mrs Franks (formerly Elizabeth Firth), 6 July 1835; SHB, *Lives and Letters*, Vol. I, p. 130.
2 No other portrait of Emily is quite beyond dispute. I have discussed them, with reference to Anne, in *The Poems of AB*, pp. 24–5. See also J. Hewish, *Emily Brontë*, pp. 32–3.
3 Introduction to 'Selections from the Literary Remains of Ellis . . . Bell'.
4 A good description is in WGAB, pp. 81–2.
5 Uncollected letter, perhaps from June or August 1836 (despite accompanying note) CB to EN, *BST* 90 (1980), pp. 353–4.
6 WGEB, p. 53.
7 WGCB, p. 65.
8 WGEB, p. 53.
9 Introduction to 'Selections from the Literary Remains of Ellis . . . Bell'.
10 Ibid.
11 'Preface' (untitled) to 'Selections from Poems by Ellis and Acton Bell'.

Notes to Chapter 8

1 I accept the evidence for dating set out in WGBB, p. 95.
2 PBB to *Blackwood's*, SHB, *Lives and Letters*, Vol. I, pp. 133–4.
3 SHB, *Lives and Letters*, Vol. I, pp. 143–4.
4 CB's 'Roe Head Journal', quoted WGCB, p. 107.
5 BB, 'Augusta', in T. J. Winnifrith, *The Poems of Patrick Branwell Brontë*, pp. 190–2, and note, p. 318.
6 F. Ratchford, *Gondal's Queen*, p. 32.
7 1837 diary paper, excellently reproduced in B. Wilks, *The Brontës*, p. 55.
8 'All day I've toiled', stanzas 1 and 5.
9 Weather records, e.g., at Cliffe Castle, Keighley.
10 WGBB, p. 132.
11 1837 diary paper in Wilks, *The Brontës*.
12 For detailed discussion and evidence, see E. Chitham, *The Brontës' Irish Background*, pp. 29–31, 105, 107.
13 1837 diary paper in Wilks, *The Brontës*.
14 'Alone I sat; the summer day/ Had died in smiling light away', stanzas 2, 4, 5.
15 BPM 1717C, facsimile in *BST* 72(1962), facing p. 49.
16 *Shirley*, Vol II, Ch. 11.
17 'O wander not so far away', stanza 7.
18 'For him who struck thy foreign string', stanza 3.

Notes to Chapter 9

1 Chitham & Winnifrith, *Brontë Facts and Brontë Problems*, pp. 20 ff; J. A. Cox, 'Emily at Law Hill, 1838: Corroborative Evidence' in *BST* 94 (1984), pp. 267–70.
2 Gaskell, p. 96.
3 *The Bookman*, March 1893, pp. 183–5; C. Simpson, *Emily Brontë*, includes a watercolour of the house; H. Marsden, 'The Scenic Background of *Wuthering Heights*' in *BST* 67 (1957).
4 E. Raymond, *In the Steps of the Brontës*, facing p. 81.
5 Cox, *BST* 94 (1984), pp. 267–70.
6 A. M. F. Robinson, *Emily Brontë*, p. 60.
7 Chadwick, p. vi.
8 Ibid., pp. 123–4.
9 Ibid., p. 127.
10 Ibid., p. 128. Miss Patchett may have been 49; she was probably baptized at Luddenden on 27 December 1789.
11 E. Raymond, *In the Steps of the Brontës*, gives a good account of his visit to Law Hill and propounds a love affair there (pp.

98–9), but his thesis cannot be supported by the poems he quotes, written before Law Hill.

12 T. Keyworth, *The Bookman*, March 1893, p. 184.
13 Ibid., p. 183.
14 Chadwick, p. 124.
15 T. Keyworth, *The Bookman*, March 1893, p. 184.
16 Chadwick, p. 128.
17 A. Lister's diary, microfilm, Halifax Public Library.
18 This cannot be tested visually now, since High Sunderland no longer exists. I have tried to check the view from the Law Hill site, and lines drawn on a map seem to show that Emily would see the house slightly to the left of Beacon Hill. High Sunderland is on the same contour as Law Hill.
19 See H. Marsden, *BST* 67 (1857).
20 Horner's lithographs are very accurate. Not so an engraving entitled 'Ancient Mansion at High Sunderland', by R. L. Wright after W. Briggs, which appears in some biographies.
21 H. Marsden, *BST* 67 (1957).
22 *Wuthering Heights*, Ch. 1.
23 Ibid., Ch. 9.
24 On the details of geography at *Wuthering Heights* interestingly based on internal evidence, see J. F. Goodridge, in *Emily Brontë: Wuthering Heights*, (London, 1964). A reconstructed map is printed on p. 72.
25 T. Keyworth, *The Bookman*, March 1894.
26 *Wuthering Heights*, Ch. 3.
27 *Wuthering Heights*, Ch. 11
28 H. Marsden, *BST* 67 (1957).
29 Author's observation.
30 *Wuthering Heights*, Ch. 6.
31 Ibid., Ch. 9.
32 BL, B manuscript.
33 Shackleton's weather records, Cliffe Castle, Keighley.
34 *Fraser's Magazine*, June 1838, pp. 661 ff.
35 1841 Census, microfilm, examined at Halifax Public Library.
36 Chadwick, p. 124.
37 J. Cox, *BST* 94 (1984).
38 Leyland, p. 153.
39 Apart from Raymond, proponents of this include Romer Wilson and Virginia Moore. While they are not able to substantiate their suggestion, all make a case that seems tenable on psychological grounds.
40 *All Alone*, p. 166.
41 Shackleton, weather records, Cliffe Castle, Keighley.
42 Most of this evidence comes from a careful study of the D group of manuscripts, chiefly at BPM.

43 Shackleton, weather records.
44 T. Hanson, 'The Local Colour of *Wuthering Heights*' in *BST* 34 (1924), pp. 201 ff.
45 Halifax Public Library Misc. 80:6, unfortunately undated, but earlier than 1838.
46 Ultimately, a good deal of this material comes from Caroline Walker's diary, in the Lister MSS at Halifax Public Library. Extracts were printed in *Halifax Archaeological Society Transactions*, 1908, pp. 208–66, and it is from this that I obtained the background. It is possible that a complete transcript of the diary might add marginally to the background picture.
47 Law Hill House is called 'otherwise Mount Pleasant' in a mortgage of 23 April 1778 (Halifax Public Libraries: Calderdale District Archives No. 672).
48 E.g. E. Raymond, as mentioned above.
49 Anne Lister's diary, microfilm at Halifax Public Library.

Notes to Chapter 10

1 For further comment on the writing of the poem, see Chitham & Winnifrith, *Brontë Facts and Brontë Problems*, p. 40.
2 Information from Mrs Joanna Hutton, Haworth.
3 See N. Rogers, *Shelley at Work* (London, 1967), pp. 68–9.
4 Leyland, pp. 238–9 links Hartley Merrall with the expedition by strong implication. It is worth noting that Merrall paid 'weekly' visits to the parsonage in 1839. He may possibly have been one of Emily's models for foppish youths such as Lockwood. Another incident involving Merrall is the source of Anne's poem 'Z's dream'. We might wish to know a lot more about Hartley Merrall.
5 It is at the British Library, where it can be seen that the writing is clearly Branwell's.
6 See Chitham & Winnifrith, *Brontë Facts and Brontë Problems*, pp. 58–75 for further discussion.
7 Ch. 13, p. 179.
8 See J. Kellett, *Haworth Parsonage*, p. 68 for a reproduction of one of Branwell's shooting invitations.
9 C. K. Shorter, *CB and her Circle*, pp. 178–9.
10 E. Chitham, *The Poems of AB*, pp. 18–19.
11 A. M. F. Robinson, *Emily Brontë*, p. 69.
12 Ibid.
13 D. R. Isenberg, 'A Gondal Fragment' in *BST* 72 (1962), pp. 24–6 and excellent facsimile facing p. 32.

14 These suggestions are based on D. R. Isenberg, with additions. For example, the two thumbnail sketches seem to me to be castles, and suggest the residence of the two characters.
15 Winifred Gérin (WGEB, p. 259) quotes William Wood, who made Emily's coffin, for this information. The record does not seem to be in Wood's accounts.
16 Reproduced in Chitham, *The Poems of AB*, pp. 189–90.
17 WGCB, pp. 152–9 documents the seaside holiday. Dates remain a little controversial.
18 A poem beginning 'Maiden, thou wert thoughtless once' in the manuscript, altered for publication in 1846.
19 Manuscript identificators are those of Hatfield. For more detail on the poems in question, see Chitham & Winnifrith.
20 'Thy sun is near meridian height', 6 January 1840.
21 P. B. Shelley, 'Prometheus Unbound', Act II, Scene IV, ' . . . as light from the meridian sun', quoted in *Fraser's*, June 1838.
22 'At such a time in such a spot'. The poem exists in copy manuscript B only, so there is no question of change in writing style.
23 For dating of Thorp Green employment, see Chitham, *The Poems of AB*, pp. 10–11.
24 The present location of the manuscript is unknown. Shorter's facsimile (p. 149) is the earliest known, but is blurred.
25 *Wuthering Heights*, Ch. 6.
26 CB to Elizabeth Branwell, SHB, *Lives and Letters*, Vol. I, pp. 242–3.
27 Reproduced B. Wilks, *The Brontës*, p. 64. WGEB, p. 116, discovered the relation with Bewick picture.
28 CB to EB, SHB, *Lives and Letters*, Vol. I, pp. 246–7.

Notes to Chapter 11

1 Gaskell, p. 147.
2 Ibid.
3 Ibid.
4 WGEB, p. 121 ff., based on Gaskell, 3rd edition, p. 146.
5 CB to EN, SHB, *Lives and Letters*, Vol. I, pp. 259–61.
6 Gaskell, p. 151.
7 CB to EN, SHB, *Lives and Letters*, Vol. I, p. 261.
8 Introduction to 'Selection from Poems by Ellis and Acton Bell', reprinted e.g. in 19th-century Smith, Elder editions of *The Professor*, p. 409.
9 Gaskell, pp. 152–4

10 It sounds much like a typical Classical approach to literary style: that it was to be imitated until perfection was achieved.

11 W. Wright, *The Brontës in Ireland*, (London, 1893), pp. 142 ff. I have been unable to discover positive evidence to corroborate Wright's account, but the link between the family and the 1798 rebellion is sure enough.

12 Facsimile of devoir in *BST* 90 (1980) pp. 366–7. In *BST* 92 (1982), Robert. K. Wallace published a carefully researched article on Emily Brontë and music (pp. 136–141). He is unable to discover precisely what music she may have freshly encountered in Belgium, nor has he traced the name of the '*meilleur*' piano teacher mentioned later in my chapter. However, he studies the contents of *The Musical Library*, purchased by Emily in 1844 and makes valid inferences from this.

13 SHB, *Lives and Letters*, Vol. I, pp. 229–30. Charlotte uses terms which seem to imply that Emily did write from time to time.

14 J. Hewish, *Emily Brontë*, (London, 1969), p. 69.

15 See M. Allott, *The Brontës: The Critical Heritage* (London, 1974), e.g. pp. 32, 376–7, for early attempts to pin down the Germanic influence on *Wuthering Heights*. WGEB, pp. 215–17 also deals with this topic, but there is scope for an authoritative investigation.

16 Chadwick, p. 226.

17 *CB and her Circle*, p. 111.

18 Chadwick, p. 228.

19 WGEB, p. 130, quoting J. J. Green, 'The Brontë–Wheelwright Friendship' in *Friends' Quarterly Examiner*, 1916.

20 Ibid.

21 *BST* 23, (1913) p. 28, also quoted in WGEB, p. 131.

22 The drawing, at BPM, may be based on a copy book, but its execution is typical of Emily Brontë.

23 The picture appears facing p. 254, and is discussed.

24 In *The Exploring Word*, pp. 131–9, David Holbrook the educationalist discusses a poem 'The Lilac Tree' by a twelve-year-old girl. He shows how the poem is a symbol of the child herself 'seeking to love herself' (p. 139). I accept this view, and consider it might be applied to Emily Brontë, *failing* to love herself, and here expressing despair. One might ask further why she gave *this* picture to Louise, and might postulate that she was actually seeking, tentatively, a friendly understanding of herself from the sixteen-year-old. If so, this throws some light on Emily's view of herself as still a girl in 1842. This is indeed corroborated by Louise's letter in *BST* 23, where she says that there could, of course, be no friendship between her and Charlotte, since Charlotte was twenty-five. This implies that she felt Emily to be younger, still girlish. In turn, this has

implications for Emily's view of childhood, as strongly influencing *Wuthering Heights*.

25 SHB, *Lives and Letters*, Vol. I, p. 267.
26 Chadwick, p. 233.
27 SHB, *Lives and Letters*, Vol. I, pp. 272–3.
28 Ibid., pp. 278–80.

Notes to Chapter 12

1 On 4 October 1843 (quoted in Lock & Dixon, p. 375) Patrick wrote to the church trustee, Mr Greenwood, hoping to counter rumours that he was drinking too freely. He claims he is using a lotion for his eyes, 'which are very weak'. The question whether he drank heavily or at all is bound to remain open, but the weak eyes are thus authenticated three years before his operation in Manchester.
2 SHB, *Lives and Letters*, Vol. I, p. 137, quoting Mary Taylor.
3 Lock & Dixon, p. 369, apparently quoting John Greenwood.
4 Gaskell, pp. 183–5.
5 Ibid.
6 CB to EN, 25 March 1844, SHB, *Lives and Letters*, Vol. II, p. 5.
7 This and several similar passages occur in *Shirley*, Vol II, Chapter 11. The relation between the fiction and Charlotte's observations of Emily is discussed below.
8 EB to EN, possibly 22 May 1843, SHB, *Lives and Letters*, Vol. I, p. 298.
9 Greenwood's 'Diary', BPM.
10 Ibid.
11 Lock & Dixon, p. 369.
12 Greenwood's 'Diary', quoted in WGEB, p. 146.
13 Chitham, *The Poems of AB*, p. 95.
14 Ibid., p. 115.
15 Ibid., p. 97 and note, p. 179.
16 The original version was 'Unmourned the body well may go'. The manuscript is Hatfield's E 20, at the Berg Collection, New York Public Libraries.
17 For an example of fiction masquerading as fact, see D. McCracken, *Wordsworth and the Lake District*, (London, 1985), pp. 192–3.
18 The propensity to fuse the meanings of Gondal and non-Gondal poems stems in part from F. Ratchford's *Gondal's Queen*.
19 *Shirley*, Vol III, Ch. 4, which also contains many other thoughts and views possibly derived from Emily, but too far from authentication to be included here.

20 *BST* 72 (1962), pp. 27–35.
21 Gaskell, p. 277.
22 Holgate, *BST*, p. 32.
23 Cf. 'No coward soul', 2 January 1846.
24 See WGEB, p. 389.
25 *Shirley*, Vol III, Ch. 4 SHB, *Lives and Letters*, Vol. II, p. 256.
26 *Shirley*, Vol III, Ch. 4.
27 For a possible chronology of Charlotte's writing of *Shirley*, see WGCB, pp. 389 ff.
28 AB to EN, 4 October 1847, SHB, *Lives and Letters*, Vol. II, p. 144.
29 'That wind, I used to hear it swelling', 28 November 1839; cf. also 'Aye, there it is!', 6 July 1841.
30 *Shirley*, Vol III, Ch. 5.
31 Cf. '. . . we rose as the dusk heaven/ Was melting to amber and blue', from 'Loud without the wind was roaring', November 1838.
32 J. Kellett, *Haworth Parsonage*.
33 Gaskell, p. 180.
34 Ibid., p. 214.
35 Ibid., p. 90.
36 Whiteley Turner, *A Spring-Time Saunter*, p. 214.
37 *Gaskell*, p. 215.
38 See Chitham, *The Brontës' Irish Background* for discussion and tentative suggestions.
39 A. M. F. Robinson, *Emily Brontë*, pp. 211–12.

Notes to Chapter 13

1 A. M. F. Robinson, *Emily Brontë*, p. 116: 'Anne's letters told of health worn out by constant, agonising suspicion'; we do not know precise dates.
2 E.g. WGEB, p. 176.
3 C. P. Sanger, 'The Structure of *Wuthering Heights*, originally a paper read to the Heretics, Cambridge. He shows that Lockwood's visit to Heathcliff, and the appearance of the ghost, are dated late November 1801. The face at the window is described as 'a child'. Catherine Earnshaw was born in 1765 and by 1781 had been proposed to by Edgar. In this chapter (Ch. 9) she is called 'Our young lady'; it is said 'she esteemed herself a woman'.
4 Shackleton's weather records, Cliffe Castle, Keighley.
5 Anne's 1845 diary paper.

6 A. M. F. Robinson, *Emily Brontë*, p. 117.
7 D. du Maurier, *The Infernal World of BB*, Chs 12–13.
8 See illustration in J. Kellett, *Haworth Parsonage*, p. 68.
9 D. du Maurier, *The Infernal World of BB*, pp. 160–2.
10 CB to EN, 31 July 1845, SHB, *Lives and Letters*, Vol. II, p. 43.
11 Reproduced, e.g., in SHB, *Lives and Letters*, Vol. II, pp. 49–51.
12 Reproduced, e.g., in SHB, *Lives and Letters*, Vol. II, p. 53. Whereabouts of original unknown.
13 Ibid. The transcript was presumably made by Shorter at an early stage, and we cannot rely on punctuation or capitals.
14 M. Visick, *The Genesis of Wuthering Heights*, p. 15.
15 Ibid., p. 14.
16 'Geraldine, the moon is shining', 17 October 1838.
17 'The wide cathedral aisles are lone', March 1838.
18 *BST* 82 (1982), pp. 85 ff.
19 Charlotte's 'Biographical Notice'.
20 Ibid.
21 SHB, *Lives and Letters*, Vol. II, p. 256; date uncertain.
22 D. Roper, 'The Revision of Emily Brontë's poems of 1846' in *The Library*, June 1984, pp. 153 ff.
23 CB, 'Biographical Notice'.
24 G. D. Hargreaves, 'The Publishing of "Poems by Currer, Ellis and Acton Bell"' in *BST* 79 (1969), pp. 294 ff.
25 Discussed by Winnifrith in Chitham & Winnifrith, *Brontë Facts and Brontë Problems*, Ch. 8.
26 The next section is based on M. Visick, *The Genesis of Wuthering Heights*.
27 'The soft unclouded blue of air', 28 April 1839.
28 CB, 'Preface'.
29 AB 'Why should such gloomy silence reign': stanzas 1, 2, 4, 5 and 7.
30 Chitham, *The Brontës' Irish Background*, pp. 105–7.
31 The remnant has sharp, straight edges, apparently hacked rather than cleanly cut.
32 The will, proved 28 December 1842, left virtually all Elizabeth Branwell's property to be equally divided between the three Brontë sisters and Jane Kingston, their Penzance cousin. SHB, *Lives and Letters*, Vol. I, pp. 277–8.

Notes to Chapter 14

1 Gaskell, p. 213.
2 Ibid.

3 Ibid., p. 215.
4 A. M. F. Robinson, *Emily Brontë*, pp. 50–1.
5 Chitham, *The Brontës' Irish Background*, p. 171.
6 J. F. Goodridge, 'A New Heaven and a New Earth', in A. Smith, *The Art of Emily Brontë* (London, 1976), pp. 170–1.
7 J. Hewish, *Emily Brontë*, p. 116.
8 Sung by Mrs C. Costello. In R. Vaughan Williams and A. L. Lloyd, *The Penguin Book of English Folk Songs* (London, 1959), p. 52.
9 K. M. Petyt, *Emily Brontë and the Haworth Dialect* (Yorkshire Dialect Society, 1970).
10 CB, 'Preface' to *Wuthering Heights*.
11 WGEB, p. 45.
12 J. Hewish, *Emily Brontë*, p. 121.
13 Ibid., pp. 122–3.
14 Ibid., pp. 124 ff.
15 H. Dingle, *The Mind of Emily Brontë*, (London, 1974), p. 33. But cf. M. Schorer, 'Fiction and the Matrix of Analogy' in *The Kenyon Review*, Vol XI, September 1949, where some examples of comparison and analogy are given. These do not, I think, invalidate Dingle's point.
16 CB, 'Preface' to *Wuthering Heights*.
17 'The Two Children' ('Heavy Hangs the Raindrop'), 28 May 1845.
18 AB, 'Self-Communion', lines 184 ff.
19 'Written in Aspin Castle', 20 August 1842–6 February 1843.
20 'I see around me tombstones grey', 17 July 1841.
21 'Aye, there it is,' 6 July 1841.
22 *Wuthering Heights*, Ch. 21.
23 'I saw thee child, one summer's day', July 1837, lines 37 ff. *Wuthering Heights*, Ch. 34,

> Now, I perceived he was not looking at the wall, for when I regarded him alone, it seemed, exactly, that he gazed at something within two yards' distance. And, whatever it was, it communicated, apparently, both pleasure and pain, in exquisite extremes; at least, the anguished, yet raptured expression of his countenance suggested that idea.

24 'To Imagination', 3 September 1844.
25 *Early Victorian Novelists* (London, 1935), pp. 173 ff.
26 *Wuthering Heights*, Ch. 34, quoted fully in n. 23 above.
27 S. Davies, *Emily Brontë*, pp. 101-2.

Notes to Chapter 15

1 Anne's 1845 diary paper, first published in C. K. Shorter, *CB and her Circle*, p. 152.
2 See Chitham, *The Poems of AB*, pp. 13–14 for details of the relationship between Anne and her pupils.
3 Ibid., pp. 15-19.
4 A record in Mr Brontë's notebook, mentioned in J. Kellett, *Haworth Parsonage*, p. 64, deals with the cleaning of the well in September 1847. 'The water tinged yellow by eight tins in a state of decomposition. It had not been cleaned for twenty years or more.' It looks as if someone in the parsonage used the bottom of the well as a rubbish dump.
5 Anne's 1845 diary paper; see note 1 above.
6 'Often rebuked' stanza 2. For its authenticity, see E. Chitham, '"Often Rebuked" . . . Emily's after all' in *BST* 93, (1983).
7 *BST* 82 (1972) and 92 (1982).
8 *BST* 82 (1972) pp. 85 ff. The article should be read carefully, as one of the few which gives Wordsworth his rightful place in influencing Emily Brontë.
9 A. M. F. Robinson, *Emily Brontë*, p. 143.
10 WGEB quotes an occurrence in 1649 when three suns were seen side by side, though this was at Colne. Revd T. W. Story saw an almost similar phenomenon at Haworth in 1907. WGEB, pp. 207–8.
11 J. Hewish, *Emily Brontë*, p. 97, seems to give the most authoritative account of Newby and lists his address after 1846 as 72, Mortimer Street, not 172 as sometimes suggested. Hewish's evidence is from London street directories. See also *BST* 80 (1970) pp. 400–7.
12 CB to WSW, SHB, *Lives and Letters*, Vol. II, p. 162; CB to George Smith, probably 18 September 1850, SHB, *Lives and Letters*, Vol. II, p. 160; CB to George Smith, 7 January 1851, SHB, *Lives and Letters*, Vol. II, p. 197.
13 CB to WSW, 10 November 1847, SHB, *Lives and Letters*, Vol. II, pp. 153–4.
14 CB to EN, 25 September 1847, SHB, *Lives and Letters*, Vol. II, p. 143.
15 J. Hewish, *Emily Brontë*, p. 162; M. Allott, *The Brontës, The Critical Heritage*, (London, 1974), p. 59.
16 C. Simpson, *Emily Brontë*, (London, 1929).
17 M. Allott, *The Brontës: Critical Heritage*, pp. 220 ff. Other summaries and quoted words from early critics are also from the same work.
18 See the article by G. Larken, already referred to, 'The Shuffling Scamp', in *BST* 80 (1970), pp. 400 ff.

19 C. Simpson, *Emily Brontë*, p. 182.
20 One might possibly argue that the outer envelope would have to have been addressed to 'E. Brontë' or 'A. Brontë'. If it was to E. Brontë, and there was some fiction that 'Ellis Bell' was a friend, the outer envelope might have been kept in the desk too; if to 'A Brontë' the major argument remains the same. Total certainty is obviously not obtainable.
21 Chitham & Winnifrith, Ch. 9.
22 'Self-communion', lines 196 ff.
23 'B' manuscript, British Library.

Notes to Chapter 16

1 Quoted, e.g., in E. Raymond, *In the Steps of the Brontës*, p. 226.
2 D. du Maurier, *The Infernal World of Branwell Brontë*, p. 52. She also suggests schizophrenia. The book is well worth reading as a very sympathetic interpretation of Branwell's life.
3 F. Leyland, *The Brontë Family*, preface.
4 Greenwood's 'Diary', quoted in *BST* 61 (1951), p. 38. Like most events in the diary, this one cannot be dated, but as Anne is mentioned in the account, it probably took place after 1845. When Emily had soused her brother, her first words were 'Don't alarm Papa'.
5 CB in the 'Biographical Notice' prefaced to the second edition of *Wuthering Heights*.
6 CB to EN, 3 March 1846, SHB, *Lives and Letters*, Vol. II, p. 84, reporting a comment of Emily's on Branwell's borrowing money from his father and spending it on drink.
7 D. du Maurier, *Infernal World of BB*, p. 222.
8 Lock & Dixon, pp. 377 ff.
9 A. M. F. Robinson, *Emily Brontë*, pp. 221–2, probably basing her account on Martha Brown.
10 AB to EN, 4 January 1848, SHB, *Lives and Letters*, Vol. II, p. 175.
11 CB to Mary Taylor, 4 September 1848, SHB, *Lives and Letters*, Vol. II, p. 251.
12 Ibid., p. 254.
13 CB to WSW, 15 February 1848, SHB, *Lives and Letters*, Vol. II, p. 189.
14 CB to WSW, 31 July 1848, SHB, *Lives and Letters*, Vol. II, p. 240.
15 CB to EN, 29 October 1848, SHB, *Lives and Letters*, Vol. II, p. 268.

16 CB to WSW, 2 November 1848, SHB, *Lives and Letters*, Vol. II, p. 269.
17 CB to WSW, 22 November 1848, SHB, *Lives and Letters*, Vol. II, p. 286.
18 Ibid., p. 287.
19 CB to WSW, 7 December 1848, SHB, *Lives and Letters*, Vol. II, p. 289.
20 Ibid.
21 CB, report to Dr. Epps, SHB, *Lives and Letters*, Vol. II, p. 292.
22 CB to EN, Date uncertain, SHB, *Lives and Letters*, Vol. II, p. 289. The date ascribed, 9 December, may be correct, but there are some indications of an earlier date.
23 A. M. F. Robinson, *Emily Brontë*, p. 227.
24 Ibid., pp. 229–30.
25 CB to EN, 23 December 1848, SHB, *Lives and Letters*, Vol. II, p. 294.
26 CB to EN, 12 April 1849, SHB, *Lives and Letters*, Vol. II, p. 324.

Notes to Chapter 17

1 W. Scruton, *Thornton and the Brontës*, p. 115.
2 'I am the only being whose doom', stanza 6.
3 A. M. F. Robinson, *Emily Brontë*, p. 51.
4 Cf. W. Craik, *The Brontë Novels* (London, 1968), pp. 24–5.
5 'Oh, thy bright eyes must answer now', 14 October 1844, stanza 8.
6 'Enough of thought, Philosopher', 3 February 1845, lines 45 ff.

Appendices

Appendix I Emily Brontë's Account Book

At front of book] *notes*

Side A – pasted to endpaper, blank?]
Side B] ______________________________

Credit[
Owe of that 160 pounds
5
_________ 40 _____ _____ for S Old[1

total 210 pounds
____

Side C] Sold more SR and M ranger shares
[an]d [paid?] myself 8(?)[2
____

At other end of book]

Side 1 blank stub]
[blotted traces on endpaper, from foot of original page]
Aug(?) . . . . paid(?) R . . g bond(?) 0(?)–7–0
blots
______________________________ 9–6–0 3

Side 2 blank stub]
____

Side 3] 1 – 12 – 0
Had – ~~0 – 18 – 0~~ January 1845
[tops of letters,
?]k[. . undecipherable] 4
____

Side 4] Ser[vice?
Leeds by Rail – 0 – 4 – 0
2 Omnibuses – 0 – 1 – 0
____

Side	Left	Right	
Side 5]		Bradford wine – 0 – 1 – 0 Keighley 0 – 3 – 6 Tea 0 – 1 – 6	
Side 6]	Profit for North S to H scrip 3 –0–0	Specs for[Share specs 70 – 6 – 2	
	Total 116–18–4	Total 1268– 13 – 9	5
Side 7]	I exceeded my income by 12 – 0 – 0 Besides being answerable for 163 – 13 – 10		
Side 8]	January 1846	expenses [illegible] 20 – 0 – 0	
Side 9]		Ed Kerew 0 – (?) – 0 Collar for F 0 – 1 – 6 needles 0 – 1 – 3	
Side 10]		Walnuts Dates &c 0 – 3 – 0 Seeds ——— 0 – 1 – 0	
Side 11]	rec]eived[?] 2 coupons of M Railway 10 –10 –0 ~~Total 3~~		6
Side 12]	Total 305 –10 –0		
Side 13	blank stub]		
Side 14	blank stub]		
Side 15	Receipts January]5 –0 –0	Expenses 1847 Tin 0 – 1 – 0	7
Side 16]		0 – 13 – 4 9 – 13 – 6 3 – 11 –10	8
Side 17]	July	. . . . . . Call 100 – 0 – 0 H sundries 0 – 0 – 3 B —— —— 0 – 0 – 3	9

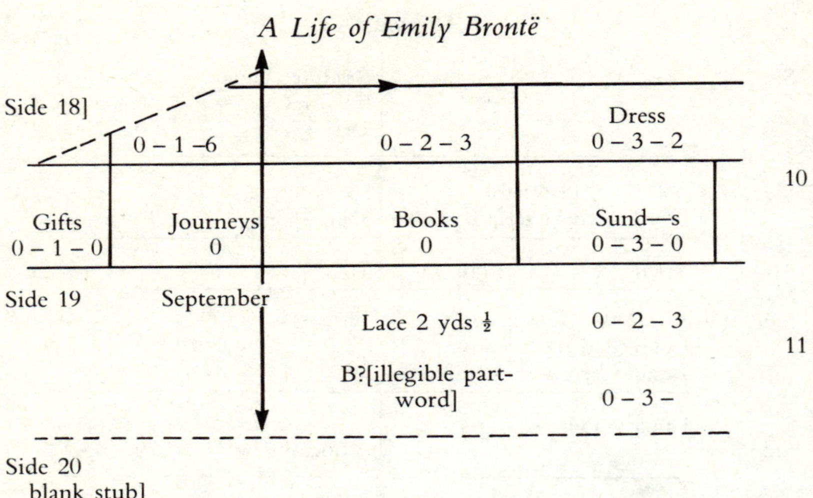

NOTES

1 It will be noted that this part of the book, presumably dating from 1844, does not have a rule differentiating income from expenditure. The changes from 4 to 5 and S to O are made by overwriting in ink.

2 In line 2, *myself* is clear; *and paid* is a possible interpretation of the blotted letters appearing in reverse on Side B.

3 These blotted letters, undivided by a vertical line, must come from late 1844.

4 Only the very tops of the letters on the expenses side are visible.

5 In the expenses total, the 6 is changed to 8 by overwriting in ink.

6 This tiny fragment hangs by a thread, and I am influenced in deciphering it by the detail in Hewish, *Emily Brontë*, p. 94.

7 Only the tops of the numbers in the receipts column have survived.

8 The figures in the expenses column are disposed thus, and there is no space for the articles to which they refer.

9 A row of small dots (six in all) may actually be tiny indecipherable letters or hints of letters.

10 The mark over the figures 0-2-3 looks like an arrow. The word Journeys is actually written on the lateral line, but its decipherment is certain.

11 The tops of the letters only have survived in the illegible word. It appears to be a dissyllable and may be something like *Bedframes*, but this is very uncertain.

Appendix II The 1841 Census at Law Hill

Elizabeth Patchett	45	Schoolmistress	Born Yorkshire
Charlotte Hartley	30	Teacher	"
Jane Aspden	25	Teacher	"
Harriet Berry	15	Pupil	"
Martha Robinson	15	"	"
Sarah Aitkin	15	"	"
Jane Berry	14	"	"
Sarah Whitehead	14	"	"
Elizabeth Marsden	14	"	"
Maria Binns	14	"	"
Ann "	13	"	"
Martha "	11	"	"
Alice Huges	13	"	"
Sarah Oldroyd	13	"	"
Mary Illingworth	13	"	"
Mary Midgley	13	"	"
Jane Brooke	13	"	"
Elizabeth H. Bramley	13	"	"
Ann Peircy	12	"	"
Julia Hemingway	12	"	"
Susan Roscom	12	"	"
Laura Robinson	11	"	"
Malvine Littlemore	11	"	"
Mary Clegg	20	F[emale] S[ervant]	"
Hannah Clegg	20	F[emale] S[ervant]	"
Jane Tillotson	15	F[emale] S[ervant]	"
Joseph Tollis	55	M[ale] S[ervant]	"
Jonas Robertshaw	40	Card mf.	"
Sarah Robertshaw	40	–	"
Martha Robertshaw	15	–	"
John Robertshaw	15	–	"
Mary Robertshaw	10	–	"
Samuel Robertshaw	9	–	"
James Robertshaw	4	–	"
Thomas Magson	65	Weaver	"
Grace Magson	50	–	"
Jennet Foster	25	–	"
Elizabeth Foster	25	F[emale] S[ervant]	"

Selected Bibliography

There are many detailed bibliographies of the Brontë family. The following therefore includes only recent books, or those which I have found especially valuable.

Alexander, C., *The Early Writings of Charlotte Brontë*, Oxford, 1983.

Allott, M., *The Brontes: The Critical Heritage*, London, 1974.

Butterfield, M. A., *The Heatons of Ponden Hall*, Stanbury, 1976.

Cecil, D., *Early Victorian Novelists*, London, 1934.

Chadwick, E. A., *In the Footsteps of the Brontës*, London, 1913.

Chitham, E., *The Brontës' Irish Background*, London, 1986.

Chitham, E. (ed.), *The Poems of Anne Brontë*, London, 1979.

Chitham, E. and Winnifrith, T. J., *Brontë Facts and Brontë Problems*, London, 1983.

Craik, W., *The Brontë Novels*, London, 1968.

Davies, S., *Emily Brontë: the Artist as a Free Woman*, Manchester, 1983.

Dingle, H., *The Mind of Emily Brontë*, London, 1974.

du Maurier, D., *The Infernal World of Branwell Brontë*, London, 1972.

Gaskell, E. C., *The Life of Charlotte Brontë*, London, 1857.

Gérin, W., *Anne Brontë*, London, 1959; 2nd edn., 1974.

Gérin, W., *Branwell Brontë*, London, 1961.

Gérin, W., *Charlotte Brontë*, London, 1967.

Gérin, W., *Emily Brontë*, London, 1971.

Hewish, J., *Emily Brontë*, London, 1969.

Kellett, J., *Haworth Parsonage*, Haworth, 1977.

Leyland, F., *The Brontë Family*, London, 1886.

Lock, J. and Dixon, W. T., *A Man of Sorrow*, London, 1965.
Ratchford, F., *Gondal's Queen*, Austin, Texas, 1955.
Raymond, E., *In the Steps of the Brontës*, London, 1948.
Robinson, A. M. F., *Emily Brontë*, London, 1883.
Scruton, W., *Thornton and the Brontës*, Bradford, 1898.
Shakespeare Head (pub.), *The Brontës, their Lives, Friendships and Correspondence*, Oxford, 1932, reissued, 1980.
Shorter, C. K., *Charlotte Brontë and her Circle*, London, 1896.
Simpson, C., *Emily Brontë*, London, 1929.
Spark, M. and Stanford, D., *Emily Brontë, her Life and Work*, London, n. d.
Stuart, J. Erskine, *The Brontë Country*, London, 1888.
Turner, J. Horsfall, *Brontëana*, Bingley, 1898.
Turner, J. Horsfall, *Haworth, Past and Present*, Brighouse, 1879.
Turner, Whiteley, *A Spring-time Saunter: Round and about Brontëland*, Halifax, *c*1905.
Visick, M., *The Genesis of Wuthering Heights*, Hong Kong, 1958.
Wilks, B., *The Brontës*, London, 1975.
Winnifrith, T. J. (ed.), *The Poems of Branwell Brontë*, Oxford, 1983.
Wilson, R., *All Alone*, London, 1928.
Wright, W., *The Brontës in Ireland*, London, 1893.

Brontë Society *Transactions*, especially Parts 23, 34, 61, 67, 69, 72, 80, 82, 85, 90, 92, 93.

The following books, pamphlets or articles have been of special value as sources:

Goodridge, J. F., in *Emily Brontë: Wuthering Heights*, London, 1964.
Goodridge, J. F., 'A New Heaven and a New Earth' in Smith, A., *The Art of Emily Brontë*, London, 1976.
Keyworth, T., in *The Bookman*, March 1893, pp. 184-5.
Petyt, K., *Emily Brontë and the Haworth Dialect*, Menston, 1970 (Yorkshire Dialect Society Publications).
Roper, D., 'The Revision of Emily Brontë's Poems of 1846' in *The Library*, June 1984, pp. 153 ff.
Shorter, C. K., 'Relics of Emily Brontë' in *The Woman at Home*, (1897) p. 909.
Williams, M., *Notes on the Clergy Daughters' School, Casterton*, Beverley, 1935.

Index

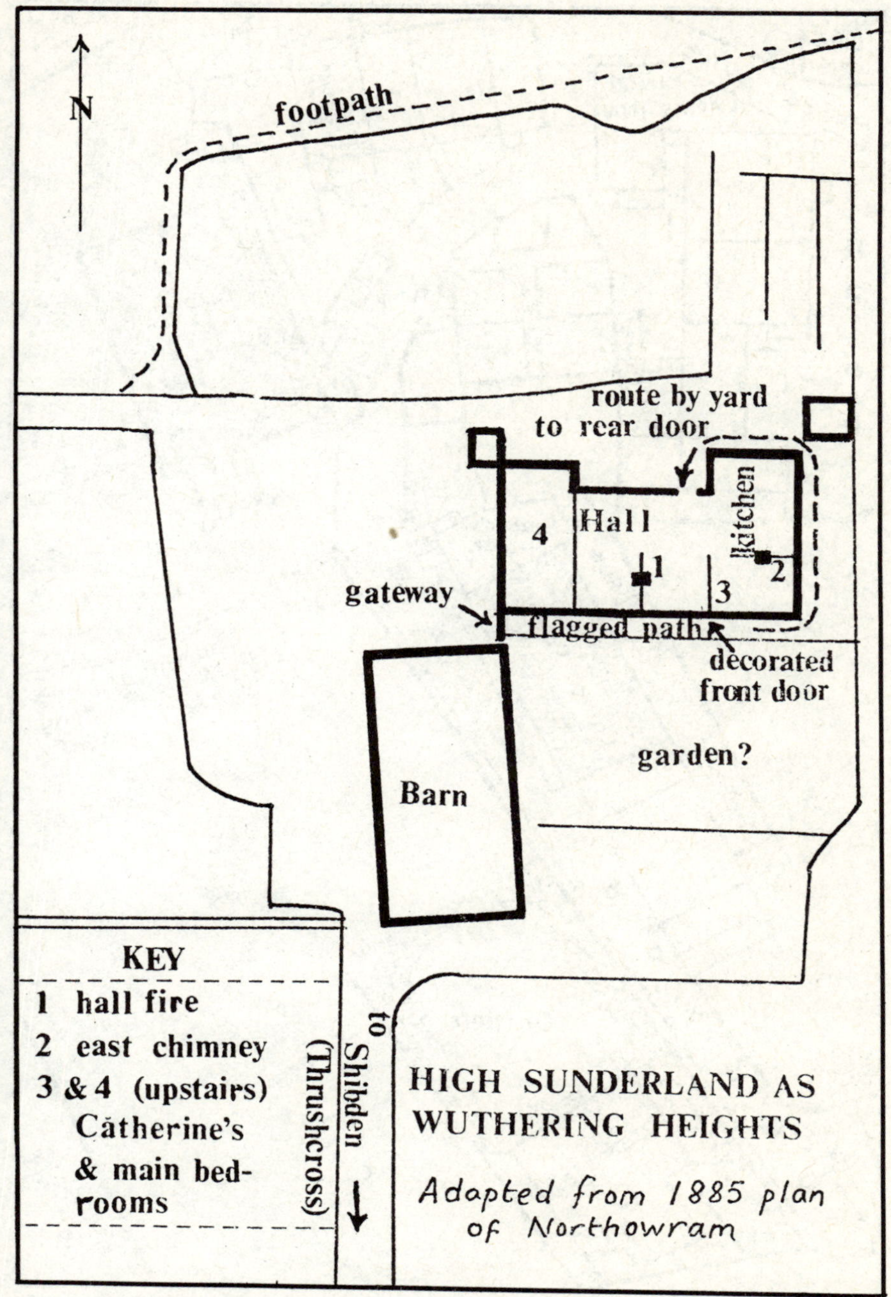

A High Sunderland as Wuthering Heights. The plan is based on a MS plan of 1885 in Calderdale District Archives, but the labels are from the novel.

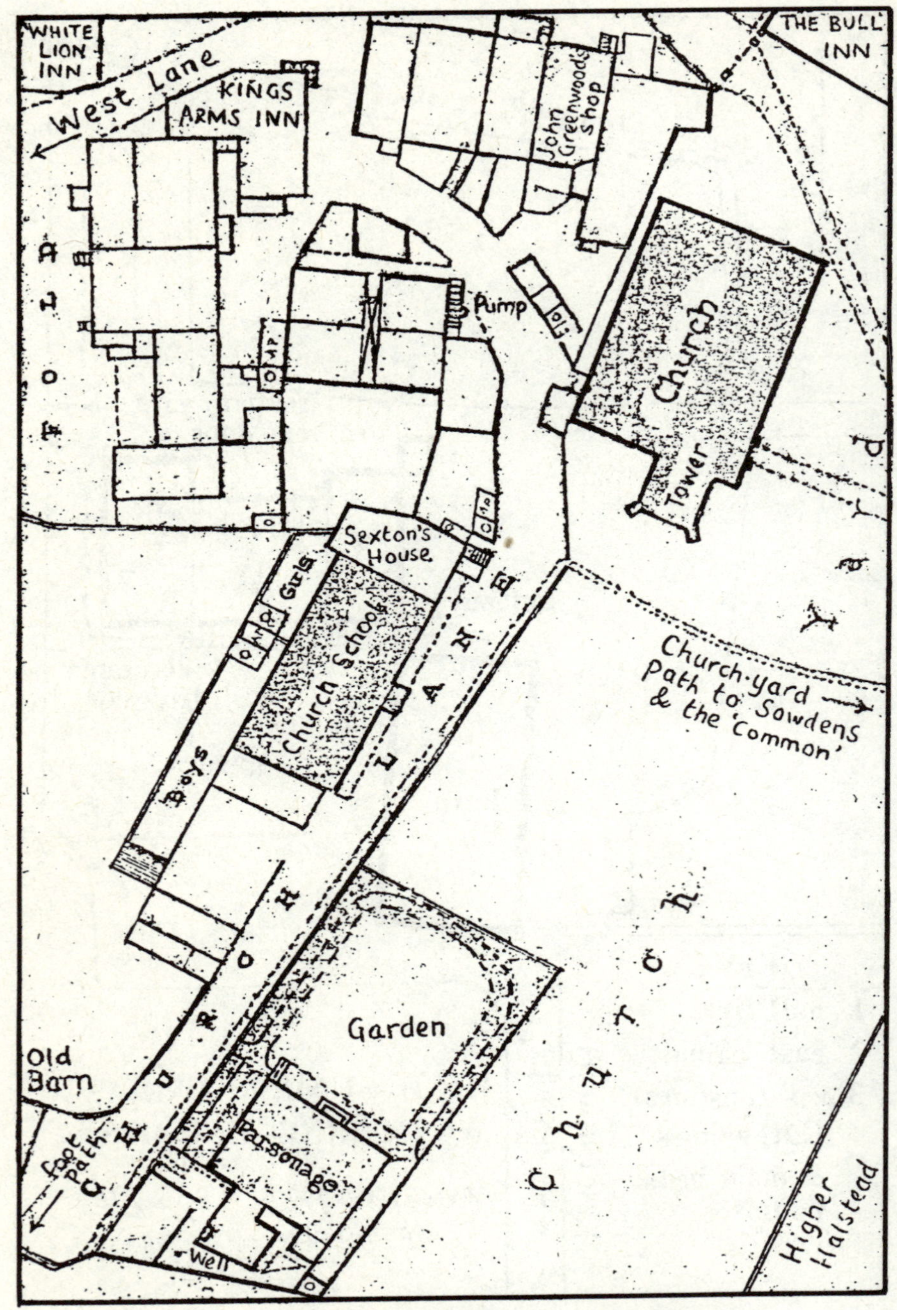

B Plan of part of Haworth, showing the parsonage and garden in 1853.

C Haworth and district, 1817.

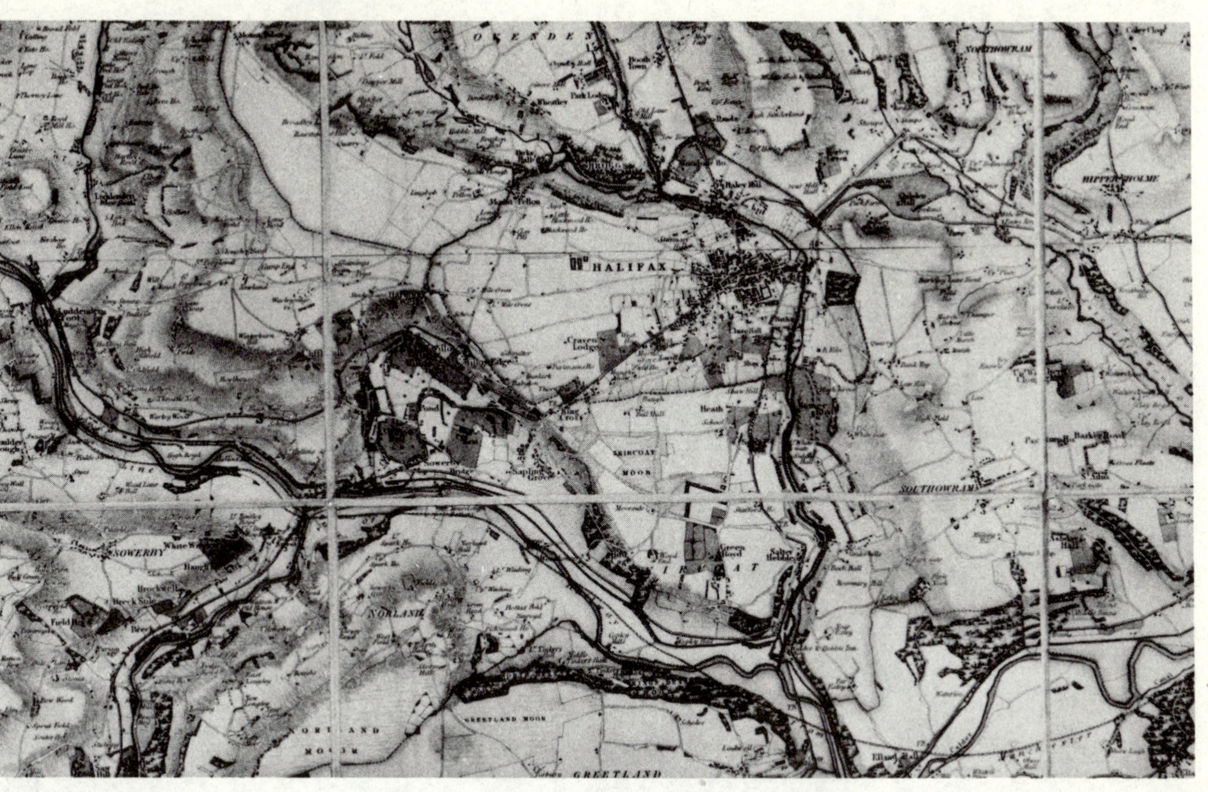

D Halifax, 1835.

PACE UNIVERSITY LIBRARIES
BIRNBAUM STACKS
PR4173.C45 1987
A life of Emily Bronte
3 5061 00517 1906